THE SOUP BIBLE

THE SOUP BIBLE

David Paul Larousse

John Wiley & Sons, Inc.

New York · Chichester · Brisbane · Toronto · Singapore · Weinheim

"Of soup and love, the first is the best."—Spanish proverb

Publisher: Margaret K. Burns
Senior Editor: Claire Thompson
Associate Managing Editor: Donna Conte
Photography: Marshall Gordon
Food Styling: D. P. Larousse
Illustrations: Carol Nunnelly

This text is printed on acid-free paper.

This publication is designed to provide accurate and
authoritative information in regard to the subject
matter covered. It is sold with the understanding that
the publisher is not engaged in rendering legal, accounting,
or other professional services. If legal advice or other
expert assistance is required, the services of a competent
professional person should be sought.

Library of Congress Cataloging in Publication Data:
Larousse, David Paul, 1949–
    The soup bible / David Paul Larousse.
      p.   cm.
    Includes index.
    ISBN 0-471-13562-3 (cloth : alk. paper)
    1. Soups. I. Title.
  TX757.L34   1997
  641.8′13—dc20   96-25881

Printed in the United States of America

10 9 8 7 6 5 4 3 2 1

CONTENTS

RECIPES

•••

CHICKEN CONSOMMÉ   68

PREFACE

● ●

Of all the items on the menu, soup is that which exacts the most delicate perfection and the strictest attention. —Auguste George Escoffier

Escoffier's commentary on soup is so apropos of his personality—a reflection of such serious intent by one of our greatest culinary administrators on a dish as elementary as soup. Yet the history of soup is as old as the history of cooking, and not all that has transpired throughout the evolution of cooking has been attended to with delicate perfection or strict attention. There are, of course, soups that require perfection and attention, and it was about these that Escoffier spoke. But there is also a relaxed and familial approach, in which soup is a thick mélange prepared with wild abandon and based on available ingredients. Both approaches have their place in the grander scheme of things.

The body of soup we know of today represents centuries of evolution from simple broths and gruel-thickened liquids to the modern system of bisques, chowders, consommés, and regional ethnic specialties. In the early stages of this evolution, the presence of two foods was significant: one was cereal-based ingredients, such as leavened and unleavened bread, pasta, and rice, which predate all other cooked dishes; the other was the common practice of boiling all available edibles in one big cauldron. In medieval Europe, grains were sometimes added to the meat, fish, and aromatics that were boiled with water or verjuice (unfermented grape juice), which added a little viscosity. This dish came to be known as a grané; however, when an English transcriber later rewrote a French manuscript and mistook the *n* for a *v*, *grané* was inadvertently changed

to *gravé* (gravy). Another practice during the Middle Ages was that of placing a slice of stale bread, called a *trencher*, on a wooden plank upon which was placed roasted or boiled joints of meat. The trencher soaked up the juices from the meat, effectively thickening those juices, which when reheated yielded a slightly thickened and rather tasty liquid dish.

Between the end of the ancient Roman Empire (fifth century) and the Florentine renaissance (fourteenth century) appeared the king of the Franks, Charles I, a.k.a. Charlemagne (742–814), dubbed by one writer as the "lighthouse of Europe." A towering figure in his physical presence (6'4") as well as in his personality and leadership qualities, he spearheaded the Carolignian renaissance, what Will Durant referred to as "one of several heroic interludes in the dark ages. Charlemagne's reign was a feat of genius . . . in an age and region of economic decline." In addition to bringing order and governance to eighth-century Europe, he was also responsible for introducing a modicum of refinement and hygiene in the realm of food. They were small refinements, but significant for their time. He instructed guests at his table to secure their food with the point of a knife instead of with their fingers; ordered estate owners to discontinue the practice of squashing the grape harvest by foot, and to stock their larders with smoked and salted meat, mustard, cheese, butter, and honey; and insisted that Frankish estates and monasteries be self-sufficient, which necessitated the presence of bakers, [beer] brewers, cheesemakers, coopers, gardeners, wine makers, and so on.

One of the earliest precursors to the formation of soup took place in the town of Pavia, Italy. There, in February 1525, a German-Spanish army sent by Italian emperor Charles V nearly annihilated the French and Swiss army in the Battle of Pavia. A servant girl assigned to bring a bowl of broth to the imprisoned French king, Francis I, had the good sense to feel embarrassed at serving such meager food to a king. She subsequently scavenged some stale bread—then referred to as a *soppe*—and an egg, and added the two ingredients to the broth, creating *Zuppa Pavese*, a simple Italian soup still prepared today.

By the seventeenth century the hodge-podge of ingredients that had been boiling in cauldrons for some centuries had now been refined to a *potage*—as in pot—consisting of meat or fish with vegetables, simmered in a clear broth (Pot-au-feu, Périgord Wedding Soup, and Olla Podrida are perfect examples of this). When the liquid from a potage was poured over a slice of bread—a *sop*—in a separate bowl, it was referred to as a *soupe*. *Soupe* can also refer to specialty regional concoctions, though in contemporary parlance *soupe* and *potage* are fairly interchangeable.

In the Orient, particularly China, where refined culture and cuisine evolved long before it had in the West, a somewhat different view of cooking evolved. As Lin Yutang eloquently points out in his essay "On Food and Medicine" (*The Importance of Living*, The John Day Company, NY, 1937), the Chinese do not draw any distinction between food and medicine: what is good for the body is medicine and at the same time food. Sun Ssemiao, a medical man of the sixth century, wrote: "A true doctor first finds out the cause of the disease, and having found that out, he tries to cure it first by food." In fact, Chinese medicines are conceived and prepared in the same manner as ordinary soups, served as one would serve a stew, and they are literally called "soup." A typical Chinese tonic might consist of a bowl of black-skinned chicken soup cooked with *rehmannia lutea*, or rich turtle soup with wood ear mush-

rooms and cinchona bark—and, in all cases, it was prepared with serious regard for the proper mixing of flavors and ingredients. There are anywhere from seven to twenty ingredients in such a brew, and its intended function is to nourish and strengthen the body as a whole, and not solely to attack a specific disease.

This is not to say that all foods were always served as medicine. For the Chinese epicure great things could be found in small blessings, and a profound respect for cooking revealed an enormous world of contemplation around the simplest of culinary experiences. Not only were good cooks revered for their ability to establish the three requisites of food—color, fragrance, and flavor—but a fine chicken soup was more than a universal panacea—it was a work of art. (It has been scientifically verified that when one is exposed to the aroma of "Jewish penicillin"—chicken soup—the flow of mucous through nasal passages increases 33 percent.) Served in a fine porcelain bowl, barely thicker than an eggshell, with fragrant flower petals floating on its surface, it was not just sustenance but an object of contemplation that by the grace of heaven and a good cook, could soothe, even transform, the inner man.

In a multi-course dining experience, soup is important as a starter dish—it stimulates the appetite and sets the tone for the rest of a meal. Grimod de La Reynière (1758–1838) described it as follows: "It is to dinner what a portico or a peristyle is to a building; that is to say, it is not only the first part of it, but it must be devised in such a manner as to set the tone of the whole banquet, in the same way as the overture of an opera announces the subject of the work."

Soup can also occupy the center of a meal, in a familial milieu where conversation and communion between friends and family is the primary event. The soup then acts as a focal point for the experience of "breaking bread," of friends and family coming together at the table—the ultimate common ground. "Stone Soup" is a concoction created from the ingredients brought by each guest to a prearranged gathering. While the dinner is being prepared, people mingle and engage in conversation, steeped in an ambiance that asserts anticipation of the forthcoming communal brew.

Within the nomenclature of soup can also be found scores of gourmands and distinguished personalities, cities and nations, attitude and social status, all honored by a fluid dish containing the very ingredients favored by its namesake. These include soups named for cities (Boston, Cincinnati, New York, and Palermo); soups named for ambiance or technique (Happy Family and Egg Drop); soups named for historical personalities (Bismarck, Cleopatra, Mary Stuart, and Zola); soups named for social status (Citizen, Household, and Housewife); and soups expressing a feeling of the moment (Perfect, Rich, and Royal).

In modern times soup is prepared from a stock, a liquid extraction of flavors from meat, poultry, or fish, herbs and aromatics. In French nomenclature, this is *fond*, literally "bottom," a reference to the indispensable and building-block function of stock, and a further indication of the primary nature of a soup. Judith Martin (a.k.a. *Miss Manners*) may have described soup the best of all: "Do you have a kinder, more adaptable friend in the food world than soup? Who soothes you when you are ill? Who refuses to leave you when you are impoverished and stretches its resources to give you a hearty sustenance and cheer? Who warms you in the winter and cools you in the summer? Yet who is also capable of doing honor to your richest table and impressing your most demanding guests? . . . Soup does its loyal best, no matter what undignified conditions are imposed upon it." Or as a Spanish proverb puts it succinctly, "Of soup and love, the first is the best."

David Paul Larousse
San Francisco, California

ACKNOWLEDGMENTS

Special thanks to: Yorgos Kladis for Greek soups; chef Henri Patey (The Culinary Institute at Greystone), Madame Gisèle Cervisi (Alliance Francaise), and chef Hervé Le Biavant (California Culinary Academy) for assistance with French translations; Ernestina Whitehouse for historical research; and chef Robb Vaughn, Occidental Grill, San Francisco, for his Duck Gumbo recipe.

I also wish to thank the following individuals in San Francisco for their gracious assistance with photography props: sous-chef Jeff Baggenstoss, hostess Karrie Grove, and food and beverage manager Fred Hansen of the Fairmont Hotel; chef de cuisine Gloria Ciccarone-Nehls of the Big Four, Huntington Hotel; Patti Gray of Silhouettes; Robert King, Robert King Associates; Margo's Antiques; Anne Olney, The Sonoma Country Store.

CHAPTER 1

STOCKS

Fine wholesome soups can be made in a great variety, but only with good basic soup stocks. Indispensable in the making of good soups are white, brown, fish and game stock [and] the careful selection of all ingredients." (Hering's Dictionary of Classical and Modern Cookery, Virtue & Co., London, 1972)

The French term for stock is *fond*, from Latin *fundus*, meaning "bottom," and this definition provides a clue to the function and importance of stocks—the bottom is where the foundation lies, upon which one builds a repertoire of culinary creations. Since stocks provide the primary medium within which nearly all varieties of soup are created, understanding how to prepare them is essential to their creation.

Stocks are divided into two primary categories: *brown stock* (fond brun) and *white stock* (fond blanc). Primarily, what distinguishes the brown stock from the white is (1) the roasting of primary ingredients before they are simmered in the stock pot, (2) the addition of a tomato ingredient—paste and/or purée, and (3) the use of red wine when deglazing the roasting pan. These three steps add brown color and a slightly different character than when the bones are simmered raw. To maximize the color in a brown stock, a peeled Spanish onion is sometimes sliced in half and placed cut side down onto the top of a flattop stove or griddle until the sugar in the onion caramelizes. The resulting dark brown color of the onion is then infused into the stock. The same procedure can be applied to the bottom three inches of a stalk of celery, or a peeled carrot split in half lengthwise.

———————————— • ————————————

In some commercial production kitchens, where cooperation is encouraged by the kitchen management, the individual responsible for stock and soup production (technically, the "potager") will be able to work in concert with other kitchen personnel and can arrange to receive on a regular basis valuable stock ingredients that might otherwise be discarded. These include the residue from other roasting pans (the *déglacage* obtained from deglazing), the trim from beef and veal loins and legs, clean vegetable trimmings, herbs stems, and so on.

INGREDIENTS

The ingredients of a stock are divided into three elements: *nutritional, aromatic,* and *liquid.* The nutritional element primarily consists of bones, though meat may also be included, effectively making the stock richer in flavor. (Technically, a stock made with both bones and meat is considered a bouillon.) The aromatics are divided into two further categories: *mirepoix*—celery, carrot, and onion—and *bouquet garni*—a collection of herbs and spices, the most common of which are known as a *standard* bouquet garni: bay leaf, thyme, parsley sprigs, and peppercorns. The liquid element consists of water, sometimes augmented with wine, pan drippings (déglacage), lemon juice (for fish stock), or tomato juice (for brown stock).

Brown stocks are typically prepared from beef, veal, lamb, and game bones; white stocks from chicken, turkey, duck, and feathered game. Occasionally white stocks are prepared from beef, veal, or lamb, while poultry may be used to prepare brown stock—in both cases this is primarily a matter of personal preference. Fish bones are typically used for creating a white stock only, with the exception of matelotes, which are freshwater fish stews made with red wine that makes them fairly dark.

There are often occasions when it is logical to combine several different varieties of meat bones to create one all-purpose stock. When a single variety of nutritional ingredient (bones) is used, it is because a large quantity is required, or because a stock with a single flavor is needed, which will lead to the creation of a specific soup. There are a handful of soups that require a specific stock, such as white lamb stock for Scotch Broth; fish stock for Bouillabaisse; chicken stock for Queen's Style Soup (Potage à la Reine); game stock for Danish Style Game Soup (Potage de gibier à la Danoise); and so on. Most soups, however, can be made with any variety of basic stock, depending on the potager's preference.

Regardless of the type of bones used, they should always be washed well with cold water before being subjected to heat. It is also important to begin a stock with cold water, which allows for maximum extraction of flavor from the ingredients. Beginning with hot water prematurely coagulates the albumin in the bones, inhibiting its interaction with the water and the subsequent extraction of gelatin, flavor, and nutrients. After washing, the bones will be placed directly into a stock pot in the case of white stock, or roasted first, when a brown stock is being prepared.

METHOD OF PREPARATION

When making a brown stock, a thin coating of tomato paste is spread over the roasting bones (using a rubber spatula) midway through the roasting to add character and color and aid in the clarification process. When the bones and tomato reach a golden brown color, they are transferred to a stock pot and the mirepoix is placed in the same roasting pan and stirred to coat it with fat remaining from the roasted bones. This mirepoix is then roasted until it begins to caramelize, taking on a golden brown color. (A white stock requires neither tomato nor roasting.)

As a rule, for both white and brown stock, sufficient cold water is added to rise above the highest bone by approximately four inches. While the mirepoix is roasting, the bones will reach a first simmer. The top is then skimmed—a step referred to as *dépouiller* (pronounced "day-poo-yay")—which removes the first round of impurities—fat, coagulated blood, and albumin—that have collected on the top of the simmering stock.

Once the first skimming is completed, the aromatic elements are added—mirepoix (raw for white stock, roasted for brown stock) and bouquet garni. The aromatics can also be augmented with the dark green tops of leeks (and scallions), though they *must* be well washed to eliminate sand. In the case of roasted mirepoix, caramelized bits of meat or vegetables remaining in the roasting pan must also be utilized. This *déclacage* is removed by "deglazing," a technique in which a liquid is poured into the pan and heated, stirred with a wooden spoon to remove caramelized residue, and then added to the simmering stock. An all-purpose dry red wine is recommended for deglazing because it adds color and flavor and its acidity aids in the clarifying process.

---•---

A stock pot is not a receptacle for leftover vegetables or odds and ends of vegetable trimmings. The mirepoix ingredients (celery, carrots, and onions) need to be of the highest quality—onions peeled; carrots peeled, with top and bottom ends trimmed; celery trimmed and washed. The dictum here is "garbage in, garbage out"—the final stock will only be as good as the ingredients from which it is created.

Skimming is repeated periodically throughout the simmering of the stock, as fat, albumin, and impurities collect at the top. The albumin, a water-soluble simple protein found in animal bones and tissue as well as in vegetables and egg whites, is an essential part of the natural clarifying process. As the stock simmers, heat convection causes the liquid to move rhythmically around in the pot, while the naturally occurring albumin slowly coagulates, trapping minuscule impurities as the stock moves through it. For this reason, simmering is *absolutely vital* to stock preparation. It is why the stock is first brought to a simmer, as opposed to a boil. The vigorous activity of a boiling liquid prohibits the slow, careful collection of impurities, resulting in a cloudy stock, while slow, gentle simmering promotes clarification and a gentle release of flavor from the ingredients, producing a rich, clear liquid extraction.

The average simmering time for a white stock is 4 to 6 hours (with the exception of fish stock, which takes 1 to 1½ hours), and for a brown stock, 8 to 10 hours. After a white or brown stock has been strained, a second stock is sometimes produced with the same ingredients. This step is referred to as *rémouiller*, which produces a *rémouillage* (pronounced "ray-moo-yay," "ray-moo-yazh"), meaning "rewet." The resulting stock is not as strong as the first stock, but can be used as the start-up liquid for the next stock, for blanching vegetables, or for dishes that do not require a highly flavored stock. This step is generally not practiced in large commercial kitchens, where a brown stock can be prepared in a 60-gallon stationary steam kettle and allowed to simmer uninterrupted for as long as five days. Stock is drawn as needed from a built-in spigot near the bottom of the kettle, with water added at the top (in this case hot, since the stock is already hot) to replace what has been taken. When all the flavor of the stock elements has been extracted, the stock is drained, the elements removed and discarded, and the process begun all over again.

Fish stock is different from all of the other stock preparations, primarily because the bones are thinner and more delicate than other bones, consequently requiring less simmering time. The bones used for making a fish stock should be from a low-fat, white-fleshed fish such as cod, flounder, haddock, halibut, or sole. Varieties with higher fat content—bluefish, mackerel, salmon, swordfish, or tuna—tend to produce a cloudy and strongly flavored stock. The bones must be very fresh, and washed very well in cold water. The use of fish heads, gills, and skin is a matter of personal preference. They add excellent flavor, but usually are not included because they tend to cloud the stock; at the same time, certain peasant-style dishes call for these parts, particularly the head, which carries a very tasty and prized portion of flesh in the cavity of the cheek. If such parts are included, they should be very carefully and thoroughly washed.

Strict purists will employ a *white* mirepoix for fish stock that consists of onion and celery only, claiming that the carrot adds unwanted color. White wine and a small amount of lemon juice included in the liquid element aid in the clarifying process and counteract fishy aromas. The final stock should reflect a flavor and aroma of the sea, not of the fish.

Fumet (pronounced "foo-may") is a term often used in reference to fish stock. Technically, a fumet is a stock in which (1) the aromatics and nutritional elements are sweated in butter before the liquid is added; and (2) the liquid element is a stock or rémouillage, instead of water, making it a little stronger in flavor than ordinary stock.

At the end of the cooking period, all stocks are strained—carefully, since the liquid is still very hot. If there is a large quantity of stock to be strained, a large-holed strainer (conical strainer, or "chinois gros") or colander is used first, with the solids allowed to sit until all the liquid has drained. The stock can then be strained a second time through a fine screen strainer ("chinois mousseline"). Sometimes several layers of muslin are placed inside the strainer to aid in the straining.

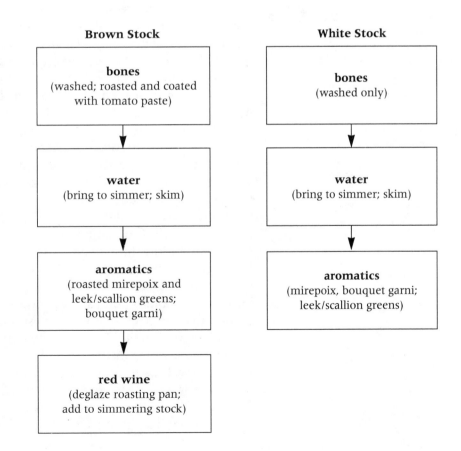

Brown Stock

bones
(washed; roasted and coated with tomato paste)

↓

water
(bring to simmer; skim)

↓

aromatics
(roasted mirepoix and leek/scallion greens; bouquet garni)

↓

red wine
(deglaze roasting pan; add to simmering stock)

White Stock

bones
(washed only)

↓

water
(bring to simmer; skim)

↓

aromatics
(mirepoix, bouquet garni; leek/scallion greens)

The stock must be cooled to room temperature before refrigerating. The warm, dark, moist environment within the stock, particularly when it is within the range of 40–140°F (4–60°C), is the optimum breeding ground for bacteria. If dealing with a quantity of five gallons or more, it will take some time for the liquid to cool off. Occasionally a hot spot develops, wherein the exterior portions of the stock cool down, leaving the interior hot and within the danger zone. For this reason, the cooling is sometimes expedited by placing the container of strained stock into a sink of cold water and ice. The stock is stirred periodically to expedite the cooling. When the stock has sufficiently cooled, it should be covered, labeled, and refrigerated.

Once it has fully chilled in the refrigerator, the stock may have a gelatinous (jellylike) consistency. This gelatin comes from the nutritional element—the bones, connective tissue, and cartilage. Its presence indicates that the stock is a flavorful one. Any fat still present in the stock will rise to the top and congeal under refrigeration. This can easily be lifted from the top and discarded.

MEATLESS STOCKS

In a perfect world, human beings might well derive sustenance solely from plant-based foods, but alas this is not the case. We are fortunate to be omnivorous, and different people thrive on different diets. For those who prefer not to employ meat-based stocks in soup production, a vegetable-derived extraction—actually, more of an essence—can be used (*see following paragraph*). Its flavor can be fortified with vegetable bouillon cubes and powders that are available in health food markets.

It is interesting to note that in many European kitchens full utilization of all ingredients is much more common than in North America. Vegetables are not only considerably more expensive there, but there have been many times during the history of European nations when, because of one tragic occurrence or another (warfare, famine, plague, and so on), vegetables and other foodstuffs were simply not available. Such a legacy over many generations has fostered the frugal practice of utilizing all food items. Hence the practice of creating a liquid vegetable extraction originated. Every vegetable scrap—from onion and shallot skins, to potato and carrot peels, to leek roots and zucchini ends—is covered with water and simmered slowly for several hours (usually 3 to 4). The resulting liquid is then used as a start-up liquid for other dishes, including meat-based stocks, soups, stews, as well as a cooking medium for rice and a reheating medium for pasta. It's not particularly flavorful alone, but fortified with the bouillon cubes or powders, or the other ingredients of a particular dish, it can serve as an aromatic medium for many a fine potage, meatless or otherwise. A meatless bouillon or consommé is a contradiction; but a minestrone or bourride, a tomato bisque or beer soup, a creamed asparagus or lettuce purée can hold up well without meat.

———————————— • ————————————

In some kitchen operations, an arrangement is made for the strained-off vegetables and other discarded food items to be picked up by a local farmer for use as livestock feed. This can be a mutually beneficial arrangement—the restaurant's garbage quantity is reduced, while the farmer has a source of good-quality feed for his animals.

GENERAL GUIDELINES FOR THE PRODUCTION OF A PROPER STOCK

- Use quality ingredients. (Recall the saying: "Garbage in, garbage out.")
- Wash ingredients well in cold water, and peel aromatics (mirepoix).
- Begin a stock with cold water.
- Perform the initial skimming before adding aromatics.
- When adding water to a simmering stock, use hot water.
- Skim regularly.
- Always simmer, never boil. (Simmering allows the natural clarifying process to manifest, producing a rich, clear stock.)
- Simmer 4 hours minimum (for fish stock, 1 to 1½ hours).
- Strain, cool, and store properly.

𝓑ROWN VEAL OR BEEF STOCK
(Fond Brun de Veau ou Boeuf)

6 pounds (2.7 kg) veal or beef shanks and knuckle bones, cut into 4-inch lengths
1 cup (240 mL) tomato paste
3 stalks celery, trimmed, rinsed, and roughly chopped

2 carrots, peeled, tops removed, and roughly cut
2 medium Spanish onions, peeled and roughly chopped
1 leek, green tops only, well rinsed, and roughly chopped

2 gallons (7.7 L) (approximately) cold water
1 garlic clove, crushed
2 bay leaves
3 sprigs fresh thyme

1 bunch parsley stems, trimmed, rinsed, and tied together
1 teaspoon (4.9 mL) black peppercorns, cracked
1 quart (960 mL) dry red wine

- Preheat an oven to 400°F (205°C).
- Wash the bones thoroughly in cold water. Place them into a roasting pan, and roast for 20 minutes. Remove from the oven, and spread a light coating of tomato paste over the bones, using a rubber spatula. Continue roasting another 15 to 20 minutes, or until golden brown.
- Remove the bones from the pan, and place in a stockpot that has been wiped out with a clean towel. Fill with cold water 4 inches (100 mm) above the highest bone, and place on a high flame. When it just begins to boil, turn down to a simmer. Skim impurities (albumin, fat, coagulated blood), from the top.
- Place the mirepoix and leeks in the pan from which the bones came, and stir it up with any fat remaining in the pan. Roast for 40 minutes, stirring occasionally, until the vegetables are well caramelized.
- Add the mirepoix and the bouquet garni to the simmering stock. Place the roasting pan over a high flame on the stove, add the dry red wine, and deglaze. Add this to the simmering stock. Simmer 8 to 12 hours, skimming periodically as needed. Strain, cool, cover, label, and refrigerate.

WHITE VEAL STOCK
(Fond Blanc de Veau)

4 pounds (18 kg) veal knuckle bones, cut into 3- or 4-inch (75- to 100-mm) pieces
4 pounds (18 kg) veal shank, cut into 3- or 4-inch (75- to 100-mm) pieces
2 stalks celery, trimmed, rinsed, and roughly chopped

2 carrots, peeled, tops removed, and roughly chopped
1 large Spanish onion, peeled, and cut into eighths
2 bay leaves
3 sprigs fresh thyme
1 bunch parsley stems, trimmed, rinsed, and tied together

1 teaspoon (4.9 mL) white
    peppercorns, cracked

2 gallons (7.7 L)
    (approximately) cold
    water

- Wash the bones thoroughly in cold water. Place them in a stockpot that has been wiped out with a clean towel. Fill with cold water 4 inches (100 mm) above the highest bone, and place on a high flame. When it just begins to boil, turn down to a simmer. Skim impurities (albumin, fat, coagulated blood) from the top, and discard.
- Add the mirepoix and the bouquet garni to the simmering stock. Place the roasting pan over a high flame on the stove, add the dry red wine, and deglaze. Add this to the simmering stock. Simmer 4 to 8 hours, skimming periodically as needed. Strain, cool, cover, label, and refrigerate.

$\mathcal{W}$HITE CHICKEN STOCK
(Fond Blanc de Volaille)

The optional chicken is included for additional flavor. In commercial kitchen production, this step is appropriate if cold poached chicken is utilized on the menu in another dish.

6 pounds (2.7 kg) fresh
    chicken bones, backs,
    necks, and wings
1 whole fresh chicken
    (optional)
2 gallons (7.7 L) water
1 large Spanish onion,
    peeled and cut into
    eighths
1 large carrot, top removed,
    scrubbed, and roughly
    chopped

2 stalks celery, rinsed and
    roughly chopped
1 leek, green tops only, well
    rinsed, and roughly
    chopped
2 bay leaves
3 sprigs fresh thyme
1 bunch parsley stems
1 teaspoon (4.9 mL) white
    peppercorns, cracked

- Rinse the bones (and whole chicken, if used) thoroughly in cold water.
- Place the bones (and chicken) into a stockpot, and cover them with cold water (should be 3 to 4 inches/75- to 100-mm above the highest bone). Heat over a high flame, just until the stock comes to a boil. Turn down to a simmer.
- Skim the top, removing, then discarding, fat and impurities.
- Add the vegetables, herbs, and spices.
- Simmer 1 hour, then lift out the whole chicken (if used), and set it aside to cool. Separate the meat from the skin and bones, reserving the meat for another dish, and returning the skin

and bones to the stockpot. Continue simmering, 4 to 6 hours, skimming off and discarding impurities periodically.

• Strain, cool, cover, and refrigerate.

The clear, savory broths found in the soups in Asian restaurants may be the result of the following technique. When the water first comes to a simmer, pour the contents of the pot into a colander, discarding the liquid. Rinse the bones thoroughly again in cold water, then begin the stock all over again with fresh water. A stock made from bones rinsed in this manner will be clear and savory if it is carefully simmered throughout the remaining cooking time.

.... # $\mathcal{B}$ROWN DUCK STOCK
(Fond Brun de Canard)

5 pounds (2.3 kg) of duck carcasses with giblets (excluding livers)
½ cup (120 mL) tomato paste
2 ribs celery, rinsed, and roughly chopped
1 large carrot, peeled and roughly chopped
1 large Spanish onion, peeled, and roughly chopped
1 leek, green tops only, well rinsed, and roughly chopped

1 pint (480 mL) dry red wine
1 bay leaf
2 sprigs fresh thyme
1 sprig fresh rosemary
1 bunch parsley stems, trimmed, rinsed, and tied together
½ teaspoon (2.5 mL) black peppercorns, cracked
1½ gallons (5.8 L) (approximately) cold water

• Preheat an oven to 400°F (205°C).

• Wash the bones thoroughly in cold water. Drain and dry. Place them in a roasting pan, and roast for 25 minutes. Remove from the oven, and spread a light coating of tomato paste over the bones, using a rubber spatula. Continue roasting another 20 to 30 minutes, or until well browned.

• Remove the bones from the pan, and place in a stockpot that has been wiped out with a clean towel. Fill with cold water 4 inches (100 mm) above the highest bone, and place on a high flame. When it just begins to boil, turn down to a simmer. Skim impurities (albumen, fat, coagulated blood) from the top, and discard.

- Pour off some of the excess fat from the pan, saving for another use. Place the mirepoix and leeks in the pan from which the bones came, and stir it up with any fat remaining in the pan. Roast for 40 minutes, stirring occasionally, until the vegetables are well caramelized.
- Skim the simmering stock (duck will yield a considerable amount of fat), then add the mirepoix and the bouquet garni. Place the roasting pan over a high flame on the stove, add the dry red wine, and deglaze. Add this to the simmering stock. Simmer 8 to 12 hours, skimming periodically as needed. Strain, cool, cover, label, and refrigerate.

Duck fat is particularly good combined with flour for roux, or in sautéing the vegetables for various soups, as well as potato and rice dishes.

$\mathcal{B}$ROWN GAME STOCK
(Fond Brun de Gibier)

The pheasant is an extravagant addition to this stock, but it makes for an exceptionally flavored stock. The bones and carcasses from pheasant, rabbit, partridge, or quail can also be used, and the flavor concentrated by reduction after the stock is completed.

5 pounds (2.3 kg) venison bones, cut into 3- or-4-inch (75- to 100-mm) pieces
1 pheasant, cut into 3- or 4-inch (75- to 100-mm) pieces
½ cup (120 mL) melted butter
a small piece of fat back, cut up into ½-inch (12-mm) cubes
½ cup (120 mL) tomato paste
2 ribs celery, rinsed, and roughly chopped
2 carrots, peeled tops removed, and roughly chopped
1 large Spanish onion, peeled, and roughly chopped

1 leek, green tops only, well rinsed, and roughly chopped
1 quart (960 mL) dry red wine
1 bay leaf
2 sprigs fresh thyme
2 sprigs fresh sage
1 bunch parsley stems, trimmed, rinsed, and tied together
½ teaspoon (2.5 mL) black peppercorns, cracked
2 whole cloves
10 juniper berries
1½ gallons (5.8 L) (approximately) cold water

- Preheat an oven to 400°F (205°C).
- Wash the bones and pheasant thoroughly in cold water. Drain and dry. Place them in a roasting pan, and brush with the melted butter. Roast for 20 minutes. Remove from the oven, and spread a light coating of tomato paste over the bones, using a rubber spatula. Continue roasting another 20 to 30 minutes, or until golden brown.

- Remove the bones from the pan, and place in a stockpot that has been wiped out with a clean towel. Fill with cold water 4 inches (100 mm) above the highest bone, and place on a high flame. When it just begins to boil, turn down to a simmer. Skim impurities (albumin, fat, coagulated blood) from the top, and discard.
- Place the mirepoix and leeks in the pan from which the bones came, and stir it up with any fat remaining in the pan. Roast for 40 minutes, stirring occasionally, until the vegetables are well caramelized.
- Skim the simmering stock, then add the mirepoix and the bouquet garni. Place the roasting pan over a high flame on the stove, add the dry red wine, and deglaze. Add this to the simmering stock. Simmer 8 to 10 hours, skimming periodically as needed. Strain, cool, cover, label, and refrigerate.

$\mathscr{F}$ISH STOCK
(Fond Blanc de Poisson)

3 tablespoons (45 mL) butter
1 Spanish onion, peeled and
  cut into eighths
1 stalk celery, roughly cut
1 leek, green top only, well
  rinsed, and roughly cut
3 or 4 mushrooms, rinsed
  and roughly cut
10 pounds (4.5 kg) fresh
  white fish bones, cut into
  3-inch (75-mm) lengths
1 cup (240 mL) dry white
  wine

1½ gallons (5.8 L) cold water
the juice of 1 lemon
1 bay leaf
1 sprig fresh thyme
1 sprig fresh dill, rinsed, and
  roughly chopped
1 bunch parsley stems,
  trimmed and rinsed
½ teaspoon (2.5 mL) white
  peppercorns, crushed

- Wash and soak the bones in cold water for 1 hour. Drain and rinse.
- Place the onions, celery, leeks, and mushrooms in a stockpot with the butter. Cover, and sauté for 10 minutes over a medium flame, stirring occasionally. Add the bones, and sauté another 5 minutes.
- Add the wine, water, and lemon juice (the liquid should rise about 4 inches/100 mm above the highest bone.) Bring to a boil, and turn down to a simmer. Skim and discard the impurities from the top.

- Add the herbs and spices, and continue simmering for 1 to 1½ hours, skimming periodically. Strain, cool, cover, label, and refrigerate.

·············· ℒOBSTER STOCK
(Fond Blanc de Homard)

3 tablespoons (45 mL) butter
2 shallots, roughly chopped
1 small Spanish onion, peeled and roughly chopped
1 stalk celery, rinsed, trimmed, and roughly cut
1 leek, white part only, roughly cut, and well rinsed
5 pounds (2.3 kg) lobster bodies and shells, broken up

1 cup (240 mL) dry white wine
1½ gallons (5.8 L) cold water
the juice of 1 lemon
1 bay leaf
1 sprig fresh thyme
1 small piece of fennel root, rinsed, and roughly chopped
1 bunch parsley stems, trimmed and rinsed
½ teaspoon (2.5 mL) white peppercorns, crushed

- Wash the lobster shells well in cold water.

- Place the shallot, onion, celery, and leek in a stockpot with the butter. Cover, and sauté for 10 minutes over a medium flame, stirring occasionally. Add the shells, and sauté another 5 minutes.

- Add the wine, water, and lemon juice (the liquid should rise about 4 inches/100 mm above the shells). Bring to a boil, and turn down to a simmer. Skim and discard the impurities from the top.

- Add the herbs and spices, and continue simmering for 1½ hours, skimming periodically. Strain, cool, cover, and refrigerate.

——— • ———
This stock is used for any soup based on lobster. Shrimp, crab, or crayfish shells can also be substituted.
———————————

MEAT GLAZE (GLACE DE VIANDE)

A glaze is a 90 percent (or more) reduction of a stock, and is used as a concentrated meat, poultry, or fish flavor to fortify soups (and other dishes). They are one of the most important tools in a culinarian's repertoire. Any stock, whether brown or white, can be reduced to create a glaze. (The only exception to this is fish stock, which requires clarification to produce a proper glaze, and is described a little further on.) Commercial kitchens produce large quantities of a single stock that can then be made into a specific glaze, but even when working on a smaller scale, a stock made from several different nutritional components (varieties of bones) can also be reduced into a glaze.

The word *glace* in French also means "mirror," a linguistic connection to its reflecting qualities, which are amazingly effective in spite of the fact that it turns dark brown and syrupy as the reduction nears completion.

The commercial counterpart to glaze is commonly referred to as *soup base* and is available in beef, chicken, clam, and lobster varieties. These, too, have a concentrated flavor of the food from which they are made, but they also include a high percentage of both salt and monosodium glutamate (MSG). In the consumer market, *bouillon cubes* ("bouillon" is the noun form of the French verb *bouillir* meaning "to boil") are the home version of a concentrated stock base, and these, too, are primarily made up of salt. Though glazes are also salty, that salt is derived naturally from the ingredients used in the original stock; it is for this reason that stocks should not be salted. But in all, homemade glaze is a superior product, and more time-consuming than difficult to prepare.

One of the most important first steps in making a glaze is to begin with a very clear stock. As it is reduced, the minute solid particles that make up the flavor of the stock become so concentrated that only a clear stock will yield a smooth and flavorful glaze, without it burning or turning bitter. A clear stock can be achieved by the slow and careful simmering of the stock, which enables a *natural clarifying process* to take place, yielding a clear stock. Fish stock is an exception—because of the short simmering time, there is insufficient time for natural clarification, and it often comes out cloudy. In this case—or with any stock that comes out cloudy (sometimes "cloudy happens," no matter how carefully one works)—a stock will require a separate clarifying procedure, utilizing the same method used to create a consommé (see Fish Consommé, pages 30 and 33).

To prepare a glaze, a stock is simply simmered until reduced down to a thick, concentrated syrup. This should be done in stages—first reduced by approximately half, and strained through a fine screen strainer (chinois mousseline) or several layers of muslin (cheesecloth) into a smaller vessel. It is reduced again by half in a smaller vessel, which must be made of a heavy-gauge metal—as the stock becomes thicker, the heat must be evenly dispersed to prevent it from burning (a pan at least 1/8-inch/3-mm thick at its bottom is recommended). At this point, the stock begins to thicken noticeably, a result of the concentration of the gelatin content of the stock and the minute particles that give the stock its color and flavor. The simmering is continued, though one or two passes through a fine strainer (chinois mousseline) are sufficient. Eventually the glaze reaches a thick, dark, syrupy consistency, similar in appearance to molasses. It is cooled down, then stored in small individual containers, preferably with securely fitting lids. They will keep for approximately one month under refrigeration. Any mold that later forms on the top surface can be scraped off and discarded—the underlying glaze is so dense that it will not be adversely affected by surface growths. Glazes can also be stored in the freezer, where they will keep for up to a year.

————————————— • —————————————

When the glaze is removed from the pot or pan it is simmered in, there will be some residue left in the pot. Because it is so rich and flavor-concentrated, this residue should be deglazed with hot water and that water used to prepare the next stock. Such practices are also known to improve kitchen relations with the plongeur (dishwasher).

Type of Stock (white or brown)	Technical Name
beef	glace de boeuf
veal	glace de veau
lamb	glace d'agneau
chicken	glace de poulet
duck	glace de canard
turkey	glace de dinde
game	glace de gibier
fish*	glace de poisson

* white only

Brown stocks reduced to a glaze are slightly darker and denser than those prepared from white stock, but both produce viable glazes. Choosing which variety of stock to reduce to a glaze will depend on its use. Personally, stock and glaze production has always had the number-one priority whenever I have gone into a new kitchen. Once I had a cup or two (2.5–5 dL) each of veal, chicken, and fish glaze, I was ready to get into a production rhythm. I then used the indispensable glazes to fortify soups, sauces, rice, and so on.

CHAPTER 2

THE BASIC CUTS

Prince Huei's cook was cutting with his knife, and every chhk of the chopper was in perfect rhythm. "Well done!" cried the prince. "Yours is skill indeed!"

"Sire," replied the cook, laying down his blade, "I have always devoted myself to Tao ["dow"], which is higher than mere skill. When I first began to cut up different food items, I saw the whole item, but after three years' practice I no longer viewed them in this way. I work with my mind and not with my eye or through control of the senses. I glide through great joints or delicate vegetables according to the natural constitution of the thing being cut."

"A good cook rarely changes his blade, because he cuts. An ordinary cook must change his blade once a month, because he hacks. I have had this knife for nineteen years, and although I have cut up a thousand bulls and ten thousand cabbages, its edge is as if fresh from the whetstone." (Adapted from "The Butcher's Knife," by Chuangtse [335–275 B.C.], from The Book of Chuangtse, as seen in The Importance of Understanding, Translations from the Chinese, by Lin Yutang)

Some years ago I worked in a large multi-restaurant operation that had a central kitchen where all the basic preparations for five different restaurants were produced. David Young was the butcher who filleted, trimmed, and boned hundreds of pounds of beef, veal, poultry, and fish each week. Several times a year, I would gather up some of the other cook's knives, and drop them off at a cutlery shop that skillfully renewed the cutting edges on our tools. I always asked David if he had any knives he wanted tuned up, and he always declined. The only sharpening device he used was an old worn steel, which he used periodically throughout the day in a rather frantic manner as he tore through his day's workload. Chuangtse's parable on cutlery may sound a bit corny and metaphysical, but I have seen this principle in action. To this day I marvel at my memory of the butcher whose work symbolized an ancient Taoist principle as he worked in harmony with the item he was cutting. He was able to break down great quantities of raw culinary material in a way that never depleted the edge on his tools.

Cutlery handling is a very personal learning experience, and all the information in the world cannot take the place of time spent working with one's tools in order to understand their physicality and how to maintain a sharp edge. Sharpness is essential, of course, as is special attention paid to the cutting of garnishes for all dishes, particularly soup. When a dining patron lifts a spoonful of soup containing perhaps a half-dozen diced vegetables, the precision with which they have been cut, or not cut, becomes starkly clear. And it is at this moment of consuming the soup that the skill of the cook is laid bare. For this reason, it is of the utmost importance to cut garnishes as uniformly as possible. It is an opportunity to demonstrate the care that one has taken to transform nature's ordinary ingredients into a visually splendid and carefully attended to gastronomic effort.

There follows a table of all the cuts applicable to vegetables in the preparation of soup garnishes. (There is an additional family of cuts that apply to deep-fried potatoes, but they are not included here.) It is intended as a guide, since nomenclature and dimensions vary considerably from kitchen to kitchen.

BASIC VEGETABLE CUTS

(See Figure 2.1.)

English	French	Description
small dice	brunoise	⅛″ square
medium dice	jardinière	¼″ square
large dice	macedoine	⅓ to ½″ square
pea (also *pearl*)	pois (*perle*)	tiny ball or sphere
medium sphere	noisette	a medium ball (sphere)
Parisienne	Parisienne	a large ball (sphere)
julienne	julienne	a small rectangle
slivered (or shredded)	chiffonade	a thin ribbon, usually for green leafy vegetables
julienne	julienne	⅛″ × ⅛″ × 1″
thin sliced	Vichy	a thin circular slice

•

Jardinière means "of the garden," in reference to the origin of vegetables; macédoine has its origins in ancient Macedonia, the area comprised of modern-day Persia, Greece, and Egypt, that was ruled over by Alexander the Great (356–323 B.C.); a *julienne* refers to a small rectangle, and its size depends on its use (a very large version is known as a *batonnet* ["little stick"], which measures roughly ¼″ × ¼″ × 2 to 2½″); Vichy is a town in central France whose natural hot springs have made it a celebrated spa. The use of the term here is a bit of a stretch. It is derived from a dish typical of the region—Vichy Carrots—thin-sliced carrots simmered in mineral water and seasoned with chopped parsley (no fat, no salt).

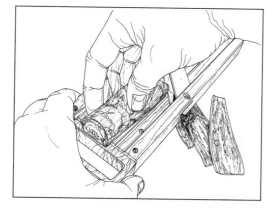

When cutting a vegetable into julienne or dice for use as a garnish, it is important that they be of uniform size—an exemplary way to demonstrate the care that went into preparing the dish to which they apply. (Some of the big country soups, such as Borscht, Garbure, and Minestrone, call for a more relaxed approach to garniture.) Such uniformity can be expedited using a mandoline, of which there are several varieties. The one shown is imported from Japan (brand name, "Benriner") and comes with a slicing guard and three sizes of julienne blades. Here a carrot is being cut into thin slices.

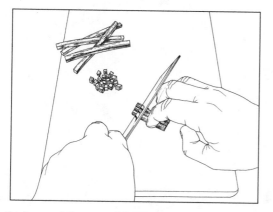

The thickness of the vegetable slices and subsequent thickness of the julienne strips will determine the size of the dice. Here, a large dice (macedoine, 1/3–1/2-inch square) and a medium dice (jardinière, 1/4-inch square) are cut from julienned strips.

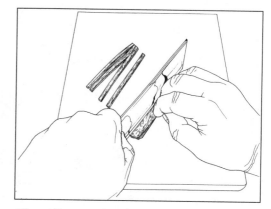

These slices can then be squared off and cut into a large julienne . . .

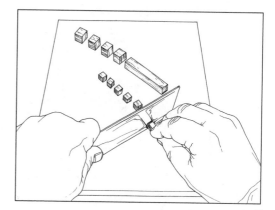

. . . which are then cut into a small dice (brunoise, 1/8-inch square).

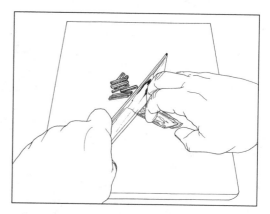

The squared-off carrot slices can also be cut into a fine julienne.

Figure 2.1

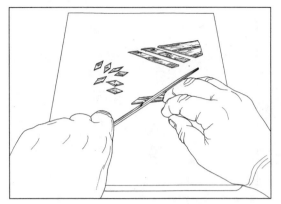

The same squared-off slices can also be cut on the bias in two directions, creating a small diamond-shaped garnish (See Maria Consommé, page 88).

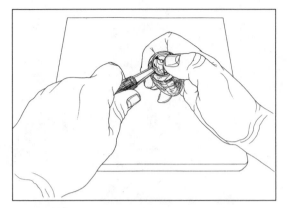

When cutting a carrot into a large sphere (Parisienne), it is advisable to keep a thumb on the cutter while the other hand works the cutter back and forth, radially, into the carrot.

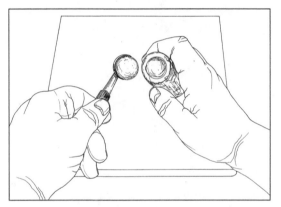

After the sphere is removed, the carrot can be trimmed back so that another sphere can be cut.

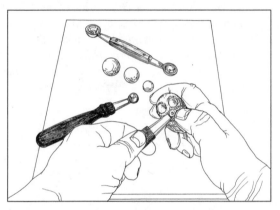

Four size variations of spherical garnish (from left to right): standard Parisienne, small Parisienne, noisette, and pois (pronounced "pwa"; also referred to as pea or pearl).

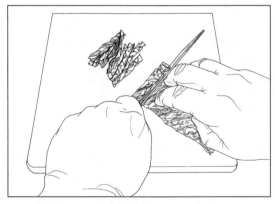

Cutting lettuce (or basil, sorrel, spinach, etc.) into chiffonade.

Figure 2.1 (Cont.)

CHAPTER 3

CLEAR SOUPS

*N*ote: Clear soups are traditionally divided up into two categories: bouillon (broths) and consommé. The problem with this categorization is that bouillon is also referred to as simple consommé (in English, broth), while a formal consommé is technically a double consommé (consommé double). Many regional soups, such as Manhattan Clam Chowder, Minestrone, Pot au Feu, Olla Podrida, and so on, fall under the heading of bouillon as well, further complicating the issue. For this reason, only a handful of bouillons are included under the following category of consommés, while the clear broth-based soups from different countries are included in the section Regional and National Soups. For further clarification, see Bouillons versus Consommés, page 29.

CONSOMMÉ

Consommé is an ultra-clear, highly flavored liquid extract, prepared from meat, game, poultry, or fish; aromatic vegetables; and herbs and spices. It has its roots in "consummate," from the Latin *consummare*—in this case, meaning "to bring to perfection." It is probably the soup genre Escoffier was referring to when he spoke of soup exacting "the most delicate perfection and the strictest attention." Consommé does require considerable time and attention for such a brief gastronomic experience at the beginning of a meal. But for those who appreciate its simplicity, crystal-clear clarity, and delectable aroma, it is an apex of achievement.

Consommé as Cultural Artifact

Many of the consommés included in the following section contain ingredients that are either very expensive or very difficult to obtain. In addition, some garnishes are quite complex, and their production in most commercial restaurant operations would be both time-consuming and hardly appreciated for all of the labor involved. They are included nevertheless, if only to reveal this large body of unique and special soups, many of which are named for personalities, occupations, or locales. We do not presume to revive classical broths entirely, but rather present these classical consommés as a lively and intriguing perspective through which to view the cultural and culinary mind-set of the day. It is here that one meets artists and authors, gourmands and gastronomes, poets and philosophers, statesmen and revolutionaries through dishes prepared in their honor or prepared with ingredients that suited their own preferences during their lifetime. As Leonard N. Beck wrote (in *Two Loaf-Givers*), "There should be no need to argue that the kitchen window is a good observatory from which to watch the course of history."

Consider then Napoléon Consommé (chicken), garnished

with triangular-shaped raviolis filled with a purée of foie gras. It is easy to imagine that these triangular ravioli are a miniature imitation of the emperor's well-known chapeau, with the goose liver representing the Corsican's political career in France. Culinarians know that Soubise indicates onion and that Soubise Consommé (beef) is garnished with onion royale (custard), reflecting eighteenth-century aristocrat Charles de Rohan's (the Prince of Soubise) affinity for onion purée. And finally, there is Leo XIII Consommé, a beef and veal consommé garnished with plain royale cut into the shapes of crosses and the papal tiara. Other intriguing dishes include Artagnan Consommé (Consommé Artagnan; beef), flavored with essence of heathcock and garnished with strips of heathcock meat and peas; Benevent Consommé (Consommé Benevent; beef), which is flavored with tomato, garnished with julienned beef tongue and small macaroni; Indian Style Consommé (Consommé à l'Indienne; chicken), flavored with curry, garnished with diced coconut royale and rice; Nelson Consommé (Consommé Nelson; fish), slightly thickened with arrowroot, garnished with rice, profiteroles stuffed with lobster hash served separately; Nesselrode Consommé (Consommé Nesselrode; game), flavored with hazelhen, garnished with chestnut royale, julienned hazel-hen meat, and diced mushrooms; Oriental Style Consommé (Consommé à l'Orientale; mutton), flavored with tomato juice and saffron, garnished with rice, brain royale cut in the shape of half moons, and hard-cooked egg yolks pressed through a sieve; Rabelais Consommé (Consommé Rabelais; game), flavored with truffle and larks, garnished with julienned celery and lark quenelles flavored with truffle; Rubens Consommé (Consommé Rubens; chicken), flavored with tomato juice, garnished with hop shoots; Spinner's Style Consommé (Consommé à la Filateur; beef), garnished with noodle dough cut into very fine strips.

There are also consommés named simply for the garnish. We have only included a handful of these, since there are plenty of consommés named for individuals and locales, and these bring considerable more personality to the dish than a simply generic variety. There are times, of course, when such simple designation is appropriate. The following is a partial list of such varieties:

Consommés with Generic Nomenclature

Consommé Brunoise (with a mixed vegetable brunoise [fine dice])

Consommé aux Abatis de Volaille (with chicken giblets)

Consommé aux Aillerons de Volaille et Riz (with chicken wings and rice)

Consommé au Cresson (with garden cress)

Consommé Diablotins (with croutons topped with cheese and glazed)

Consommé Julienne (with mixed vegetables cut into julienne strips)

Consommé Macédoine (with mixed vegetables cut into medium to large dice)

Consommé aux Nouilles (with any variety of noodle; also called *aux Pâtes d'Italie*)

Consommé aux Perles (with mixed vegetables cut into miniature spheres)

Consommé à l'Orge Perlé (with pearl barley)

Consommé aux Oeufs Pochés (with poached eggs)

Consommé Printinier (with spring vegetables)

Consommé aux Quenelles (with quenelles)

Consommé aux Profiteroles (with profiteroles)

Consommé aux Raviolis (with raviolis)

Consommé au Riz (with rice)

Consommé Royale (with squares or diamond-shaped custard)

Consommé au Vermicelli (with vermicelli)

Bouillon versus Consommé

While a stock is made from bones and aromatics, a bouillon is made with bones, aromatics, and a portion of the flesh of beef, veal, poultry, game, or fish, depending on the type of bouillon. The long, slow simmering that yields a clear stock is also essential to a bouillon, and the addition of meat simply brings more flavor than that derived solely from bones, as well as additional albumin, which aids in the natural clarification process.

The term *bouillon* comes from the French *bouillir*, meaning "to boil." In nineteenth-century France, an old-fashioned herb bouillon was made of sorrel, lettuce and chervil leaves that were simmered with sea salt, beaten with butter, and strained. There was also a vegetable bouillon made by simmering vegetable peels and trimmings, and even a cereal bouillon prepared as a nutrient-rich beverage for children. In these cases there is no meat ingredient; therefore, in modern nomenclature such preparations would be classified as essences or simply stocks.

Technically speaking, in the stock-bouillon-consommé family, *bouillon* is also referred to as "simple consommé," while *consommé* is referred to as "consommé double" (double-strength consommé). Preparing consommé from a basic stock does not imply that the stock is unclear; it is simply a separate step ensuring the utmost clarity and intense flavor. Also, when a consommé is served bourgeois style—in a home setting—what is served is a bouillon (also known as *simple consommé*); a consommé (*consommé double*) is served in a formal dining circumstance and is a clear stock re-clarified with beef, egg whites, tomatoes, and aromatics to ensure its clarity and intense flavor. While these definitions alone can be confusing (common parlance often varies from kitchen to kitchen), the important elements are the ambiance of the service setting—in the home or at a formal dinner—and the clarity, flavor, and aroma of the brew.

---•---

Many years ago, when I was a tournant (rounds cook) at the Woodstock Inn in Vermont, the practice was to fill a large tilting skillet with roasted veal shanks, bones, and aromatics, and just barely simmer it 24 hours a day for nearly a week at a time. The "simple consommé" that was drawn from a spigot at the bottom of the skillet was so clear and well-flavored that it was served in the dining room directly from the spigot as consommé. Hot water was added to replace whatever was drawn off, and when the flavor of the ingredients was spent, the skillet was drained and cleaned out, and the process was started all over again.

To Prepare Consommé

Consommé is begun with a good clear stock—very gelatinous, indicating a flavorful extraction—and with the congealed fat removed from its top. Ground beef, beaten egg whites, roughly chopped mirepoix and tomatoes, and salt are blended together, then combined with the cold stock in a heavy-gauge stockpot, stirred well, and placed over a medium-high flame. At this point it must be stirred once every few minutes to prevent the egg whites—which are heavier than the cold stock—from settling down and burning on the bottom of the stockpot. Once the temperature reaches 100°F (38°C), the egg whites and other clarifying ingredients begin solidifying and floating up towards the top of the stock. Stirring should continue, though, just until the mixture barely begins to simmer. At this point stirring is discontinued, and the heat is adjusted to bring the stock down to a bare simmer.

Although the stock the consommé is made from has already been flavored with mirepoix and bouquet garni, these aromatics are usually added again as part of the clarification ingredients, both to fortify flavor and to provide solid parts that add strength to the raft.

As the brew quietly simmers, a "raft" will begin to form on the surface. This is made up of the albumen in the egg whites and ground beef that is slowly coagulating from the heat of the simmer. For the next 2 hours the liquid stock moves rhythmically within the pot in a convection movement through this raft as it coagulates, trapping minute particles and impurities in the stock, leaving it completely clear.

The raft must then be cut open very gently, so that the broth can be ladled out. A perforated skimmer is used for this step, and the clear broth underneath the raft is poured through a fine strainer known as a bouillon strainer (chinois mousseline). In the absence of a bouillon strainer, a larger-holed strainer lined with four layers of cheesecloth will work just as well (rinse it first to be sure the cheesecloth is clean!). The straining is necessary, because no matter how carefully one cuts through the raft, some bits and pieces of it invariably break off and float off into the broth.

If the consommé is to be served soon after preparation, clean paper towels dabbed onto its surface will remove any vestige of fat before serving (a proper consommé has virtually no fat). Be sure the consommé is served very hot, and add the garnish to each serving bowl at the moment of service.

ℬEEF CONSOMMÉ
(Consommé de Boeuf)

2 gallons (7.7 L) rich brown beef stock

1 cup (240 mL) dry tomato purée

6 pounds (27 kg) ground lean beef

6 egg whites, briefly beaten with . . .

½ cup (120 mL) dry red wine

1 celery stalk, trimmed, rinsed, and finely chopped

1 carrot, peeled, top removed, and finely chopped

1 small Spanish onion, finely chopped

1 small leek, white part only, finely chopped, and well rinsed

1 bunch parsley stems, trimmed, rinsed, and finely chopped

1 bay leaf

1 sprig thyme

1 tablespoon (15 mL) black peppercorns, cracked

- Combine all the ingredients in a heavy-gauge stockpot, and blend thoroughly. Place over a medium fire, and gently stir once every five minutes, until the mixture gets warm, about 100°F (38°C).

- When the brew just barely begins to simmer, turn the fire down low enough to maintain the barest simmer. Allow to simmer for two hours.

- Using a perforated skimmer, very gently cut and lift out a portion of the "raft" that has formed on top. Remove the clear broth underneath the raft, using a ladle, straining it through several layers of muslin.

- Return the consommé to the fire, bring to a boil, and hold in a hot bain marie until ready for service.

Stocks derived from chicken, duck, game, lamb, or mutton can all be clarified by substituting the variety of stock.

CHICKEN CONSOMMÉ
(Consommé de Volaille)

2 gallons (7.7 L) chicken stock (cold)

the juice of 1 lemon

6 pounds (27 kg) coarsely ground chicken

6 egg whites, briefly beaten with . . .

1 cup (240 mL) dry white wine

1 celery stalk, trimmed, rinsed, and finely chopped

1 carrot, peeled, top removed, and finely chopped

1 small Spanish onion, finely chopped

1 small leek, white part only, finely chopped, and well rinsed

1 small bunch parsley stems, trimmed, rinsed, and finely chopped

1 bay leaf

1 sprig thyme

Prepare a game consommé in the same fashion as chicken consommé, substituting game for chicken ingredients.

- Prepare this consommé by following the same instructions used for beef consommé.

$\mathscr{F}$ISH CONSOMMÉ
(Consommé de Poisson)

2 gallons (7.7 L) fish stock
   (cold)
the juice of 1 lemon
6 pounds (27 kg) coarsely
   ground fish (such as cod,
   sole, or whiting)
8 egg whites, briefly beaten
   with . . .
1 cup (240 mL) dry white
   wine
1 celery stalk, trimmed,
   rinsed, and finely chopped

1 Spanish onion, finely
   chopped
1 small leek, white part only,
   finely chopped, and well
   rinsed
1 small bunch parsley stems,
   trimmed, rinsed, and
   finely chopped
1 bay leaf
1 sprig thyme

If the fish stock is intended to be used in a creamed or puréed shellfish soup, the addition of crab, lobster, or shrimp shells transform it into an excellent base for those soups.

- Prepare this consommé by following the same instructions used for beef consommé.

Consommé Garnishes

Profiteroles are miniature cream puffs prepared with pâte à choux—a dough commonly known as "choux paste"—the same dough used to prepare eclairs, duchesses, and cream puffs. *Choux* is also the French term for cabbage, a reference to the appearance of these pastries when baked.

    Profiteroles can be stuffed with sweet or savory fillings varying from custard, whipped cream, ice cream, and jam, to cheese and herb paste, fish salad, ham, or game mousse. In the case of soup, they are prepared very small, sometimes added to a soup plain, or stuffed with a meat, poultry, game, or fish paste.

$\mathscr{P}$ÂTE À CHOUX

½ cup (120 mL) water
½ cup (120 mL) milk
5 tablespoons (75 mL)
   unsalted butter, cut into
   1-inch (25-mm) pieces

pinch of salt
1 cup (240 mL) + 2
   tablespoons (30 mL) flour
3 eggs

- Bring the water, milk, butter, and salt to a boil in a noncorrosive pan. When the butter has melted, add the flour and blend thoroughly until it forms a ball of paste that comes away from the side of the pan (add a little additional flour if necessary). Remove from the fire.

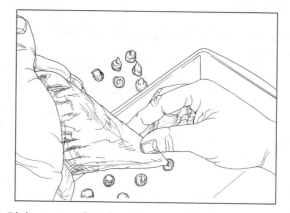

Piping out profiteroles, using a No. 2 or 3 round pastry tip (shown with six baked profiteroles). They are sometimes stuffed with a mousse or purée of some kind.

Figure 3.1

- When the paste has cooled slightly, add the eggs, one at a time, and stir until completely incorporated. Continue adding and incorporating the eggs, one at a time.
- Scoop the paste out with a rubber spatula, and place in a pastry bag fitted with a #2 or #3 round tip. Pipe out on a lightly greased pan, allowing a ½-inch space between each piece to allow for expansion. Bake in a preheated 350°F (176°C) oven for 8 minutes or until golden brown. (See Figure 3.1.)

When quenelles are called for as a garnish, but are not specified as to their type, one is free to decide which variety to use. Quenelles are most commonly made from chicken or fish, though they can also be made from veal or game; their logical use will be in the same variety of consommé, though veal and chicken quenelles work in most soups (with the exception of a fish-based soup).

*B*ASIC CHICKEN QUENELLES

1 pound (450 g) boneless, skinless chicken breast, cut into 1-inch pieces
1 shallot, minced
1 cup (240 mL) dry white wine

1 bay leaf
2 tablespoons (30 mL) butter, softened
6 tablespoons (90 mL) flour
3 eggs

⅔ cup (160 mL) heavy
cream, very cold

salt and white pepper to taste
court bouillon as needed

- Place the chicken in the freezer for 30 minutes. Simmer the shallots and wine until nearly dry. Discard the bay leaf, and allow to cool. Blend the butter and flour into a smooth paste.
- Place the chicken, shallots, butter/flour paste in a food processor, and purée, using the pulse switch.
- Add the eggs, one at a time, and incorporate, still using the pulse switch. Add the cream in a slow steady stream, again using the pulse switch. Take a small portion of the farce out, poach and taste, and check for seasoning.
- Moisten a teaspoon and the palm of one hand with cold water. Scoop out a small amount of the farce, and shape into a smooth oval in the moistened palm. Place in barely simmering bouillon, and simmer until fully cooked (about 5 minutes). (See Figure 3.2.)

To prepare small dumplings, prepare the following batter:

.... $\mathscr{A}$ **BASIC DUMPLING BATTER**

4 eggs
¾ cup (180 mL) flour
pinch of salt

pinch of nutmeg
3 tablespoons (45 mL)
 melted butter

- Beat the eggs, flour, and salt into a smooth paste. Add the butter, and blend thoroughly. Allow to rest for 30 minutes.
- Pour the batter through a small-holed colander (or a spaetzle maker) into simmering stock (or 375°F [191°C] deep fat in the case of Cavour Consommé and Doria Consommé). Remove with a slotted spoon when cooked, and place into the soup at service.

Royale is custard, a garnish commonly used in consommés. It can be served plain, as in Consommé Royale, or flavored with various ingredients, including almonds, asparagus, celery, Madeira wine, peas, puréed game, tomato, truffle, and so on. The basic recipes are as follows:

Quenelles are scooped out with a small spoon that has been dipped in water (in this case, Basic Chicken Quenelles).

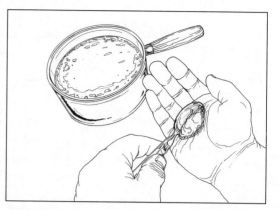

The farce is shaped into small ovals in the palm of a moistened (and well-scrubbed) hand.

They are then poached separately in stock or court bouillon and then added to the soup.

Figure 3.2
Shaping quenelles

.... 𝓑ASIC ROYALE

2 egg yolks
¾ cup consommé (or rich
   stock)

salt and white pepper to
   taste
2 eggs

• Heat the consommé until it liquifies. Beat the eggs and then pour slowly into the consommé while continuously beating the mixture. Pour into a well-buttered ovenproof container.

Set into a hot water bath, cover, and bake in a preheated 350°F (176°C) oven for 15 minutes or until a toothpick that has been inserted comes out clean. Carefully invert to unmold, allow to cool, and then cut into designated shape.

 FLAVORED ROYALE

1 cup vegetable purée
   (asparagus, celery,
   spinach, tomato, truffle,
   etc.)
½" cup very thick Béchamel
   sauce (not hot)

6 eggs
12 egg yolks
salt and white pepper to
   taste

• Follow the same directions as for Basic Royale.

———————————— • ————————————

The Béchamel can be substituted with a 75 percent reduction of heavy cream.

Royale is very soft, and must be handled with care. And whether it is called for in diced, sliced, or circular form, the pieces should be fairly large—roughly ½ inch (13 mm) square or round.

Additional Notes on Preparing Specific Consommés

The garnish of a consommé is extremely important, since it will be magnified in the crystal-clear broth. Consequently, whether the garnish is vegetable brunoise or vegetable pearls (miniature balls), lettuce chiffonade, julienned crêpe, or profiteroles, it is important to take the extra time to cut the pieces uniformly. (See The Basic Cuts, page 19).

When small lettuce or cabbage balls are called for in a soup, they can be prepared by rolling up a small leaf of poached lettuce or cabbage, or by pressing the same firmly into a Parisienne scoop, then gently tapping it out.

Vegetables, sauerkraut, vermicelli, and rice used for garnish can be blanched in a little stock or in salted water (mushrooms should be sautéed in butter and rinsed with white wine), then strained, and the liquid discarded so that no residue, fat, or starch that might cloud the soup is added. The exception to this is when a recipe calls for tapioca to thicken the consommé (tapioca is used because it thickens without clouding).

In consideration of table etiquette, when a noodle—cappellini, spaghetti, or vermicelli—is called for as a garnish, it should be broken into short pieces (1 to 3 inches/25 to 75 mm) before cooking, in order to spare dining guests the potential embarrassment of having to navigate around and/or slurp strands of pasta that may hang off their spoon. Where a small macaroni is called for (macaroni is a generic term), a small version should be used, such as ditalini—a small cylindrical noodle, about an eighth of an inch (3 mm) in length. Though pasta nomenclature varies considerably, depending on where it is produced, there are hundreds of other varieties to choose from, including conchigliette (very small shells), coralini (very small ditalini), farfallini (small bows), pennette (a small penne, an imitation of a pen quill), puntette (in the shape of rice, also called *riso*), stellette (miniature stars), and mezze tubetti (small elbow).

A number of consommés call for garnishes derived from the head of a calf. Some may find this an unpleasant thought, but "tête de veau" is considered a gastronomic delicacy in French cookery, and in truth veal bones are derived from the same source, even if they do not visibly appear to be connected with a sentient creature.

Even though some consommés call for thickening with tapioca, arrowroot, rice flour, or sago, in contemporary practice such practice is a matter of preference. A fine consommé is a labor of love and a work of culinary art—the use of instant thickeners seems to run contrary to its essential elegance and we prefer not to employ them. For the purist who prefers to adhere to traditional recipes, we suggest using such thickeners where called for, in small proportion, augmented by more quality-oriented thickeners such as roux or beurre manié, or puréed rice, potatoes, vegetables, and so on.

———————————— • ————————————

Sago is a starch derived from a tropical plant of the same name. At the end of the seventeenth century, it was one of the most popular thickening agents in Europe and was used as a garnish or thickener of soups, for making soft rolls, and thickening spiced milk. In Asia it has been used both as a thickener for dessert puddings and jellies, as well as a fabric stiffener.

———————————————————————

There are occasions involving time restraints when consommé must be prepared using hot stock. In such a case, take the meat, egg white, tomato, and vegetable mixture, and blend it with roughly double its volume in ice cubes. Beat this into the hot stock and continue with the normal method of preparation.

"Pearls" of various vegetables are miniature balls cut with a small scoop—in common parlance a "pea" or "pois" scoop, the same shape as a Parisienne scoop (also known as a melon baller), except smaller. (See The Basic Cuts, page 19.)

Chervil is an herb commonly used in consommé both for its delicate flavor and visually attractive leaves. It is a sibling of parsley; both chervil and parsley are botanical members of the carrot family. It is slightly more delicate than parsley, but when not available can be substituted for with flat-leaf parsley. It is added chopped, cut into chiffonade (small ribbons), or in leaf form.

Foie gras—fattened goose or duck liver—is an ingredient in a number of quenelle garnishes. There are two producers in the United States (see Appendix), and their foie gras is made solely from duck.

When one sees grated cheese in Italian and certain other Mediterranean-based dishes, one is inclined to think only of Parmesan. There are other varieties, including Pecorino Romano, made with goat's milk instead of cow's milk; and Dried Monterey Jack, which is unique to California.

———————————— • ————————————

During World War II, when Parmesan imported from Italy became virtually unavailable, the Monterey Jack cheese producers in northern California increased production of this semi-soft cheese, which was first produced by Scottish immigrants to Monterey Bay in the mid-nineteenth century. When the war ended and the traditional cheeses became available again, there was suddenly a huge surplus of Jack cheese. Thomas Vella, whose son Ignatius ("Ig"), currently operates the three-generation-old Vella Cheese Company in Sonoma, California, constructed storage rooms for this surplus, hoping that demand might once again reach previous levels. It never did, at least for the fresh cheese. But in the process he discovered that aged Monterey Jack created a hard and very flavorful grating cheese, similar to those of Italy. Today it is one of the finest cheeses produced in North America. The large balls of Jack are coated with a mixture of olive oil and unsweetened cocoa powder, and aged from 6 months to 2 years.

When a consommé is described as being flavored with tomato, or tarragon, or curry, one of those ingredients is simply added to the clarifying mixture to impart that additional flavor. In the case of herbs, it is fiscally wise to use only stems, utilizing the leaves for other dishes.

BEEF CONSOMMÉ

A variation of the garnish consists of filling the croustade with puréed vegetables, sprinkling with grated cheese, gratinéeing, then setting into the broth.

Aremberg, also spelled Arenberg, was a royal family whose name stems from a small town of the same name near Bonn, Germany (see Aremberg Consommé under chicken consommé, page 70).

African Style Consommé (*Consommé à l'Africaine*)

Beef consommé garnished with rice, diced artichoke bottoms, and curry-flavored profiteroles.

Ancient Style Consommé (*Consommé Croûte au Pot à l'Ancienne*)

Beef consommé poured over a small hollowed-out roll (croustade) that has been brushed with butter and toasted in the oven, then filled with an assortment of vegetables (celery, carrots, onions, leeks, string beans, etc.) cut in uniform shape. (See Figure 3.3.)

Andalusian Style Ham Bouillon (*Consommé de Jambon à l'Andalouse*)

Simple beef consommé prepared with the addition of ham hocks and bones, strained, garnished with rice and diced tomato royale (see recipe for Royale, page 37).

Angel's Hair Consommé (*Consommé aux Cheveux d'Anges*)

Beef consommé garnished with cappellini.

Aremberg Consommé (*Consommé Aremberg*)

Beef consommé garnished with green peas; carrot, turnip, and truffle pearls; and chervil.

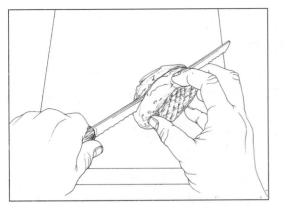

To make a croustade, slice off the top from a small hard roll.

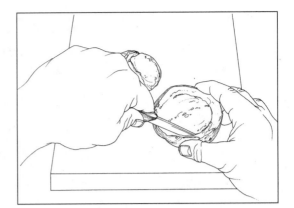

Score the inside edge of the roll with a paring knife.

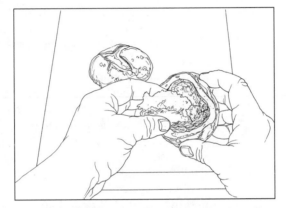

Tear out the bread from the interior of the roll, brush with butter or olive oil, and bake in a moderate oven until golden brown.

Figure 3.3
Making a croustade from a small roll

Artagnan Consommé
(Consommé Artagnan)

Beef consommé flavored with essence of heathcock, garnished with strips of heathcock meat and green peas.

Aulagnier Consommé
(Consommé Aulagnier)

Beef consommé garnished with green peas and julienned cabbage.

Aurora Consommé
(Consommé Aurore)

Beef consommé flavored with tomato juice, slightly thickened with tapioca, and garnished with julienned chicken breast.

Baron Brisse Consommé
(Consommé Baron Brisse)

Beef consommé garnished with rice and three types of diced royale: plain (basic), green (spinach), and black (truffle).

———————————— • ————————————

Baron Léon Brisse (1813–1876) became a culinary journalist after leaving a minor government position following a scandal (he was known to be rather malevolent). His recipes were published daily in *La Liberté,* moving colleagues to nickname him "the newspaper gastrophile." He wrote two cookbooks on bourgeois home cooking—*Recettes à l'usage des ménages bourgeois et des petite ménages* (1868) and *La Petite Cuisine du baron brisse* (1870)—and another on Carême—*La Cuisine en carême* (1873). His name is given to several dishes, including *Tournedos Baron Brisse,* two beef medallions topped with tomato concassé, garnished with artichoke bottoms filled with truffle pearls, soufflé potatoes, and brown truffle (Périgordine) sauce.

Basque Style Consommé
(Consommé à la Basquaise)

Beef consommé garnished with diced (or julienned) green and red bell peppers, diced tomatoes, and rice.

Benevent Consommé
(Consommé Benevent)

Beef consommé flavored with tomato, garnished with julienned beef tongue and small macaroni.

Berny Consommé
(Consommé Berny)

Beef consommé slightly thickened with tapioca, garnished with small balls of deep-fried Dauphine potatoes (mixed with chopped almonds and truffles).

Dauphine Potatoes

1 part mashed potatoes
1 part pâte à choux

- The mashed potatoes are seasoned with salt, pepper, and a little butter, then blended together thoroughly with the choux paste. They are typically shaped into ½-inch balls, deep fried at 375°F (190°C) until golden brown, then added to the soup at service.

Dauphine potatoes consist of mashed potatoes mixed with pâte à choux, formed into various shapes, and deep fried. Additional ingredients (such as the almonds and truffle above) are added as pertains to a particular dish; shapes can be changed as well.

Bismarck Consommé
(Consommé Bismarck)

Beef consommé flavored with Port, slightly thickened with arrowroot, garnished with diced mushrooms and grated cheddar cheese.

Prince Otto Eduard Leopold von Bismarck (1815–1898), nicknamed the "Iron Chancellor," was instrumental in initiating the Franco-Prussian War. Prussia's victory made him a hero, and he was appointed first chancellor of the German empire. He initiated administrative reforms, developed a common currency, a central bank, and a single code of commercial and civil law. He was also the first major statesman to establish a comprehensive plan of social security, giving workers accident and health insurance, and a retirement pension.

Brancas Consommé
(Consommé Brancas)

Beef consommé garnished with rice, lettuce and sorrel chiffonade, vermicelli, julienned mushrooms, and chervil leaves.

Fresh pimento closely resembles a red bell pepper, except that it is slightly pointed at one end. In dried and ground form it is known as paprika; it is also found preserved in small jars though it is rather tasteless in that form (roasted and peeled red bell peppers are superior).

Brasilian Style Consommé
(Consommé à la Brésilienne)

Beef consommé garnished with rice and julienned vegetables, including pimento.

Breton Style Consommé
(Consommé à la Bretonne)

Beef consommé garnished with julienned celery root, leek, and mushrooms, and chopped chervil.

Brighton Style Consommé
(Consommé à la Brighton)

Beef consommé flavored with sherry, garnished with small veal quenelles, and julienned calf's head ("tête de veau") and vegetables.

Butcher's Style Consommé
(Consommé à la Bouchère)

Beef consommé garnished with small cabbage balls and sliced poached beef marrow.

Marrow is a soft, fatty material in the center of bones, high in protein, and an essential ingredient in stocks, and certain dishes and sauces. The marrow of beef bones can be retrieved by poaching a small section of leg bone that has been cut open at both ends, by simmering it in salted water until soft enough to push gently out through one end. When cool it solidifies, making it easier to slice.

Camerani Consommé
(Consommé Camerani)

Beef consommé garnished with diced celery, carrots, and leeks braised in butter, and small macaroni.

Barthélemy-André Camerani (1735–1816), well-known gourmand and comedian, was a member of Grimod de La Reynièr's "Jury of Tasters." While performing at the Opéra Comique, his popularity was such that a baked Neopolitan-style pasta dish (layers of small macaroni, and shredded vegetables with diced chicken livers, topped with grated cheese) was concurrently served at the Café Anglais.

Camino Consommé
(Consommé Camino)

Beef consommé garnished with small dumplings made from thick crêpe batter flavored with grated cheese (see previous note on dumplings, page 35).

Carlton Consommé
(Consommé Carlton)

Beef consommé garnished with diced royale, small quenelles, and profiteroles flavored with grated cheese.

Carmen Consommé
(Consommé Carmen)

Beef consommé flavored with tomato, garnished with rice, julienned green pepper, and chervil.

Catalonian Style Consommé
(Consommé à la Catalane)

Beef consommé garnished with rice, diced tomatoes, and julienned green pepper.

Caux Style Consommé
(Consommé à la Cauchoise)

Beef consommé garnished with diced bacon and lamb fried very crisp, and finely sliced vegetables braised in butter.

Chancelor's Consommé
(Consommé Chancelière)

Beef consommé garnished with green pea royale, and julienned chicken breast, truffles, and mushrooms.

Charivari Consommé
(Consommé Charivari)

Beef consommé garnished with julienned carrot, cabbage, celery root, onions, and turnip.

Charley Consommé
(Consommé Charley)

Beef consommé slightly thickened with tapioca, garnished with asparagus tips, small poached eggs, and chervil.

Charolaise Bouillon
(Consommé de Queue de Boeuf à la Charolaise)

Simple beef-tail consommé garnished with small pearl onions, carrot pearls, the diced meat from the tail, and small balls of cooked cabbage.

———————————— • ————————————

Charolaise is the French term for a bony piece of meat cut from the elbow of the animal; oxtail is the common term for beef tail. Both cuts are highly gelatinous and make very flavorful stocks.

The cabbage garnish can be made by cutting the leaves into 1-inch (25-mm) squares, blanching them, pressing 2 or 3 squares firmly into a Parisienne scoop, and gently tapping them out into the soup.

————— • —————

Raviolis can be easily made using wonton wrappers, a very thin flour and water dough available in most Asian markets.

Charterhouse Consommé
(Consommé Chartreuse)

Beef consommé slightly thickened with tapioca, garnished with very small raviolis filled with a chicken farce flavored with goose liver, mushrooms, and spinach.

Cherbourg Style Consommé
(Consommé à la Cherbourg)

Beef consommé flavored with Madeira, garnished with julienned truffle and mushroom, ham quenelles, and small poached eggs.

Choiseul Style Consommé
(Consommé à la Choiseul)

Beef consommé garnished with asparagus tips and royale cut into fancy shapes.

Clarmont Consommé
(Consommé Clarmont)

Beef consommé garnished with fried onion rings and small circles of royale.

Clothilde Consommé
(Consommé Clothilde)

Beef consommé garnished with small pearl onions stewed in butter.

Saint Clothilde (also Clotilda, Chlothlde, Chrodechilde; d. 545), a native of Burgundy, was queen consort to Clovis I, an early Merovingian king. She bore him four sons: Ingomer, and the future kings Clodomir, Childebert I, and Chlotar I. During this time, a cultural battle ensued among the dozens of pagan tribes that existed following the end of the ancient Roman Empire. Clothilde was an ardent Catholic and unwavering in her efforts to convert Clovis to her faith. He eventually did so, following a battle against the Alemannians. After his death she retired to Tours and became famous for her generosity to the church and charity work. She was buried beside her husband in what is now the church of Sainte-Geneviève in Paris.

Colbert Consommé
(Consommé Colbert)

Beef consommé garnished with pearls or small diced spring vegetables, and small poached eggs.

Jean-Baptiste Colbert (1619–1683), the son of a merchant family and a promoter of French economic self-sufficiency, he later served as finance minister and secretary of the navy under Louis XIV. In 1651, when Cardinal Mazarin was politically forced into exile, Colbert secretly served as his agent in Paris; when Mazarin returned to power, he made Colbert his personal assistant. On his deathbed, Mazarin recommended him to Louis XIV, and he subsequently worked in service to the king for the next 25 years.

Dalayrac Consommé
(Consommé Dalayrac)

Beef consommé slightly thickened with tapioca, garnished with julienned chicken, mushrooms, and truffles.

Truffles have been famed for centuries for their mystical and aphrodisiac qualities. Brillat-Savarin called them "the diamonds of cookery"; in Italian they are called *perle della cucina*, "pearls of the kitchen"; and in the first century, the Roman satirist Juvenal told the Libyans, "Keep your wheat, and send us your truffles."

The d'Aumonts were a French noble family that produced many notable military heroes dating back to Pierre I d'Aumont (d. 1381), councilor and chamberlain to John II and Charles V.

Daumont Consommé
(Consommé Daumont)

Beef consommé slightly thickened with tapioca, garnished with rice, and julienned beef tongue and mushrooms.

Deslignac Consommé
(Consommé Deslignac)

Beef consommé garnished with royale cut into circles, small lettuce balls, and chervil.

Don Carlos Consommé
(Consommé Don Carlos)

Beef consommé garnished with squares of royale, diced tomato, and chervil.

Dubarry Consommé
(Consommé Dubarry)

Beef consommé slightly thickened with tapioca, garnished with squares of cucumber royale and cauliflower flowerettes.

———————————— • ————————————

Marie-Jeanne Bécu, the Comtesse du Barry (1743–1793), Louis XV's influential confidant and last courtesan (dishes thus named always contain cauliflower). The illegitimate child of lower-class parents, she received a convent education, and became the mistress of Jean du Barry, a Gascon nobleman who had made a fortune as a war contractor. Her beauty attracted a series of nobly born lovers, but in order to qualify as official royal mistress, a position vacant since the death of Madame de Pompadour (1764), a marriage was arranged between her and du Barry's brother Guillaume. In 1769 she joined Louis XV's court; shortly after he died (1774) she was banished to a nunnery. In 1793 she was condemned as a counter-revolutionary by the Revolutionary Tribunal for having provided financial assistance to French émigrés in London, and was guillotined in December 1793.

Dumesnil Consommé
(Consommé Dumesnil)

Beef consommé garnished with julienned vegetables, sliced beef bone marrow, and chervil.

Dumont Consommé
(Consommé Dumont)

Beef consommé garnished with julienned beef tongue, cabbage, and mushrooms.

François Dumont (1751–1831) was a celebrated miniature painter who painted portraits of Louis XVI, Marie Antoinette, Louis XVIII, Charles X, and many celebrated personalities of his day.

Elisabeth Consommé
(Consommé Elisabeth)

Beef consommé garnished with julienned artichoke bottoms and leek, vermicelli, and grated cheese.

Farmer's Style Consommé
(Consommé à la Fermière)

Beef consommé garnished with julienned root vegetables and diced potatoes.

Farmer's Wife's Style Consommé
(Consommé à la Belle Fermière)

Beef consommé garnished with julienned cabbage, diced green beans, and small square noodles.

Flower Girl Style Consommé
(Consommé à la Bouquetière)

Beef consommé garnished with green peas, diced green beans, asparagus tips, and small-diced carrot and turnip.

Frankforter Style Consommé
(Consommé à la Francfortoise)

Beef consommé flavored with juniper berries, garnished with julienned red cabbage (poached in stock) and sliced Frankfurter sausage; grated cheese served separately.

Franklin Consommé
(Consommé Franklin)

Beef consommé flavored garnished with carrot and turnip pearls, profiteroles, and diced vegetable royale.

Garibaldi Consommé
(Consommé Garibaldi)

Beef consommé garnished with diced tomatoes and spaghetti.

———————————————— • ————————————————

Giuseppe Garibaldi (1807–1882) was a passionate general known for his use of guerrilla-fighting tactics that he learned while leading the Uruguayan navy against Argentina in 1842. An internationally known champion of Italian nationalism, he also believed strongly in racial equality, women's emancipation, and the abolition of capital punishment. President Abraham Lincoln offered him a command (1861) during the American Civil War, but he declined in part because Lincoln's condemnation of slavery was not broad enough and because Lincoln refused to grant him supreme command of the Federal troops.

German Style Consommé
(Consommé à l'Allemande)

Beef consommé garnished with julienned red cabbage and sliced frankfurters.

Germinal Consommé
(Consommé Germinal)

Beef consommé flavored with tarragon, garnished with green peas, diced beans, asparagus tips, and small chicken quenelles seasoned with tarragon and chervil.

Girondine Consommé
(Consommé Girondine)

Beef consommé garnished with diced ham royale and julienned carrots.

Green Vegetable Consommé
(Consommé Vermandoise)

Beef consommé slightly thickened with tapioca, garnished with asparagus tips, diced string beans, lettuce and sorrel chiffonade, and green peas.

Grenade Consommé
(Consommé Grenade)

Beef consommé garnished with ham royale cut in the shape of grenades, diced tomatoes, and chervil.

Grimaldi Consommé
(Consommé Grimaldi)

Beef consommé flavored with tomato, garnished with tomato royale and julienned celery.

Joseph Grimaldi (1778–1837) came from a family of dancers and entertainers, and his talent and influence were such that to this day clowns are sometimes nicknamed "Joey." His performance as a comic mime in *Harlequin and Mother Goose* (1806) is considered his greatest success, for his having portrayed rogue, simpleton, criminal, and innocent dupe in one character.

Gutenberg Consommé
(Consommé Gutenberg)

Beef consommé garnished with asparagus tips, green peas, diced mushrooms, and root vegetables, and sliced Frankfurter sausages.

Johann Gutenberg (1397–1468), German goldsmith and printer, was one of the first Europeans to develop and print with moveable type. In 1448, Gutenberg obtained capital funding from Johann Fust, a wealthy financier. Looking for a quick return on his investment, Fust became impatient and successfully sued Gutenberg in 1455. Fust then funded Peter Schöffer, Gutenberg's son-in-law and former employee, who produced the Psalters (Book of Psalms). Their magnificent scroll borders and multicolored initial letters were all the result of Gutenberg's innovations. Gutenberg died penniless, losing his eyesight, supported by a local official who took pity on the destitute inventor.

Harlequin Consommé
(Consommé Arlequin)

Beef consommé garnished with vermicelli, and three types of small quenelles: yellow (bound with egg yolks), green (spinach), and red (tomato paste).

Housewife Style Consommé
(Consommé à la Bonne Femme)

Beef consommé garnished with diced potatoes, julienned carrots and leeks, and small croutons.

Imperial Style Consommé I
(Consommé à l'Imperial)

Beef consommé garnished with very small cock's combs, cock's kidneys, rice, green peas, and finely julienned vegetables.

Irish Style Consommé
(Consommé à l'Irlandaise)

Beef consommé garnished with diced mutton, pearl barley, small diced mirepoix vegetables, and chervil leaves.

Irma Consommé
(Consommé Irma)

Beef consommé garnished with curry-flavored quenelles and julienned mushrooms.

Italian Style Consommé
(Consommé à l'Italienne)

Beef consommé garnished with diced spinach and tomato royale, macaroni, and grated cheese.

Jacobine Consommé
(Consommé Jacobine)

Beef consommé garnished with diced carrots, green beans, turnips, truffles, and green peas.

The Jacobines were a middle-class (bourgeois) political faction formed in 1789, and named after the monastery of the Jacobins (the Parisian name of the Dominicans) where they first held their meetings. Under Maximilien Robespierre, they instituted the bloody Reign of Terror, although they fell from popular grace when Robespierre himself was guillotined (1794).

Jean-Baptiste Kléber (1753–1800) was a French general of the revolutionary wars, who later fought for Napoléon in his Egyptian campaign (1798–99). Assigned to governing duties in Cairo, he was assassinated by a fanatic.

Kléber Consommé
(Consommé Kléber)

Beef consommé garnished with green peas, diced celery root, goose liver quenelles, and chervil.

Leo XIII Consommé
(Consommé Leo XIII)

Beef and veal consommé garnished with royale cut into the shapes of crosses and the papal tiara.

———————— • ————————

Vincenzo Giocchino Pecci (1810–1903) demonstrated great promise in his early years in the Catholic Church, but his independence and modern thinking led to his confinement to a small diocese in Perugia for 32 years (1846–78). After the death of Pius IX, he was elected Pope on the third ballot, and though many believed his delicate health would precipitate a brief reign, he held the post for a quarter of a century. He is remembered for bringing a new spirit to the papacy, as shown by an awareness of the pastoral and social needs of his day, and for advocating that the church not oppose scientific progress.

————————————————

Ferdinand Marie, the Vicomte de Lesseps (1805–1894), was a French diplomat and the engineer who supervised the building of the Suez Canal (1859–69). He intended to participate in the building of the Panama Canal, but his company went bankrupt in 1888, and he was convicted of misappropriation of funds.

Lesseps Consommé
(Consommé Lesseps)

Beef consommé garnished with diced calf's brain royale and chervil.

Leverrier Consommé
(Consommé Leverrier)

Beef consommé slightly thickened with tapioca, garnished with plain royale cut into the shapes of stars, and chervil leaves.

Urbain Jean Joseph Leverrier (1811–1877), was a French astronomer whose work led to the discovery of the planet Neptune (1846).

Lille Style Consommé
(Consommé à la Lilloise)

Beef consommé flavored with tarragon and chervil, garnished with diced calf's brain royale and chervil.

Londonderry Consommé
(Consommé Londonderry)

Beef consommé flavored with Madeira, slightly thickened with tapioca, and garnished with quenelles and diced calf's brain.

Robert Stewart, Marquess of Londonderry (1769–1822), as secretary of war (1805–1809) coordinated the British effort against Napoléon I's effort to gain control of the Iberian peninsula (The Peninsula Wars). Though considered a great statesman, he was personally cold and never popular. He inherited the marquess title upon his father's death (1821) and committed suicide the following year.

Basil, chervil, fennel, marjoram, and savory are known as turtle herbs and are used to flavor turtle soup; and also turtle sauce, typically served with calf's head and boiled beef tongue.

Dishes so titled are named for Mary Stuart (1542–1587), Queen of Scotland (1561), who was charged with complicity in a plot to murder Elizabeth I, and subsequently beheaded. Her beauty and courage have made her a romantic historical figure and the subject of much literature.

London Style Consommé
(Consommé à la Londonienne)

Beef consommé flavored with turtle herbs, and garnished with quenelles and diced calf's head and rice.

Marquise Consommé
(Consommé Marquise)

Beef consommé flavored with celery, garnished with sliced poached bone marrow, and chicken quenelles mixed with finely chopped hazelnuts.

Mary Stuart Consommé
(Consommé Marie Stuart)

Beef consommé slightly thickened with tapioca, garnished with truffled chicken quenelles.

Médici Consommé
(Consommé Médici)

Beef consommé slightly thickened with tapioca, garnished with green pea royale and carrot royale, and sorrel leaves cut into chiffonade and cooked in butter.

The Médici family, which gained immense wealth in Florence from the fifteenth to early eighteenth centuries, also produced three popes and two French queens. The best known of the clan was Lorenzo ("The Magnificent," 1449–1492), statesman and generous patron of the Florentine Renaissance. His daughter Catherine de Medici (1519–1589) gained notoriety by marrying the Duke of Orléans, the future King Henry II, in 1533. In spite of his attachment to his mistress Diane de Poitiers, Catherine gave birth to ten children, of whom four boys and three girls survived; and she personally supervised their education. She has been variously described as artistic (she designed the Tuileries chateau in Paris), energetic, extroverted, and courageous, as well as a glutton—probably unfairly as a result of many political entanglements—her preferences running to cock's combs, kidneys, and artichoke hearts.

Meissonier Consommé
(Consommé Meissonier)

Beef consommé garnished with diced artichoke bottoms and tomatoes, green peas, and chervil.

Mercédès Consommé
(Consommé Mercédès)

Beef (or chicken) consommé flavored with sherry, garnished with red pepper rings and sliced cock's combs cut into the shape of stars.

Mirette Consommé
(Consommé Mirette)

Beef consommé garnished with small chicken quenelles, lettuce and chervil chiffonade; cheese straws served separately.

Mock-Turtle Consommé
(Consommé Fausse Tortue)

Beef consommé flavored with cayenne pepper, celery, turtle herbs (basil, chervil, fennel, marjoram, and savory), and Madeira, and garnished with diced calf's head and quenelles.

Molière Consommé
(Consommé Molière)

Beef consommé garnished with small bread dumplings; poached bone marrow on toast served separately.

Molière is the pen name of Jean-Baptiste Poquelin (1622–1673), French actor, director, and playwright. The son of a well-to-do upholsterer, he left home at the age of 21 to become an actor. With the success of *Précieuses ridicules* (*The Affected Young Ladies*; 1659) in Paris, his career was under way. He later wrote under the patronage of Louis XIV, producing farces and comedies of manners for the entertainment of the court. *Le Tartuffe* (*The Impostor*), produced in 1664 (revived in 1950), outraged religious authorities and was banned until it was revised. He collapsed on-stage during a performance of his last play, *Le Malade imaginaire* (*The Imaginary Invalid*), and died the same night.

Mona Lisa Consommé
(Consommé Mona Lisa)

Beef consommé garnished with small chicken quenelles and green peas.

Monselet Consommé
(Consommé Monselet)

Beef consommé garnished with julienned beef tongue, sliced poached beef marrow, green peas, chervil, and fried croutons.

Charles Pierre Monselet (1825–1888) was the author of *Le Gourmet*, a weekly gastronomic journal published in 1858. It was republished as *Almanach des gourmands*, a title borrowed from Grimod de La Reynière, whose work it endeavored to continue. His other published works included *Gastronomie* (1874), *Les Lettres gourmandes* (1877), and *Les Mois gastronomiques* (1880). Acquainted with many restaurateurs of his time, a number of dishes were named for him, including steamed quartered artichokes, poached oysters, skewered sliced truffles breaded and fried, an artichoke and truffle omelet, and a dessert bombe.

Monte Carlo Style Consommé
(Consommé à la Monte Carlo)

Beef consommé garnished with diablotins.

Montesquieu Consommé
(Consommé Montesquieu)

Beef consommé garnished with julienned chicken, ham, and mushrooms, and small cauliflower flowerettes.

Charles Louis de Secondat, Baron de la Brède et de Montesquieu (1689–1755) wrote *The Spirit of Laws*, which is considered a major contribution to political theory. In it he advocates a separation and balance of government powers as a means of guaranteeing freedom of the individual, and it helped form a philosophical basis for the U.S. Constitution. His satire on French culture and Parisian institutions, *Persian Letters* (1721), supposedly seen through the eyes of two Persian travelers, mocks the reign of Louis XIV, makes fun of social classes and Roman Catholic doctrines, and reflects a new spirit of vigorous, disrespectful, and iconoclastic criticism. His contemporaries considered him affable and modest, a faithful friend, and helpful to young unestablished writers.

Nansen Consommé
(Consommé Nansen)

Beef consommé flavored with vodka; very small caviar canapés served separately.

Naples Style Consommé
(Consommé à la Napolitaine)

Beef consommé flavored with tomato juice, garnished with julienned ham and celery root, macaroni, and chervil; grated cheese served separately.

Navarin Consommé
(Consommé Navarin)

Beef consommé garnished with small crayfish tails, green pea royale, and chopped parsley.

New York Style Consommé
(Consommé à la New Yorkaise)

Beef consommé garnished with game quenelles, diced onion royale and tomato royale, and chervil.

Olga Consommé
(Consommé Olga)

Beef consommé flavored with Port, garnished with julienned truffle, leek, carrot, and celery root.

Orléans Style Consommé
(Consommé à l'Orléanaise)

Beef consommé garnished with chicory royale, diced green beans, flageolets (small lima beans), and chervil.

Orléans is a royal French family name that was prominent for six centuries, and also the name of a small ancient city in France. Today the town of Orléans is an important industrial and transportation center, but in ancient times it first gained notoriety in 52 B.C. by revolting against Julius Caesar, who burned it down. Orléans also repelled Atilla in 451, but fell to Clovis of the Merovingian clan in 498. During the Hundred Year's War, Joan of Arc lifted the British siege in 1429; and in World War II many historic buildings were destroyed, and later rebuilt incorporating traditional architectural styles.

Oxtail Consommé
(Consommé de Queues de Boeuf)

Beef consommé flavored with herbs and sherry, garnished with diced oxtail and root vegetables.

Palestinian Style Consommé
(Consommé à la Palestinienne)

Beef consommé garnished with carrot and turnip pearls, green peas, and diced green beans.

Palestro Consommé
(Consommé Palestro)

Beef consommé garnished with julienned root vegetables, lettuce chiffonade, rice, and diced tomato royale.

Parisian Style Consommé
(Consommé à la Parisienne)

Beef consommé garnished with fine julienned vegetables (cooked in butter), round slices of royale, and chervil leaves.

Peasant Style Bouillon
(Consommé à la Paysanne)

Simple beef consommé garnished with small thin slices of root vegetables braised in butter, and served with fried croutons.

Peter the Great Consommé
(Consommé Pierre le Grand)

Beef consommé garnished with julienned celery and turnip, lettuce chiffonade, and minced tarragon.

Petrarch Consommé
(Consommé Petrarch)

Beef consommé garnished with leek chiffonade, roasted pistachios (shelled and skinned), and diablotins.

Picard Consommé
(Consommé Picard)

Beef consommé garnished with leek chiffonade and plain croutons.

Peter I (1672–1725) was the son of Czar Alexis and ruled as Czar from the age of ten until his death. When he returned from a tour of Europe in 1697–98, he initiated a series of modernizing reforms, which included personally cutting off the beards of his nobles and ordering them to wear Western dress.

Petrarch is the common name of Francesco Petrarca (1304–1374), Italian humanist poet and influential Renaissance literary figure, who is known for perfecting the sonnet as a poetic form.

Piedmont Style Consommé
(Consommé à la Piémontaise)

Beef consommé flavored with saffron, garnished with rice, diced ham, Piedmont truffle, and diced tomatoes; grated cheese served separately.

————————•————————

Piedmont truffles, the famed white truffle from Northern Italy, is an exquisite gastronomic delicacy. Unfortunately, they are very difficult to obtain, and even when available, very expensive. There is really no substitute for this product, though diced and sautéed boletus or oyster mushrooms come from the same botanical family (fungus).

Polignac Consommé
(Consommé Polignac)

Beef consommé garnished with chicken farce (cut as desired), minced truffle, and small, round slices of beef tongue.

———•———

Portuguese Consommé is often served cold (with garnish omitted).

Portuguese Style Consommé
(Consommé à la Portugaise)

Beef consommé flavored with tomato and cayenne pepper, garnished with diced tomatoes and rice.

Raphael Consommé
(Consommé Raphael)

Beef consommé garnished with diced celery root.

Raspail Consommé
(Consommé Raspail)

Beef consommé garnished with chicken quenelles and asparagus tips.

Remusat Consommé
(Consommé Remusat)

Beef consommé garnished with two varieties of quenelles: one flavored with tomato purée, the other with spinach purée; diced root vegetables and chervil.

Richelieu Consommé
(Consommé Richelieu)

Beef consommé garnished with julienned carrot and turnip, and small chicken quenelles wrapped in lettuce leaves.

———————— • ————————

Armand Jean du Plessis, duc de Richelieu (1585–1642), was a French cardinal and statesman, and chief minister to Louis XIII. Richelieu virtually ran the government behind the scenes from 1624 until his death. Though politically a hawk—he was instrumental in involving France in the Thirty Years' War (1635)—he also promoted trade and the arts, and was the founder of the French Academy, a society of scholars.

———— • ————

Maximilien François Marie Isidore de Robespierre (1758–1794) was a significant player in the peasant rebellion that toppled the government of Louis XVI. The revolution that he helped ignite, though, took many twists and turns, and he himself was guillotined during the Reign of Terror that he had been instrumental in starting.

Risi-Bisi Consommé
(Consommé Risi-Bisi)

Beef consommé garnished with rice and green peas; grated cheese served separately.

Robespierre Consommé
(Consommé Robespierre)

Beef consommé flavored with tomato.

Royale Consommé
(Consommé Royale)

Beef consommé garnished with plain royale cut into diamond (losange) shapes.

Rustic Style Consommé
(Consommé à la Villageoise)

Beef consommé garnished with julienned leek and small square noodles.

St. Charles Consommé
(Consommé St. Charles)

Beef consommé garnished with small poached eggs and chopped chervil.

St. Germain Consommé
(Consommé St. Germain)

Beef consommé garnished with small quenelles, green peas, lettuce chiffonade, and chopped chervil.

Salvator Consommé
(Consommé Salvator)

Beef consommé flavored with tomato juice, garnished with diced tomatoes and chervil.

Savarin Consommé
(Consommé Savarin)

Beef consommé garnished with sweetbread quenelles flavored with onion purée.

Saxon Style Consommé
(Consommé à la Saxonne)

Beef consommé garnished with julienned ham, beef tongue, sauerkraut (cooked in broth and drained), and small square croutons.

———————— • ————————

The Saxons were a fierce pagan tribe, originally from South Jutland, that raided the North Sea coasts in the third and fourth centuries, and later settled in Britain and Frankish Gaul (what is now northwestern Germany). Against Charlemagne and the Franks—who were determined to conquer and convert them to Christianity, or totally annihilate them—they battled for 32 years. A turning point for the Franks took place at Verden on Christmas Day in 782, when Charlemagne rounded up 4,500 Saxons and beheaded them before attending Mass.

Sevillian Style Consommé
(Consommé à la Sevillane)

Beef consommé flavored with tomato juice, slightly thickened with tapioca, garnished with diced tomato royale.

Sheperd's Style Consommé
(Consommé à la Bergère)

Beef consommé slightly thickened with tapioca, garnished with asparagus tips, diced mushrooms, tarragon, and chervil.

Solange Consommé
(Consommé Solange)

Beef consommé garnished with pearl barley, diced chicken breast, and lettuce chiffonade.

Solferino Consommé
(Consommé Solferino)

Beef consommé garnished with carrot, potato, and turnip pearls.

Soubise Consommé
(Consommé Soubise)

Beef consommé garnished with diced onion royale.

Spinner's Style Consommé
(Consommé à la Filateur)

Beef consommé garnished with noodle dough cut into very fine strips (resembling sewing thread).

Charles de Rohan, Prince of Soubise, was an eighteenth-century aristocrat and marshal of France who had a particular affinity for onion purée.

Strasbourg is an important industrial city on the Rhine, famous for its goose liver pâté and choucroûte (a special sauerkraut and pork dish), and Rhenish architecture, particularly its cathedral. A political football ever since its early governance under imperial Rome, it was destroyed by the Huns in the fifth century. In modern times it was ceded to Germany in 1871 and returned to France in 1919.

Strasbourg Style Consommé
(Consommé à la Strasbourgeoise)

Beef consommé flavored with juniper berries, slightly thickened with rice flour, garnished with julienned red cabbage, sliced and skinned Strasbourg sausage; prepared horseradish served separately.

Turtle Consommé
(Consommé Tortue Clair)

Consommé made with beef and veal bones, calf's feet, turtle meat, flavored with turtle herbs and sherry, garnished with diced turtle meat.

Two variations of Turtle Consommé are Turtle Consommé, Lady Curzon (Consommé Tortue Clair, Madame Curzon), served in a small bowl, and topped with curry-flavored whipped cream, and Sir James Consommé, flavored with Cognac and Madeira wine.

Tuscan Style Consommé
(Consommé à la Toscane)

Beef consommé garnished with diced egg plant, mushrooms, and tomatoes, and small macaroni (e.g., ditalini).

Vaudoise Style Consommé
(Consommé à la Vaudoise)

Beef consommé garnished with diced beef and root vegetables; crusts of dried baguettes (French bread) and grated Swiss cheese served separately.

Venetian Style Consommé
(Consommé à la Vénitienne)

Beef consommé flavored with tarragon, chervil, and basil, garnished with rice; small deep-fried Dauphine potatoes served separately.

Verdi Consommé
(Consommé Verdi)

Beef consommé garnished with tomato and cream quenelles, small macaroni, and spinach.

———————————— • ————————————

Giuseppe Fortunino Francesco Verdi (1813–1901) was one of the foremost Italian opera composers, creator of numerous celebrated operas and operettas, notably *Aïda, Rigoletto, Il Trovatore*, and *La Traviata*. With the help of Antonion Barezzi, a merchant from the nearby town of Bussetto, who recognized the boy's musical gifts, he secured a scholarship at the conservatory in Milan. He was rejected, however, as being over the age limit at 18, but remained in Milan for three years to study with Vincenzo Lavigna, a musician on the staff of La Scala. He then returned to Bussetto, where at the age of 23 he married Barezzi's daughter Margherita. That same year, Verdi's first opera, produced at La Scala in 1839, was successful enough for the theater to commission him for three more operas. The first of these was so poorly received that it was closed after one performance. That same year his wife tragically died, only a year after losing an infant son, and he was so overcome with grief during this time that he vowed to never write another opera. Some of Verdi's later work initiated major scandals: *Rigoletto*, based on Victor Hugo's *Le Roi s'amuse* (roughly, *The King Who Had a Good Time*), included a royal assassination attempt—a politically taboo subject—and a curse, considered blasphemous. After concessions to the authorities, the libretto was approved. (Interestingly, in the modern version the assassination attempt is gone, while the curse remains.)

Véron Consommé
(Consommé Véron)

Beef consommé flavored with truffle (peelings) and Port, garnished with julienned red pepper and diced flagolet royal.

———————————— • ————————————

Louis Désiré Véron (1798–1867) was a French doctor who practiced medicine in fashionable circles, and later worked as an administrator of the Opéra and as a literary and political journalist. Véron's table was legendary, thanks to Sophie, his cook, and many celebrated actors, actresses—including his mistress Élisabeth Félix (her stage name was "Rachel")—and politicos were among his guests. Though Véron had a reputation for being ostentatious, he was a sober and moderate man. "He eats only two courses, and his normal drink is very old Bordeaux, greatly diluted with water," wrote a journalist of his time, for which Véron personally thanked him.

Victor Emmanuel (1820–1878) was the king of Sardinia from 1849 to 1861, and thereafter until his death the first king of a united Italy.

Victor Emmanuel Consommé
(Consommé Victor Emmanuel)

Beef consommé garnished with diced tomatoes and macaroni; grated cheese served separately.

Viennese Style Consommé
(Consommé à la Viennoise)

Beef consommé flavored with smoked beef, bacon, and root vegetables, garnished with rice, pearl barley, peas, very small white beans, and green peas.

Westmoreland Consommé
(Consommé Westmoreland)

Veal and calf's head consommé slightly thickened with arrowroot, flavored with Madeira, garnished with finely sliced cornichons (sour gherkins), truffles, chicken quenelles, and diced calf's head.

Windsor is the family name of the royal house of Britain; it was changed from Wettin in 1917.

Windsor Consommé
(Consommé Windsor)

Beef consommé flavored with turtle herbs and sherry, slightly thickened with arrowroot, garnished with julienned calf's foot.

Xavier Consommé
(Consommé Xavier)

Beef consommé flavored with Madeira, slightly thickened with arrowroot, garnished with julienned plain crêpe.

Zola Consommé
(Consommé Zola)

Beef consommé garnished with small cheese dumplings flavored with white truffle; grated cheese served separately.

———————————— • ————————————

Émile Zola (1840–1902) was a French novelist well known for his article *J'accuse*, in which he accused the judicial courts of complicity with the military in falsely convicting French army officer Alfred Dreyfus (1859–1935) for giving Major von Schwartzkoppen, the German military attaché in Paris, a list of secret French documents. Zola was prosecuted for libel, but fled to England until amnestied a few months later. Three years later (1898), when it was learned that most of the evidence against Dreyfus was forged by Colonel Henry of French army intelligence, Henry took his own life. At the military retrial, the court was unwilling to admit error, and though they found Dreyfus guilty and sentenced him to 10 years in prison, President Loubet directly issued a pardon. Dreyfus retired the next year, was formally acquitted by the supreme court of appeals in 1906, and further exonerated with the publication of von Schwartzkoppen's papers in 1930.

CHICKEN CONSOMMÉ

Adèle Consommé
(Consommé Adèle)

Chicken consommé garnished with green peas, carrot pearls, and chicken quenelles.

Adelina Patti Consommé
(Consommé Adelina Patti)

Chicken consommé garnished with green peas, carrot pearls, and large diced chestnut royale.

———————————— • ————————————

Adela Juana Maria Patti (1843–1919), the daughter of Italian parents in Wales, was one of the greatest coloratura sopranos of her day. She made her singing debut in New York City at the age of 16 (1859), and soon became quite popular.

Rossini arranged much of the music for *The Barber of Seville* for her part as Rosina. Her voice was small by operatic standards, but was considered remarkable for its range and purity.

Albion II Consommé
(Consommé Albion II)

Chicken consommé garnished with asparagus tips, chicken and duck liver quenelles, cockscombs, and grated truffle.

Alexandra Consommé
(Consommé Alexandra)

Chicken consommé slightly thickened with tapioca, garnished with lettuce chiffonade, and julienned chicken breast.

Dishes so titled are named for Alexandra (1844–1925), daughter of Christian IX of Denmark, and queen consort of Great Britain's Edward VII.

Alsacian Style Consommé
(Consommé à l'Alsacienne)

Chicken consommé garnished with sauerkraut simmered in stock and strained, and thin slices of poached and skinned Strasbourg sausages.

Ambassador's Style Consommé
(Consommé à l'Ambassadeur)

Chicken consommé garnished with truffle royale cut in round slices, diced mushrooms cooked in butter with a little lemon juice, and diced chicken breast.

Ambassador's Wife's Style Consommé
(Consommé à l'Ambassadrice)

Chicken consommé garnished with tri-color royale—red (tomato), green (peas), and black (truffle); diced mushrooms cooked in butter with a little lemon juice; and diced chicken breast.

Andalusian Style Consommé
(Consommé à l'Andalouse)

Chicken consommé garnished with diced tomato royale, rice, julienned ham, and thick crêpe batter poured through a colander into simmering stock, then added to the soup.

Andalusia is a southern Spanish region that borders on the Mediterranean and the Atlantic Ocean. It is rich in agriculture, so many Spanish dishes are named for this region. It is also rich in history, having been settled by the Phoenicians in the eleventh century B.C., and variously ruled by Carthage, Rome, the Visigoths, the Moors, and Great Britain.

Aremberg Consommé
(Consommé de Volaille à l'Aremberg)

Chicken consommé (simple) garnished with pearls of carrot, turnip, and truffle; miniature chicken quenelles; and asparagus royale cut in small rounds.

Aremberg was a royal family whose name stems from a small town of the same name (spelled Arenberg) near Bonn, Germany. Their extensive lands, in what is now Belgium and northwestern Germany, date back to 1299 with the marriage of Engelbert II of the house of La Marck and Matilda, an heiress of the area's former lords. Later marriages to other aristocratic families continued to expand the family's empire, which was made into a countship in 1549, a principality in 1576, and a duchy in 1664. During the Napoléonic reorganization of Europe, Prosper Louis, then head of the family's holdings, was deprived of the duchy in 1810 but was able to recover it at the Congress of Vienna in 1815.

Assas Consommé
(Consommé Assas)

Chicken consommé garnished with small balls of lettuce and diced carrot royale.

Beauharnais Consommé
(Consommé Beauharnais)

Chicken consommé garnished with lettuce paupiettes poached in stock and sliced, asparagus tips, and julienned truffles.

———————————— • ————————————

Alexandre, Vicomte de Beauharnais (1760–1794) was a French general who fought in the American Revolution, and later was guillotined for being a member of the nobility during the Reign of Terror. His widow married Napoléon I and became Empress Josephine; his son Eugène de Beauharnais (1781–1824) also had a distinguished military career, serving under his stepfather Napoléon.

A paupiette is technically a thin slice of meat spread with a farce, rolled up, secured with string or wooden toothpicks, then braised or poached. It may or may not be wrapped with a thin slice of bacon. Veal is the meat most commonly used, though beef, lamb, turkey, or chicken can also be used. In a literal use of the word, a paupiette can refer to any little package, in this case well-trimmed Boston lettuce leaves, stacked, then rolled into tight half-inch wide cylinders, poached, drained, and sliced.

Béhague Consommé
(Consommé Béhague)

Chicken consommé garnished with small poached eggs and chervil leaves.

Bizet Consommé
(Consommé Bizet)

Chicken consommé slightly thickened with tapioca, garnished with very small chicken quenelles flavored with tarragon, and chervil leaves.

———————————— • ————————————

Alexandre-César-Léopold Bizet (1838–1875), better known as Georges Bizet, was so extraordinarily gifted musically that he was admitted to the Paris Conservatoire at the age of 10. His most popular work, the opera *Carmen*, initially caused a scandal when it was first produced in 1875; and sadly he died just as the public began to appreciate the work. Bizet produced eight operas, thirty-seven published songs, and three orchestral compositions, one of which accompanied Alphonse Daudet's *L'Arlesienne*.

Boïeldieu Consommé
(*Consommé Boïeldieu*)

Chicken consommé garnished with three types of small quenelles: foie gras, chicken, and truffle.

Bonaparte Consommé
(*Consommé Bonaparte*)

Chicken consommé garnished with small chicken quenelles.

The Buonaparte family dates back to twelfth century Florence. Napoléon I's ancestor emigrated to Corsica in the mid-sixteenth century. His parents, Carlo Maria and Maria Letizia Buonaparte, spawned a family that produced five major political leaders—three of them in France—who were active over the period of a century (mid-eighteenth to mid-nineteenth century).

Borghese Consommé
(*Consommé Borghèse*)

Chicken consommé garnished with asparagus tips and julienne of chicken breast.

The Borghese were a family of Roman nobles who first gained fame in the thirteenth century as magistrates, ambassadors, and other public officials. Camillo Borghese became Pope Paul V in 1605, and appointed his nephew Scipione Caffarelli (1576–1633) cardinal. Scipione's interest was more in the arts than in religious matters, and he was instrumental in restoring and constructing many churches and palaces in Rome, including the Villa Borghese, where he assembled important paintings and sculptures. He also encouraged the talent of young Gian Lorenzo Bernini (1598–1680), who later became an outstanding sculptor and architect. Three other family members became cardinals, and another nephew became viceroy of Naples.

Bourdalou Consommé
(Consommé Bourdalou)

Chicken consommé garnished with four different flavors of royale: tomato, asparagus, chicken, and carrot.

Briand Consommé
(Consommé Briand)

Chicken consommé garnished with diced chicken, ham, and veal, and chopped chervil.

———————————— • ————————————

Aristide Briand (1862–1932) served as French premier eleven times between 1909 and 1921, holding a total of twenty-six ministerial posts between 1906 and 1932. Following World War I, he championed international peace by advocating the League of Nations, and towards the end of his life advocated a plan for a United States of Europe. Two of his great successes were the Pact of Locarno (1925), an effort to normalize relations between Germany and its former enemies, and the Kellogg-Briand Pact of August 27, 1928, in which sixty nations agreed to outlaw war as an instrument of national policy. He and Gustav Stresemann of Germany shared the Nobel Peace Prize in 1926.

Bride's Consommé
(Consommé Petite-mariée)

Chicken consommé garnished with chicken and almond royale, and chervil chiffonade.

Brillat-Savarin Consommé
(Consommé Brillat-Savarin)

Chicken consommé flavored with celery, slightly thickened with arrowroot, garnished with julienned carrot, mushroom, and truffle.

Britannia Style Consommé
(Consommé à la Britannia)

Chicken consommé garnished with foie gras quenelles, asparagus tips, finely julienned truffle, and tomato royale cut into triangles.

Capuchin Consommé
(Consommé Capucine)

Chicken consommé garnished with lettuce and spinach chiffonade; profiteroles filled with chicken purée served separately.

Carême Consommé
(Consommé Carême)

Chicken and veal consommé garnished with round slices of carrot and turnip, lettuce chiffonade; and asparagus tips.

---•---

Antonin Carême (also Marie-Antoine or Marc-Antoine; Paris, 1784–1833) was sent off into the world at the age of eleven by his father, a poor handyman. He was later encouraged by his employer (Bailly, a celebrated caterer) to develop his innate ability to draw. Carême studied Parisian architectural drawings at night in the National Library. "The fine arts are five in number, to wit: *painting, sculpture, poetry, music, architecture—whose main branch is confectionery.*" His subsequent pièces montées, created from pastries, puff paste, preserved fruits, creams, and sherbets, will influence centuries of pâtissiers.

Among Carême's employers were Talleyrand, England's Prince Regent (future King George IV), Tsar Alexander I, the Viennese Court, the British Embassy, Princess Bagration, and Baron de Rothschild. Among his five published works were *Le Pâtissier Pittoresque* (1815) and *Le Pâtissier Royal Parisien* (1825). He spent his last moments dictating notes to his daughter, and died "burnt out by the flame of his genius and the heat of his ovens." (Laurent Tailhade).

Carolina Style Consommé
(*Consommé à la Caroline*)

Chicken consommé garnished with rice, diced almond royale, and chopped chervil.

Cavour Consommé
(*Consommé Cavour*)

Chicken consommé garnished with green peas, macaroni, and small fried dumplings.

---•---

This dish is named after Camillo Benso, conte di Cavour (1810–1861), whose family dates back to sixteenth-century soldiers of the House of Savoy, and who served as premier of Sardinia, 1852–59 and 1860–61. His exploitation of international rivalries and revolutionary movements led to the unification of Italy in 1861, with himself serving as the first prime minister.

---•---

This soup (as well as a chicken dish and an omelet) are dedicated to the owner of the nineteenth-century restaurant Le Cercle in Lyon.

Celestine Consommé
(*Consommé Celestine*)

Chicken (or beef) consommé garnished with julienned crêpes flavored with chervil or parsley.

Châtelaine Consommé
(*Consommé Châtelaine*)

Chicken consommé slightly thickened with tapioca, garnished with diced onion and artichoke royale, and small chicken quenelles flavored with chestnut purée.

Chevreuse Style Consommé
(*Consommé à la Chevreuse*)

Chicken consommé garnished with julienned chicken royale and plain royale, and julienned chicken breast and truffles.

Christopher Columbus Consommé
(Consommé Christophe Colomb)

Chicken consommé flavored with tomato, slightly thickened with tapioca, garnished with diced tomato royale and chicken quenelles.

———————————————— • ————————————————

Christopher Columbus (1451–1506) was a master mariner who, after eight years of soliciting support from the Spanish monarchs Ferdinand V and Isabella I, set sail from Spain with the intention of arriving in India. He reached the Bahama Islands in 1492, explored Cuba and Hispaniola, and on his return to Spain was made an admiral and governor of all new lands. He returned to the New World in 1493 and established a colony at Hispaniola where he was governor. In 1500, because of disreputable conditions there, he was arrested and returned to Spain in chains; he died penniless and unknown.

Cincinnati Style Consommé
(Consommé à la Cincinnatienne)

Chicken consommé garnished with carrot, turnip, and potato pearls, and profiteroles filled with chicken purée.

Cleopatra Consommé
(Consommé Cleopatra)

Chicken consommé garnished with diced tomatoes.

———————————————— • ————————————————

Cleopatra (69–30 B.C.) was the daughter of Ptolemy XI, who gained political control of Egypt with the help of Julius Caesar. After Caesar's death, she married Marc Antony in an effort to restore her throne's power. Octavian, then head of Rome, defeated their forces in a naval battle at Actium (31 B.C.), and they returned to Egypt. Antony committed suicide the next year, as did Cleopatra soon afterward.

Colombine Consommé
(Consommé Colombine)

Chicken consommé garnished with carrot and turnip pearls, julienned pigeon breast, and poached pigeon's eggs.

Countess Style Consommé
(Consommé à la Comtesse)

Chicken consommé slightly thickened with tapioca, garnished with asparagus royale, small chicken quenelles flavored with truffle, and lettuce chiffonade.

Dante Consommé
(Consommé Dante)

Chicken consommé flavored with pigeon, garnished with fine julienned truffle and beef tongue, and saffron-flavored quenelles.

Dante Alighieri (1265–1321) was an Italian poet and author of *The Divine Comedy*, a 14,000-line poem about a poet's journey through purgatory and hell guided by Virgil, and through heaven guided by Beatrice (Bice Portinari, 1266–1290), a model of spiritual perfection which he used in much of his work. Although he is considered one of the greatest and last medieval poets, a shifting political climate in Florence in 1301 forced him into exile, from which he was never able to return. In 1315 he was twice offered pardons, but because they were under humiliating conditions, he refused. His last years were spent with his children, happily and peacefully, under the patronage of Guido de Polenta.

Daudet Consommé
(Consommé Daudet)

Chicken consommé garnished with diced ham and chicken royale, lobster quenelles, and julienned celery root.

Léon Daudet (1867–1942) often bragged that when he had been a student in a medical school he invented a dish consisting of a layer of white beans, a layer of fried potatoes, followed by two fried eggs, and named it *kaulback* in memory of a Russian general. He went on to become a respected gastronomic journalist, arguing about such issues as whether chicory salad lightly sprayed with absinthe should or should not be served with foie gras (he opined that the taste of the oil kills the foie gras).

Delavergne Consommé
(Consommé Delavergne)

Chicken consommé garnished with diced plain royale, asparagus tips, and very small soft-boiled eggs (e.g., quail eggs).

Delriche Consommé
(Consommé Delriche)

Chicken consommé garnished with vermicelli, sliced beef marrow, and croutons.

Demidow Consommé
(Consommé Demidow)

Chicken consommé garnished with carrot, turnip, and truffle pearls; small chicken quenelles flavored with fine herbs; and chopped chervil.

Dijon Style Consommé
(Consommé à la Dijonnaise)

Chicken consommé slightly thickened with tapioca, and garnished with game quenelles and julienned beef tongue.

Diplomat Consommé
(Consommé Diplomate)

Chicken consommé garnished with round slices of chicken roulade and round thin slices of truffle.

Diva Consommé
(Consommé Diva)

Chicken consommé garnished large chicken quenelles flavored with truffle, and diced lobster royale.

Divette Consommé
(Consommé Divette)

Chicken consommé garnished with round slices of crayfish royale, small fish quenelles, and truffle pearls.

Dolores Consommé
(Consommé Dolores)

Chicken consommé garnished with julienned chicken breast and saffron-flavored rice.

Doria Consommé
(Consommé Doria)

Chicken consommé garnished with small oval-shaped cucumbers, chicken quenelles, fried dumplings (choux paste flavored with cheese), and chopped chervil. (See Figure 3.4.)

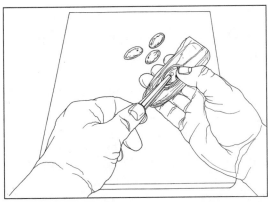

When a small tournéed vegetable is called for, an oval scoop helps cut them expeditiously and uniformly. (Notice that the thumb presses the cutter down, while the opposite hand turns the scoop on a rotating axis.)

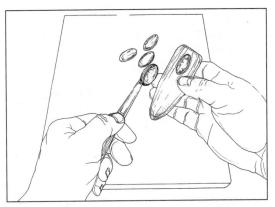

The cucumbers can be warmed in simmering stock or water before adding them to the soup.

Figure 3.4

Douglas Consommé
(Consommé Douglas)

Chicken consommé garnished with diced artichoke bottoms, asparagus tips, and diced poached sweetbreads.

Dounou Consommé
(Consommé Dounou)

Chicken consommé flavored with turtle herbs, slightly thickened with tapioca, garnished with chicken quenelles, diced artichoke bottoms, and truffles; small puff pastry bouchées filled with chicken purée served separately.

Dubourg Consommé
(Consommé Dubourg)

Chicken consommé garnished with rice, diced chicken royale, and chopped chervil.

Duchess Style Consommé
(Consommé à la Duchesse)

Chicken consommé garnished with lettuce chiffonade and plain royale.

Eleanora Duse (1859–1924) was an Italian actress who established her popularity at the age of 14 with a performance as Juliet. An actress with tremendous emotional power, she made a farewell appearance in Ibsen's *Lady from the Sea* (1923).

Dupré Consommé
(Consommé Dupré)

Chicken consommé garnished with carrot and turnip pearls, small quenelles, and croutons.

Duse Consommé
(Consommé Duse)

Chicken consommé garnished with small chicken quenelles flavored with tomato and tortellinni (or other fancy-shaped pasta).

Easter Style Consommé
(Consommé à la Pascale)

Chicken consommé garnished with green peas, diced carrots, diced turnip royale, and chopped fennel greens.

Edward VII Consommé
(Consommé Edouard VII)

Chicken consommé lightly flavored with curry and garnished with rice; small puff pastry bouchées filled with chicken purée served separately.

———————————— • ————————————

Edward VII (1841–1910) was the eldest son of Britain's Queen Victoria and Prince Albert. From his early childhood, he showed more interest in people and conversation than in scholarly or intellectual pursuits. After the death of his father (1861), Edward quietly endured his mother's snubs and criticisms on official matters, since she was never able to reconcile herself to her son's lack of proper royal deportment. But beneath his gregarious and foppish demeanor (he was a popular habitué of fashionable restaurants in Paris), Edward had deep concern for international matters, if evidenced only by his fluency in French and German, and a tolerable command of Italian. As a result, he was able to forge an alliance with France and initiate friendships with other nations at a time when anti-British sentiment following the South African Boer War was high. Overall, he was a popular sovereign, and numerous dishes were named after him.

Emanuel Consommé
(Consommé Emanuel)

Chicken consommé garnished with spaghetti, julienned chicken breast, and diced tomato royale; grated cheese served separately.

Epicurean Style Consommé
(Consommé à l'Épicurie)

Chicken consommé garnished with toasted julienned almonds and chopped chervil.

Fanchonette Consommé
(Consommé Fanchonette)

Chicken consommé garnished with small pancakes stuffed with chicken purée and chopped truffles.

Favorite Style Consommé
(Consommé à la Favorite)

Chicken consommé slightly thickened with tapioca, garnished with potato pearls, julienned artichoke bottoms and mushrooms, and chervil.

Federal Style Consommé
(Consommé à la Fédéral)

Chicken consommé flavored with cayenne pepper, garnished with very thin-sliced truffles, and diced plain royale.

Fleury Consommé
(Consommé Fleury)

Chicken consommé garnished with small, flat, round chicken quenelles and green peas.

Floreal Consommé
(Consommé Florêale)

Chicken consommé garnished with carrots and turnips cut in the shape of small daisies, peas, asparagus tips, small quenelles flavored with pistachios, and chervil.

Florence Style Consommé
(Consommé à la Florentine)

Chicken consommé garnished with three varieties of quenelles: beef tongue (red), chicken (white), and spinach (green).

Francatelli Consommé
(Consommé Francatelli)

Chicken consommé garnished with chicken royale, foie gras quenelles, cock's combs, and kidneys.

Francillon Consommé
(Consommé Francillon)

Chicken consommé (very hot) poured over a (thin) ring of chicken farce piped into the bottom of a soup bowl, garnished with poached eggs.

André Hercule de Fleury (1653–1743) was a French Roman Catholic cardinal and chief minister to Louis XV. Though a promoter of peace, he was unable to avoid the wars of the Polish and then the Austrian secession.

French Style Consommé
(Consommé à la Française)

Chicken consommé garnished with lettuce chiffonade, chicken quenelles, and chervil.

Frou-frou Consommé
(Consommé Frou-frou)

Chicken consommé garnished with carrot pearls, profiteroles, and chopped chervil.

Gabrielle Consommé
(Consommé Gabrielle)

Chicken consommé garnished with diced chicken royal and diced crayfish tails.

Gaul Style Consommé
(Consommé à la Galloise)

Chicken consommé garnished with diced cock's combs, kidneys, and ham royale.

Germaine Consommé
(Consommé Germaine)

Chicken consommé garnished with chicken quenelles, diced green pea royale, and chervil.

Gouffé Consommé
(Consommé Gouffé)

Chicken consommé slightly thickened with tapioca, garnished with julienned chicken breast, beef tongue, truffles, and hard-cooked egg whites pressed through a sieve.

Jacques Ange Gabriel (1689–1782) worked for 30 years as an architect for Louis XV at Versailles, Compiègne, and other royal residences. He designed Place Louis XV (now Place de la Concorde) and worked on the design of the Louvre.

Jules Gouffé (1807–1877) was the son of a Parisian pastry cook, with whom he apprenticed. At the age of 17, he worked under Carême in the kitchens of the Austrian Embassy in Paris. He ran a successful restaurant for fifteen years on the rue Saint-Honoré, later orchestrating banquets for Emperor Napoléon III. At the urging of Alexander Dumas and Baron Brisee, in what turned out to be the last year of his life, he took over the management of the kitchens at the Jockey Club. His *Livre de Cuisine* (1867), republished several times, is considered his most important work and was widely plagiarized in its time.

Gourmet Style Consommé
(Consommé du Gourmet)

Chicken consommé garnished with diced game meat, foie gras, and beef tongue, small round sliced of poached chicken farce, and chopped pistachios.

Grand Duchess Style Consommé
(Consommé à la Grande Duchesse)

Chicken consommé garnished with julienned chicken breast and beef tongue, asparagus tips, and small chicken quenelles.

Gypsy Style Consommé
(Consommé à la Zingara)

Chicken consommé garnished with three varieties of royale: ham, tongue, and mushroom.

Imperial Style Consommé II
(Consommé de Volaille à l'Imperial)

Chicken consommé slightly thickened with tapioca, garnished with small round slices of poached chicken farce, sliced cock's combs and kidneys, green peas, and chervil.

Indian Style Consommé
(Consommé à l'Indienne)

Chicken consommé flavored with curry, garnished with diced coconut royale and rice.

Isoline Consommé
(Consommé Isoline)

Chicken consommé garnished with small chicken quenelles flavored with asparagus, julienned mushrooms, chicken breast, and truffles.

Jockey Club Consommé
(Consommé Jockey Club)

Chicken consommé garnished with small round slices of carrot, green pea and chicken royale.

Johore Consommé
(Consommé Johore)

Chicken consommé flavored with curry, garnished with julienned chicken breast, rice, and curry royale.

Juanita Consommé
(Consommé Juanita)

Chicken consommé garnished with rice royale, diced tomatoes, and hard-cooked egg yolks pressed through a sieve.

Judic Consommé
(Consommé à la Judic)

Chicken consommé garnished with truffle rings, rosette-shaped chicken quenelles; small braised lettuces served separately.

Dame Judic was the stage name for comedienne Anna Damiens, for whom several dishes were created, including a Tournedos Judic, sautéed beef medallions garnished with braised lettuce and cock's comb, kidney, and truffle ragout; and Sole Judic, poached fillets garnished with braised lettuce and fish quenelles and glazed with Mornay Sauce.

Julia Consommé
(Consommé Julia)

Chicken consommé slightly thickened with tapioca, garnished with diced plain royale, and profiteroles.

Juliette Consommé
(Consommé Juliette)

Chicken consommé garnished with small round chicken quenelles, diced spinach royale, and julienned hard-cooked egg whites.

King's Style Consommé
(Consommé des Rois)

Chicken consommé flavored with quail, garnished with quail quenelles, julienned quail breasts, asparagus tips, and truffle pearls.

Ladies Delight Consommé
(Consommé aux Délice de Dames)

Chicken consommé flavored with celery, garnished with fine julienned celery and hard-cooked egg whites, and diced tomatoes.

Laffite Consommé
(Consommé Laffite)

Chicken consommé flavored with Madeira, garnished with julienned cock's combs, cock's kidneys, mushrooms, and truffles, cucumber pearls, and small pitted olives.

————————— • —————————

Jean Laffite (also Lafitte; 1780–1826) was the leader of a band of privateers and smugglers who preyed on Spanish ships from his bases in Texas and Louisiana. He and his band colonized the secluded islands of Barataria Bay south of New Orleans, and because of their logistical importance, during the War of 1812 the British offered him $30,000 and a captaincy in the Royal Navy for his allegiance. Laffite pretended to cooperate, but surreptitiously warned Louisiana officials of the impending peril to New Orleans. Governor

W.C.C. Claiborne doubted his intent, and sent the U.S. Navy to wipe out the colony. Still devoted in his loyalty to the U.S., Lafitte offered aid to the hard-pressed forces of General Andrew Jackson in exchange for a full pardon. Jackson agreed, and the Baratarian's help was significant in the Jackson's defeat of the British in the battle of New Orleans (1815). In 1817 Lafitte organized a commune with nearly 1,000 followers on the island site of the future city of Galveston, Texas, from where he continued to prey on Spanish vessels. When several of his lieutenants attacked U.S. ships in 1820, Lafitte was again considered an enemy of the U.S. In 1821, he burned down the commune, and sailed off to continue his pirating to the end of his days.

Lagrandière Consommé
(Consommé Lagrandière)

Chicken consommé flavored with Madeira, garnished with julienned cock's combs, cock's kidneys, mushrooms, and truffles, cucumber pearls, and small pitted olives.

Lorette Consommé
(Consommé Lorette)

Lorette potatoes are the same as Dauphine with the addition of grated Parmesan cheese.

Chicken consommé flavored with paprika, garnished with asparagus tips, julienned truffle, and chervil; small Lorette potato balls served separately.

Louisiana Style Soup
(Consommé à la Louisiannaise)

Simple chicken consommé flavored with saffron, garnished with sliced okra, rice, crabmeat, and diced shrimp and bell peppers.

Madeleine Consommé
(Consommé Madeleine)

Chicken consommé garnished with diced celery, shredded lettuce, and small chicken quenelles; profiteroles served separately.

Madrid Style Consommé
(Consommé à la Madrilène)

Chicken consommé flavored with tomato, garnished with diced tomatoes and/or diced red peppers. (Usually served chilled.)

Maecenas Consommé
(Consommé Mécène)

Chicken consommé garnished with celery root, small game quenelles, and chicken royale.

———————— • ————————

Calius Maecenas (d. 8 B.C.) was a Roman statesman and patron of letters under Caesar Augustus. His famous literary circle included Horace, Virgil, and Propertius, and his name is the symbol of the wealthy benefactor of the arts.

Magenta Consommé
(Consommé Magenta)

Chicken consommé slightly thickened with arrowroot, garnished with truffle quenelles, julienned mushrooms and truffle, and diced tomatoes.

Margot Consommé
(Consommé Margot)

Chicken consommé garnished with two varieties of quenelles: chicken, and chicken blended with spinach.

Maria Consommé
(Consommé Maria)

Chicken consommé slightly thickened with tapioca, garnished with diced white bean royale, carrot and turnip pearls, peas, and string beans cut into diamond shapes (losange).

Marie-Louise Consommé
(Consommé Marie-Louise)

Chicken consommé garnished with diced plain royale and green peas.

Marigny Consommé
(Consommé Marigny)

Chicken consommé garnished with chicken quenelles, peas, and julienned cucumber and chervil.

Enguerrand de Marigny (1260–1315), a powerful chamberlain to the French king Philip IV ("The Fair"), was once described as the man who knew all the king's secrets. After rising to the position in charge of the royal treasury, his policies of taxation and debasement of the coinage, as well as his personal power over the king, made him unpopular. The king's brother, Charles de Valois, charged him with corruption, for which he was initially cleared and then imprisoned. The new sovereign, Louis X, was inclined to merely banish de Marigny, but de Valois charged him with sorcery and he was immediately executed.

Martinière Consommé
(Consommé Martinière)

Chicken consommé garnished with slices of stuffed and braised cabbage, peas, chervil, and square diablotins.

Messaline Consommé
(Consommé Messaline)

Chicken consommé flavored with tomato, garnished with cock's kidneys, julienned pimentos, and rice.

Mikado Style Consommé
(Consommé à la Mikado)

Chicken consommé flavored with tomato, garnished with cock's kidneys, julienned pimentos, and rice.

Milanese Style Consommé
(Consommé à la Milanaise)

Chicken consommé garnished with small macaroni croquettes (bound with thick Béchamel, coated with bread crumbs, and deep fried); grated cheese served separately.

Mimosa Consommé
(Consommé Mimosa)

Chicken consommé garnished with several varieties of royale: carrot, green pea, plain, and egg yolk.

Mireille Consommé
(Consommé Mireille)

Chicken consommé garnished with sliced chicken farce flavored with tomato purée, and saffron rice.

Mogador Consommé
(Consommé Mogador)

Chicken consommé slightly thickened with tapioca, garnished with foie gras royale; and chicken breast, beef tongue, and truffle cut into diamond shapes (losange).

Monaco Style Consommé
(Consommé à la Monaco)

Chicken consommé garnished with truffle, carrot, and turnip pearls, and profiteroles.

Monte-Carlo Style Consommé
(Consommé à la Monte-Carlo)

Chicken consommé garnished with very small chicken quenelles, lettuce chiffonade, and chopped chervil; profiteroles served separately.

Montmorency Consommé
(Consommé Montmorency)

Chicken consommé slightly thickened with tapioca, garnished with asparagus tips, small chicken quenelles, rice, and chervil.

Montmort Consommé
(Consommé Montmort)

Chicken consommé garnished with sliced carrots and turnips cut into the shape of half-moons, small slices of chicken farce flavored with chopped truffle and beef tongue, diced green pea royale, and chervil.

Murillo Consommé
(Consommé Murillo)

Chicken consommé garnished with vermicelli, diced tomatoes, and chervil.

Nantes Style Consommé
(Consommé à la Nantaise)

Chicken consommé garnished with green peas, pearl barley, and julienned chicken breast.

Napoleon Consommé
(Consommé Napoléon)

Chicken consommé garnished with triangular raviolis filled with a purée of foie gras.

———————————————————— • ————————————————————

Ravioli is derived from "rabiole," meaning scraps of little value, in reference to leftover food chopped up and wrapped in small pasta pillows by the sailors of Genoa during their voyages. The triangular ravioli may be an imitation of the emperor's well-known chapeau, with the goose liver representing the Corsican's French political career.

Nice Style Consommé
(Consommé à la Niçoise)

Chicken consommé garnished with diced tomato and green bean royale, diced potatoes, and chopped chervil.

Nilson Consommé
(Consommé Nilson)

Chicken consommé slightly thickened with tapioca, garnished with peas and chervil, and three varieties of chicken quenelles: with chopped ham, chopped truffle, and chopped chives.

Ninon Consommé
(Consommé Ninon)

Chicken consommé garnished with carrot, turnip, and truffle pearls; miniature chicken hash tartlets decorated with a truffle star served separately.

Noailles Consommé
(Consommé Noailles)

Chicken consommé garnished with julienned beef tongue and chicken breast, diced artichoke bottom royale, and chervil.

————— • —————

A variation on this recipe consists of a garnish of three types of chicken quenelles of the same flavors as the royale.

—————————

Orléans Style Consommé
(Consommé à l'Orléans)

Chicken consommé slightly thickened with tapioca, garnished with chervil and three varieties of diced royale: plain, spinach, and tomato.

Orsay Consommé
(Consommé Orsay)

Chicken consommé garnished with poached egg yolks, pigeon quenelles, julienned pigeon meat, and chervil.

Palermo Style Consommé
(Consommé à la Palermo)

Chicken consommé garnished with spaghetti, diced tomato royal and chicken breast; grated cheese served separately.

Parisian Style Consommé
(Consommé à la Parisienne)

Chicken consommé garnished with poached egg yolks, pigeon quenelles, julienned pigeon meat, and chervil.

$\mathcal{A}$remberg Consommé *(Consommé Aremberg) (p. 40)*

$\mathcal{F}$aubonne Soup *(Potage Faubonne) (p. 137)*

$\mathcal{L}$ithuania Style Soup *(Potage à la Lithuanienne) (p. 140)*

*C*atherine Soup *(Potage Catherine) (p. 153)*

$\mathcal{B}$resse Style Soup *(Potage à la Bressane)* upper left *(p. 162)*; Duchess Style Soup *(Potage à la Duchess) (p. 168)*

$\mathcal{T}$omato Bisque *(Bisque de Tomate) (p. 205)*

*M*ulligatawny Soup *(p. 224)*

*H*ousehold Garlic Soup, Provence Style *(Aïgo Bouïdo à la Ménagère) (p. 243)*

*M*ulligatawny Soup *(p. 224)*

$\mathcal{H}$appy Family *(shown with hot pepper oil and soy sauce) (p. 228)*

*C*zechoslovakian Potato Soup *(Bramborová Polevká) (p. 231)*

$\mathcal{H}$ousehold Garlic Soup, Provence Style *(Aïgo Bouïdo à la Ménagère) (p. 243)*

*C*abbage Soup *(Laghanosupa) (p. 249)*

*G*oulash Soup *(Magyar Gulyás Leves) (p. 250)*

*I*talian Fish Soup *(Brodetto di Pesce) (p. 253)*

$\mathcal{C}$ream of Corn, George Washington *(p. 260)*

$\mathscr{P}$olish Duck and Beet Soup *(Borschtsch Polski) (p. 267)*

*S*panish Pot Soup *(Olla Podrida) (p. 279)*

Patti Consommé
(Consommé Patti)

Chicken consommé slightly thickened with tapioca, garnished with diced artichoke bottoms and truffles.

Pépita Consommé
(Consommé Pépita)

Chicken consommé flavored with tomato, seasoned with paprika, garnished with diced tomato royale.

Perfect Consommé
(Consommé Parfait)

Chicken consommé slightly thickened with tapioca, flavored with Madeira, and garnished with diced plain royale, diced red peppers, and chervil leaves.

Pigeon Bouillon
(Consommé au Pigeon)

Simple chicken consommé flavored with pigeon and ham, garnished with diced vegetables and julienned pigeon breast.

Pojarsky Consommé
(Consommé Pojarsky)

Chicken consommé made with hazel-hen bones; small hazel-hen or chicken cutlets served separately.

Pojarski was an innkeeper whose ground beef and veal cutlets were much favored by Czar Nicolas I. In modern times, Veal Chop Pojarsky is a mixture of predominately veal, sometimes blended with pork and/or beef, bound with fresh white bread crumbs, fitted with a rib bone, and shaped into a chop. It is then standard breaded (flour, egg wash, bread crumbs), pan-fried, and served with a simple butter sauce, such as beurre noisette or a Piccata-style beurre blanc (with capers and lemon).

Princess Style Consommé
(Consommé à la Princesse)

Chicken consommé garnished with pearl barley, diced green pea royale, and julienned chicken breast.

Princess Alice Consommé
(Consommé Princesse Alice)

Chicken consommé slightly thickened with tapioca, garnished with lettuce chiffonade, vermicelli, and julienned artichoke bottoms and chicken breast.

Rachel Consommé
(Consommé Rachel)

Chicken consommé slightly thickened with tapioca, garnished with julienned artichoke bottoms; poached beef marrow on toast served separately.

———————— • ————————

Rachel was the stage name of Élisabeth Félix (1821–1858), a great tragic actress, and the mistress of Dr. Louis Véron (1798–1867). Véron's table was legendary, thanks to Sophie, his cook, who reputedly surpassed herself with such dishes as *Canard aux olives* (Duck braised with olives) and *Gigot d'agneau aux flageolets* (Roast Lamb Leg with flageolets).

Récamier Consommé
(Consommé Récamier)

Chicken consommé garnished with sago, truffle pearls, and small chicken quenelles.

———————— • ————————

The following tale was related to René de Beauvoir by Chevrier, a popular maître d'hôtel in the early nineteenth century, and which appeared in *Monde Illustré* in May 1857: "'Madame Recamier,' says Chevrier, 'had lost all interest in food and we could see her fading away. No one dared disobey the doctor's orders for her—a diet. Very well, I said to myself, she likes peaches—I'll serve her some in my own way. And I put one, the best I could find, to cook in a bain-marie; I smothered it with exquisite sugar syrup, poured some cream over it—and there it was.' "

Réjane Consommé
(Consommé Réjane)

Chicken consommé flavored with chervil, garnished with carrot and filbert royale cut to look like confetti (small rounds, squares, and triangles), and raw eggs strained through a sieve into the hot broth.

Rembrandt Consommé
(Consommé Rembrandt)

Chicken consommé garnished with diced green pea royale, and diced chicken breast.

---•---

Rembrandt Harmenszoon van Rijn (1606–1669) was a Dutch painter, etcher, and draftsman who attained significant success for a period, and whose work makes dramatic use of light and shadow. During the last 20 years of his life he had financial difficulties, and though he withdrew from society, he created many of his masterpieces during this time (e.g., *Aristotle Contemplating a Bust of Homer*). He produced more than 600 paintings, 300 etchings, and nearly 2,000 drawings, many of which can be found in the Rijks Museum in Amsterdam.

Renaissance Style Consommé
(Consommé à la Renaissance)

Chicken consommé garnished with spring vegetable pearls, diced fine herb royale, and chervil.

Rich Style Consommé
(Consommé à la Riche)

Chicken consommé garnished with large truffled chicken quenelles.

Richepin Consommé
(Consommé à la Richepin)

Chicken consommé garnished with chicken quenelles, julienned carrot and turnip, and lettuce chiffonade.

Rossini Consommé
(Consommé Rossini)

Chicken consommé flavored with truffles, slightly thickened with tapioca; very small profiteroles stuffed with truffled foie gras purée served separately.

———————————— • ————————————

Gioacchino Antonio Rossini (1792–1868), the prolific opera composer and gastronome, once offered the following philosophy of life: *"To eat, to love, to sing, and to digest; in truth, these are the four acts in this opéra bouffe that we call life, and which vanishes like the bubbles in a bottle of champagne."* One of his most important gastronomic contributions came out of an incident at the Café Anglais one evening, where he reportedly declared, "I am tired of the everlasting piece of beef listed on every menu." "Take something else," replied the waiter. "No, I don't like anything but beef." He gave the maître d'hôtel instructions for the meat to be prepared another way, to which he responded, "Never would I dare to offer a thing as . . . unpresentable." "Well," responded Rossini, ". . . then arrange not to let it be seen." Hence the name, *tournedos* (turn one's back).

———————————————————————

Royal Consommé
(Consommé Royale)

Chicken consommé slightly thickened with tapioca, garnished with diced plain royale.

Rubens Consommé
(Consommé Rubens)

Chicken consommé flavored with tomato juice, garnished with
hop shoots.

———————————— • ————————————

Hop is a climbing plant whose female flowers are used to
give beer its bitterness; the male flowers (hop shoots) are
prepared as a vegetable, blanched in acidulated water, then
cooked in butter, cream, or stock. Hop shoots are commonly
used in Belgian cooking, indicated here by the name of Peter
Paul Rubens (1577–1640), the foremost Flemish painter of
the seventeenth century. Rubens was a uniquely fulfilled
artist, prodigious in his painting (in excess of 2,000
paintings), and successfully passing on his legacy through
apprenticeships that spawned the work of Van Dyke and
Jordaens. His work for the diplomatic corps led to a
commission to paint a portrait of the Spanish royal family,
and he was knighted by the British for his peacemaking
efforts.

———— • ————

Charles Camille Saint-Saëns
(1835–1921) was a French
composer of symphonies and
concertos, whose works
include the opera *Samson et
Dalila* (1877).

Saint-Saëns Consommé
(Consommé Saint-Saëns)

Chicken consommé garnished with pearl barley, and noisette
(medium ball) potatoes.

San Remo Style Consommé
(Consommé à la San Remo)

Chicken consommé garnished with rice and round carrot slices;
grated cheese served separately.

Sans-gêne Consommé
(Consommé Sans-Gêne)

Chicken consommé garnished with julienned truffle, cock's
combs, and cock's kidneys.

Santa Maria Consommé
(Consommé Santa Maria)

Chicken consommé flavored with tarragon, garnished with quenelles and cappellini; profiteroles filled with mushroom duxelle served separately.

Santos-Dumont Consommé
(Consommé Santos-Dumont)

Chicken consommé slightly thickened with tapioca, garnished with carrots and turnip pearls, and julienned green beans.

Sarah Bernhardt Consommé
(Consommé Sarah Bernhardt)

Chicken consommé slightly thickened with tapioca, garnished with chicken quenelles flavored with crayfish butter, sliced beef marrow, asparagus tips, and julienned truffle.

———————————— • ————————————

Sarah Bernhardt (1844–1923), born Henriette Rosine Bernard, was a celebrated French actress who made many tours of Europe, Canada, and the United States. Some of her most memorable roles included the title role in Jean Racine's *Phèdre;* the redeemed courtesan in Alexandre Dumas' (*fils*) *La Dame aux camélias;* the title role in Eugène Scribe's *Adrienne Lecouvreur;* and the title role in *Hamlet*, performed at her Théâtre Sarah Bernhardt in 1899. During the Franco-Prussian War (1870), she organized a military hospital in the Odéon theater; and during World War I, in spite of losing her right leg to gangrene—after wrenching the knee in 1915 during the last scene of *La Tosca*—in 1916 she performed for front-line soldiers. She published her autobiography in 1907 (*Ma double vie: Mémoires de Sarah Bernhardt*), and *L'Art du théâtre* in 1923, with a section on voice training, since the actress had always considered voice to be the key to dramatic character.

Ségurd Consommé
(Consommé Ségurd)

Chicken consommé garnished with julienned chicken breast and smoked beef tongue.

Severin Consommé
(Consommé Severin)

Chicken consommé garnished with small slices of chicken roulade.

Sévigné Consommé
(Consommé Sévigné)

Chicken consommé garnished with chicken quenelles wrapped in lettuce, green peas, and chervil.

Soubrette Consommé
(Consommé Soubrette)

Chicken consommé flavored with tomato and a little cayenne pepper, garnished with small chicken quenelles, truffle rings, and miniature (titi) shrimp.

Sovereign Style Consommé
(Consommé à la Souveraine)

Chicken consommé garnished with pearl-sized chicken quenelles, green peas, diced root vegetables, and chervil.

Spring Style Consommé
(Consommé à la Printinière)

Chicken consommé garnished with carrot and turnip pearls, green peas, diced green beans, asparagus tips, lettuce chiffonade, and chervil.

Spring Style Consommé, Colbert
(Consommé à la Printinière, Colbert)

Chicken consommé garnished with carrot and turnip pearls, green peas, diced green beans, asparagus tips, lettuce chiffonade, poached eggs, and chervil.

Spring Style Consommé, Royale
(Consommé à la Printinière, Royale)

Chicken consommé garnished with carrot and turnip pearls, green peas, diced green beans, asparagus tips, lettuce chiffonade, diced plain royale, and chervil.

Surprise Consommé
(Consommé Surprise)

Chicken consommé flavored and colored with beet root, garnished with chicken quenelles.

Talleyrand Consommé
(Consommé Talleyrand)

Chicken consommé flavored with sherry, garnished with finely diced truffle.

As a young man, Charles-Maurice de Talleyrand-Périgord (1754–1838) was sent to America to get over his stormy liaison with Madame de Flahaut. While visiting Niagara Falls, he was so seized with nausea at the sight of so much water that he and two friends got drunk on corn whiskey to the point of signing up with a gang of beaver trappers. Though he has been condemned by historians as corrupt, lazy, and arrogant, these were just the kind of characteristics that would have allowed him to stay in office through the revolution. "Two things are essential in life: to give good dinners and to keep on fair terms with women," he liked to say, and towards that end he preferred heavy dishes and light women at dinner; his table was considered to be one of the very best to which to be invited as a guest. He did, however, possess a sense of humor, as indicated by a dinner party given in Paris during the winter of 1803, when fish was extremely hard to come by. He arranged for his butler to bring in an enormous sturgeon on a silver platter, then stumble and drop it to the floor, much to the horror of his guests; then at his request another was promptly brought in.

Talma Consommé
(Consommé Talma)

Chicken consommé garnished with rice and almond royale.

Theodor Consommé
(Consommé Theodor)

Chicken consommé garnished with diced chicken breast, asparagus tips, and flageolets.

Theodora Consommé
(Consommé Theodora)

Chicken consommé garnished with julienned chicken breast and truffle, asparagus tips, and diced plain royale.

Theresa Consommé
(Consommé Thérèse)

Chicken consommé garnished with julienned chicken breast and truffle, asparagus tips, and diced plain royale.

———————— • ————————

Thérèse Martin (1873–1897) was a French Carmelite nun, nicknamed Little Flower of Jesus. She entered a convent at Lisieux at the age of 15 and died of tuberculosis nine years later. Endowed with great personal charm, tact, and good nature, her reputation was enhanced by her writings, notably *Life* and *Way of Perfection*, considered among the best of mystical literature.

———— • ————

La Tosca was one of several operas by one of the most revered Italian composers, Giacomo Puccini (1858–1924).

Tosca Consommé
(Consommé Tosca)

Chicken consommé slightly thickened with tapioca, garnished with chicken quenelles flavored with foie gras and truffle, julienned carrots; profiteroles filled with chicken purée served separately.

Trévise Consommé
(Consommé Trévise)

Chicken consommé slightly thickened with tapioca, garnished with julienned chicken breast, truffle, and beef tongue.

Trianon Consommé
(Consommé Trianon)

Chicken consommé slightly thickened with tapioca, garnished with three varieties of sliced royale: carrot, chicken, and spinach.

Turbigo Consommé
(Consommé Turbigo)

Chicken consommé garnished with julienned carrots and chicken breast, and vermicelli.

Valencian Style Consommé
(Consommé à la Valencienne)

Chicken consommé garnished with chicken quenelles, lettuce chiffonade, and chervil.

Valentino Consommé
(Consommé Valentino)

Chicken consommé garnished with julienned chicken breast and truffles, and small heart-shaped chicken quenelles.

Rodolfo Alfonzo Raffaello Pietro Filiberto Guglielmi di Valentina d'Antonguolla, better known as Rudolph Valentino (1895–1926), came to the United States in 1913 and worked for a while as a dishwasher and gardener. In 1918 he went to Hollywood, where he played small parts in films with little success. In 1921 he appeared in *The Four Horsemen of the Apocalypse*, and he immediately became a celebrity, ultimately starring in nine films. When he died in New York City, an eleven-block-long crowd lined up to view his remains.

Victoria Consommé
(Consommé Victoria)

Chicken (or beef) consommé garnished with julienned chicken breast and truffles, small chicken quenelles, peas, and chervil.

Villeneuve Consommé
(Consommé Villeneuve)

Chicken consommé garnished with crêpes filled with ham purée and cut into small triangles, small squares of chicken and beef tongue purée wrapped in lettuce, and diced plain royale.

Villeroi Consommé
(Consommé Villeroi)

Chicken consommé garnished with chicken quenelles, small round slices of carrots and onions, and diced tomatoes.

Viveur Consommé
(Consommé Viveur)

Chicken consommé flavored and colored with beet root, garnished with julienned celery root, and diablotins.

Vivian Consommé
(Consommé Viviane)

Chicken consommé garnished with sliced chicken breast and truffle.

Voltaire Consommé
(Consommé Voltaire)

Chicken consommé garnished with diced chicken breast and tomatoes, and small chicken quenelles.

Dishes so titled are named after the Marshal de Villeroi, mentor of Louis XV.

———— • ————

Voltaire was the pen name of François-Marie Arouet (1694–1778), French poet, dramatist, satirist, and historian. Twice unjustly imprisoned and later banished to England, he came to admire English liberalism, and became fluent in English so that he could read John Locke. Of his copious literary output, his most enduring work is his satirical masterpiece *Candide* (1759).

White Lady Style Consommé
(Consommé à la Dame Blanche)

Chicken consommé slightly thickened with tapioca, garnished with diced almond royale, and julienned chicken breast.

Yvette Consommé
(Consommé Yvette)

Chicken consommé flavored with turtle herbs, and garnished with chicken quenelles and puréed spinach.

Zorilla Consommé
(Consommé Zorilla)

Chicken consommé flavored with tomato juice, and garnished with rice and chick peas (garbanzos).

DUCK CONSOMMÉ

Cyrano Consommé
(Consommé Cyrano)

Duck consommé; small duck quenelles coated with suprême sauce, sprinkled with cheese and gratinéed (glazed), served separately.

———————————— • ————————————

Savinien Cyrano de Bergerac (1619–1655) was a writer known for his vigorous efforts to defend Cardinal Mazarin during the Fronde (1648–1653), a legendary political battle in which the French Parliament, driven by the ambitions of discontented French nobles, attempted to limit royal authority (it ultimately failed, and actually strengthened the power of the monarchy). Cyrano also wrote fiction, and though he was masterful in his original use of metaphors, his contemporaries considered his work absurd. Edmond Rostrand's play *Cyrano de Bergerac* (1897) made him famous, though it is considered an exaggeration of de Bergerac's life and work.

Danish Style Consommé
(Consommé à la Danoise)

Wild duck consommé flavored with Marsala, garnished with small game quenelles and diced mushrooms.

Irish Style Consommé
(Consommé à l'Irlandaise)

Duck consommé garnished with small duck quenelles, diced root vegetables, and julienned cabbage.

LAMB (MUTTON) CONSOMMÉ

Egyptian Style Consommé
(Consommé à l'Egyptienne)

Mutton consommé flavored with saffron, garnished with rice, diced eggplant, and okra.

Oriental Style Consommé
(Consommé à l'Orientale)

Mutton consommé flavored with tomato juice and saffron, garnished with rice, brain royale cut in the shape of half moons, and hard-cooked egg yolks pressed through a sieve.

Pondicherry Consommé
(Consommé Pondicherry)

Mutton broth flavored with curry, garnished with rice, and plain crêpes filled with mutton hash and cut into julienne strips.

Tewki Pasha Consommé
(Consommé Tewki Pasha)

Mutton consommé flavored with tomato and peppers, garnished with rice and julienned red and green peppers.

Tunisian Style Consommé
(Consommé à la Tunisienne)

Mutton consommé flavored with saffron, garnished with chick peas (garbanzo beans), rice, and diced tomatoes and green peppers.

—— • ——

Pilaf (also spelled pilau, pilav, or pilaw) is a rice dish and a staple of the Turkish diet. It can be made with any number of ingredients—including anchovies, chicken, meatballs, nuts, pumpkin, saffron, and so on—but the basic version is made by sautéing onions and rice in butter or fat (in this case mutton fat), adding stock, and simmering until the liquid is absorbed.

Turkish Style Consommé
(Consommé de Mouton à la Turque)

Mutton consommé garnished with rice pilaf (*see sidebar on p. 105*) prepared with mutton fat and broth.

**GAME
CONSOMMÉ**

Anjou Style Consommé
(Consommé à l'Anjou)

Game consommé garnished with asparagus tips, rice, and game quenelles.

Berchoux Consommé
(Consommé Berchoux)

Game consommé garnished with diced quail and chestnut royale, and diced mushrooms and truffle.

Joseph Berchoux (1768–1839) was a French solicitor who made a name for himself in gastronomic literature with a poem entitled *Gastronomie ou l'Homme des champs à table*, published in 1801. It was very popular during the Directory period that followed the Reign of Terror and during which the French rediscovered the joys of good food. In the first canto, Berchoux describes the death of Vatel and Spartan gruel; in the second he praises good cooking; and in the third he praises dessert.

Castle Style Consommé
(Consommé à la Castellane)

Game consommé flavored with woodcock, garnished with julienned woodcock breast, and woodcock and lentil royale.

Cussy Consommé
(Consommé Cussy)

Game consommé garnished with partridge quenelles; diced chestnut and partridge royale, and julienned truffle; flavored with sherry and Cognac just before serving.

Louis, the Marquis de Cussy (1766–1837) was Prefect of the palace under Napoléon I (steward of the emperor's household, wardrobe, and provisions of the court), and according to Grimod de La Reynière, Cussy was also the inventor of 366 different ways of preparing chicken. When Louis XVIII succeeded Napoléon, he planned on releasing Cussy from his former position, but after learning that he was the creator of *Les fraises à la Cussy*, he gave him a post of responsibility. Cussy is the author of *Les Classiques de la table* (1843), which includes a large section on gastronomic history.

A hazel-hen is a small game bird found in central Europe, throughout Siberia, and in Japan. It can be prepared as though it were a partridge or quail, roasted if young, or braised if old.

Czarevitch Consommé
(Consommé Tsarevitch)

Game consommé flavored with sherry, garnished with hazel-hen quenelles and julienned truffle.

Diana Consommé
(Consommé Diane)

Partridge consommé flavored with sherry, and garnished with game quenelles and sliced truffle cut into half-moons.

Don Miguel Consommé
(Consommé Don Miguel)

Game consommé garnished with game quenelles and diced plain royale.

Hunter Style Consommé
(Consommé à la Chasseur)

Game consommé flavored with Port, garnished with julienned mushrooms and chopped chervil; small cream puffs filled with puréed partridge served separately.

Jenny Lind Consommé
(Consommé Jenny Lind)

Game consommé flavored with quail, garnished with quail breasts and diced mushrooms.

Jenny Lind is the stage name for Johanna Maria Lind-Goldschmidt (1820–1887), Swedish-born coloratura soprano. She was popular in the United States, and she was a frequent visitor to Delmonico's for after-theater suppers following her concerts in New York City in 1850 and 1851.

Laguipière Consommé
(Consommé Laguipière)

Game consommé garnished with game royale and poached pigeon's eggs.

---•---

Former mentor to Carême, who considered him ". . . the most remarkable chef of our times," Laguipière froze to death in Vilna during the retreat from Moscow in 1812, a disaster that cost France 100,000 men and fifty cooks. Carême dedicated his book *Le Cuisinier parisien* to the departed spirit of Laguipière. "Oh, my master," wrote Carême, "you suffered persecution in life, and to add insult to injury, you died in the midst of the most cruel agonies in the glacial northern cold."

Mancelle Consommé
(Consommé Mancelle)

Game consommé garnished with very small poached chestnuts and diced game royale.

Nesselrode Consommé
(Consommé Nesselrode)

Game consommé flavored with hazel-hen, garnished with chestnut royale, julienned hazel-hen meat, and diced mushrooms.

Rabelais Consommé
(Consommé Rabelais)

Game consommé flavored with Vouvray white wine and larks, garnished with julienned celery and lark quenelles flavored with truffle.

---•---

François Rabelais was a physician and humanist, and the author of two comic satires: *Pantagruel* (1532) and *Gargantua* (1534), both written under the pseudonym Alcofribas Nasier. Both works were unique and reveal both the author's mastery of comic situations and his storytelling genius that enables him to create worlds of fantasy. He produced three other works, one of which, *Quart Livre*, so mocked bloodthirsty bishops and referred to the Council of Trent (set up in 1545 by Pope Paul III to address the crisis of the Protestant Reformation) as a council of nitwits, that it was condemned by the Sorbonne and banned by the French Parliament in 1552.

Rohan Consommé
(Consommé Rohan)

Game consommé garnished with poached plover's eggs and lettuce chiffonade; game purée on small round croutons served separately.

Rothschild Consommé
(Consommé Rothschild)

Game consommé flavored with pheasant and Sauterne wine, garnished with pheasant and chestnut royale, and julienned ortolan breast and truffle.

---•---

The Rothschild family became one of the most famous European banking dynasties, due to the efforts of Mayer Amschel Rothschild (1744–1812). Although he initially studied for the rabbinate, Mayer's parents' early death forced him into an apprenticeship in a banking house in his native Frankfurt. Beginning as dealers in luxury items and traders in coins, the Rothschilds moved into banking in time to fund the French Revolution (1789) and the Napoléonic Wars (1792–1815).

Rotraud Consommé
(Consommé Rotraud)

Game consommé flavored with white wine, garnished with pheasant and chestnut royale, and julienned pheasant breast and truffle.

Saint George Consommé
(Consommé Saint George)

Hare consommé flavored with claret, garnished with hare quenelles, and julienned truffle and hare meat.

Saint Hubert Consommé
(Consommé Saint Hubert)

Game consommé garnished with diced game royale and julienned mushrooms cooked in butter and Madeira (strained before adding).

FISH CONSOMMÉ

Admiral Style Consommé
(Consommé à l'Amiral)

Fish consommé garnished with fish quenelles, diced lobster and mushrooms, and rice.

Albion I Consommé
(Consommé Albion I)

Fish consommé slightly thickened with tapioca, garnished with lobster quenelles and julienned truffle.

Angler's Style Consommé
(Consommé des Pêcheurs)

Fish consommé garnished with mussels, green peas, and diced tomatoes.

British Style Consommé
(Consommé à l'Angleterre)

Fish consommé garnished with julienned truffle and diced lobster royale.

Cancal Style Consommé
(Consommé à la Cancalais)

Fish consommé garnished with julienned truffle and diced lobster royale.

Cardinal Style Consommé
(Consommé à la Cardinal)

Fish consommé flavored with lobster, garnished with lobster quenelles.

Carmelite Consommé
(Consommé Carmelite)

Fish consommé slightly thickened with arrowroot, garnished with diced fish farce and rice.

Dufferin Consommé
(Consommé Dufferin)

Fish consommé lightly flavored with curry, garnished with curried fish quenelles, rice, and julienned sole fillet.

George Sand Consommé
(Consommé George Sand)

Fish consommé garnished with fish quenelles flavored with crayfish butter; diced morels, rice, and carp roe on small fried croutons served separately.

Dishes thus named refer to the Carmelite nuns' white habit and black veil. In a cold chicken dish (chicken breast) the white is represented by a chaud-froid sauce, the black by truffle.

George Sand is the pen name of Amandine-Aurore-Lucie Dupin, Baroness Dudevant (1804–1876), a French romantic novelist. Married to Casimir Dudevant at the age of 18, his insensitivity drove her away after a few short years and she began a long series of liaisons with many lovers (among them Frédéric Chopin, with whom she stayed 8 years). In 1832 she adopted the pseudonym George Sand for *Indiana,* her first novel, which brought her considerable fame. It was a passionate protest against the social conventions of a wife bound to a husband in an unhappy marriage. Inspiration for her novels came from a love of the countryside and sympathy for poor peasants and workers. A natural storyteller, her characters were innocent, charming, and kind, and the endings happy. "The novel," she once said, "need not necessarily be the representation of reality."

Lady Morgan Consommé
(Consommé Dame Morgan)

Fish consommé flavored with oysters, garnished with crayfish quenelles, julienned truffle, mushrooms, sole fillet, and small oysters.

Mignon Consommé
(Consommé Mignon)

Fish consommé garnished with fish quenelles, truffle pearls, and shrimp.

———— • ————

Moldavia is an historic province in East Romania known for its oil reserves and fertile soil that produces fruits and grains, among other crops.

Moldavian Style Consommé
(Consommé à la Moldave)

Fish consommé flavored with pickled cucumber brine and Madeira, garnished with julienned mushrooms, diced sturgeon, and peeled and sliced lemon.

Murillo Consommé
(Consommé Murillo)

Fish consommé flavored with tomato, garnished with fish quenelles.

Nelson Consommé
(Consommé Nelson)

Fish consommé slightly thickened with arrowroot, garnished with rice; profiteroles stuffed with lobster hash served separately.

Ostend Style Consommé
(Consommé à l'Ostendaise)

Fish consommé flavored with oysters, garnished with small poached oysters.

Polignac Consommé
(Consommé Polignac)

Fish consommé garnished with lobster quenelles and diced mushrooms.

Potemkin Consommé
(Consommé Potemkin)

Fish consommé flavored with pressed caviar and white wine, garnished with asparagus tips and julienned carrot and celery.

———————————— • ————————————

Prince Grigory Aleksandrovich Potemkin (1739–1791) was a Russian army officer and statesman, Empress Catherine II's lover for 2 years, and for 17 years the most powerful man in the empire. Variously described as an able administrator, as well as extravagant, generous, licentious, loyal, and magnanimous, he was instrumental in bringing Catherine to power, for which she gave him a small estate.

Pressed caviar is made from very ripe sturgeon eggs taken near the end of the fishing season. Five parts fish eggs yields one part pressed caviar, and its strong, oily flavor is appreciated by caviar aficionados.

Rampolla Consommé
(Consommé Rampolla)

Fish consommé flavored with crayfish and Rhenish wine, garnished with julienned eelpout, crayfish tails, oysters, and diced mushrooms.

Regina Consommé
(Consommé Regina)

Fish consommé flavored with lobster, garnished with asparagus tips and truffle pearls; small puff pastry bouchées filled with lobster ragoût served separately.

Russian Style Consommé
(Consommé de Poisson à la Russe)

Fish consommé garnished with cucumber pearls and fish quenelles.

Vatel Consommé
(Consommé Vatel)

Fish consommé garnished with diced sole fillets, and diced lobster royale.

Fritz Karl Watel (1635–1671; last name pronounced "Vatel") worked as steward to the financier Fouquet and later to the house of Chantilly. In April 1671, the Prince de Condé charged him with the organization of a party for 3,000 guests in honor of Louis XIV. On April 24, roasts ran out prematurely, and that evening a fireworks display was spoiled by a cloudy sky. After a storm over the English channel delayed the shipment of Dover sole for the next evening's banquet, Vatel was heard to utter, "I have lost my fame . . . I cannot bear this disgrace," whereupon he withdrew to his room and impaled himself on a sword. More than two centuries later, a British reporter, while interviewing August Escoffier, asked him if he would have acted the same in such a situation. "No," he replied, "I would have made a mousse of young chicken breasts, covered it with a fish velouté, and no one would have known the difference."

CHAPTER 4

THICKENED SOUPS

*T*he three traditional varieties of thick soups—
puréed, creamed, and velvet—may be defined as
follows:

Puréed: vegetables, fish, poultry, or game sweated in butter, simmered in stock, sometimes with beans, bread, lentils, potatoes, or rice,
rubbed through a sieve, enriched with butter.

Creamed: Béchamel Sauce (white roux and seasoned milk) blended
with puréed vegetables, fish, meat, or game, sometimes finished with
cream.

Velvet: white roux and stock (veal, chicken, or fish), blended with
puréed vegetables, fish, poultry, meat, or game, thickened with egg
yolks and cream.

SHIFTING CLASSICAL SOUPS TO MEET MODERN STYLES

There is no question that styles have changed since the days
when these classical soups began their evolution. Individual style
and contemporary trends are also significant in these changes,
since they represent a culinary practitioner's own personal inter-
pretation and philosophical approach, as well as the dining public's preferences. The approach here is to adhere to the tradition
of classical soups, while upgrading elements of them that fit into
the demands of modern production. That there are often minor
variations in classic recipes from different sources is all the more
reason to approach the issue in this fashion. Thus, even when the
thickening or finishing steps vary, the essential content of specific
soups is generally agree upon by all sources—a Potage à la Reine
is always a creamed soup based on chicken; a Potage Saint-
Germain or Potage Clamart is always a purée based on green
peas; a Potage Dubarry always includes cauliflower; and so on.

Before the advent of food processors, rubbing finely minced
and puréed foods through a screen sieve was a common method
of removing vestiges of fibers and other indigestible matter,
while passing it through a manually turned food mill was often
the manner in which puréeing was accomplished. Food processors have speeded up this process, though there are still occasions when straining will be necessary. Soups in which artichoke
leaves, asparagus trimmings, or celery are simmered in order to
extract their flavor are often puréed in a food processor, then
strained in order to remove any fibrous remnants. In the case of
starch and starchy vegetables (such as beans, peas, potatoes, and
rice), however, straining is often unnecessary, since it is the
puréed solids that give the soup its body.

Cream soups, originally created from a foundation of Bécha-mel Sauce, have long passed out of fashion, since roux-thick-ened seasoned milk is fairly passé. A creamed soup based on roux-thickened stock and finished with cream is far more prac-tical in modern production—not only is stock less expensive than milk, it is also easier to handle than milk (it will not curdle), lower in fat (at this point), and superior in taste (stock is a more palatable primary medium than milk). And when cream is added to the finished soup, it renders a product just as smooth and rich as the classical version made with a base of béchamel, yet it is su-perior in flavor. The type of stock may depend on the nature of the ingredients or the specifics of a recipe, though a neutral white stock is acceptable for most dishes. My preference is for chicken stock, regularly available in nearly all commercial kitchens of any size. It works surprisingly well with all soups, even when the garnish is of seafood or lamb. White veal or beef can also be used as a neutral base, though one is free to use fish or lamb as appropriate for soups with those types of components.

As for velvet soups—a thickened potage finished with a cream and egg yolk liaison—these are truly relics from the past, and are rarely employed in our time. It requires careful temper-ing to prevent the yolks from turning into scrambled eggs, though even when completed and held in a bain marie, there is a risk of the soup curdling from the heat of the bain marie. The reason this technique worked well in the past was because it was prepared *à la minute* ("à la carte"), that is, the liaison was added to the soup minutes before it was served. In today's pro-duction kitchens, we rarely have the luxury of spending that kind of time on a single dish. Instead, soup finished with cream is prepared once, placed in the bain marie, and ladled out throughout the evening's service as it is ordered—the fat content of cream gives it the strength to hold up to the prolonged heat of a hot steam table (bain marie). Consequently, velvet soups are shifted to the subheading of Creamed Soups. (It should be pointed out that "velvet" is the English equivalent of *velouté*, a mother sauce family of the same name. The name is simply de-rived from the ultra-smooth and rich texture created by the cream and egg yolk liaison.)

———————————— • ————————————

There was an ancient and stubborn Gallic chef at a small fine restaurant in southern New England who was compelled to add a liaison to each and every Soupe à l'Oignon, Gratinée after it had been glazed. He would pull back the crouton and melted cheese, pour out some of the broth into a bowl, and beat in two tablespoons of cream and an egg yolk while holding the bowl over a burner. This enriched soup would then be returned to the bowl, the crouton and melted cheese would be laid back over the top, and the soup would be sent out to the dining room. It was unequivocally a silly extravagance, though one could imagine his mentor thirty years earlier, making his young apprentice swear that he would continue the practice to the end of his career.

Our adjustment to the school of classical potage philosophy, then, will shift the three archaic categories into two, with the following adjustment of definitions:

puréed: vegetables, fish, poultry, meat, or game sweated in fat, simmered in stock, sometimes augmented with beans, potatoes, rice, or roux, blended (puréed), and enriched with butter (an optional step).

creamed: a stock simmered with beans, potatoes, rice, or roux, puréed, garnished with cut (or partially puréed) vegetables, fish, poultry, meat, or game, and finished with cream.

AUGMENTING THICKENED SOUPS WITH STARCH

The thickening element in nearly all puréed soups consists primarily of the puréed solids (legumes, vegetables, poultry, game); in the creamed soups it is generally some form of starch. The most common starch thickener is roux, often added in the form of beurre manié—two to three parts flour to one part whole unsalted butter kneaded into a paste. Other soups are thickened by the starch in beans, potatoes or rice, cooked to a very soft stage, then puréed.

A puréed soup, though, should be more than a coarse vegetable purée; it should have some starch-derived body for cohesiveness. In soups thickened with barley, beans, or rice, there is generally sufficient starch to give the soup appropriate body and smoothness. Potatoes also possess enough starch to thicken sufficiently, but the texture will be a little grainy. And in soups thickened with purées of vegetables like cauliflower, green peas, or squash, since such vegetables have proportionately less starch content to thicken a soup, some of the recipes for these are augmented with a little roux in order to add additional body. Green peas, for example, which are composed of 60 percent carbohydrate content, are well suited for puréed soup, but the starch content varies, and the peas may not have enough starch to give the soup sufficient body. My preference in terms of roux is beurre manié, since it can be added as needed and requires brief simmering—only long enough to expand the starch in the flour. An overview of common thickeners follows:

white roux: flour + fat, precooked without coloring, and the most common form of adjunct thickener. It is often created directly in the cooking vessel: flour sprinkled onto the primary ingredients being sautéed in butter (or other type of fat). It can also be added in the form of beurre manié: two to three parts whole unsalted butter to flour kneaded into a paste.

rice: an effective thickener, particularly if it is basmati, texmati (basmati produced in Texas), jasmine, or some other subtly perfumed rice grain.

potato: called for in certain soups (such as Watercress Soup and Potato Soup Jackson); it imparts a mildly grainy texture.

tapioca: a starch extracted from the roots of the manioc plant found in parts of South America and the West Indies; sometimes used whole as a soup garnish (1 to 2 tablespoons quick-cooking tapioca per cup of liquid).

arrowroot: a starch extracted from the roots of several varieties of tropical American plants; and so named for therapeutic qualities attributed to it by native tribes in the treatment of arrow wounds (cornstarch is virtually the same type of thickener, except it is derived from corn).

A BASIC APPROACH TO PREPARING THICKENED SOUPS

The following is a basic approach to preparing thickened soups that can remain constant in preparing all thickened soups.

fat (butter, chicken/duck fat, salt pork, etc.)	heat or render (melt)
aromatic vegetable(s)	sauté (or sweat)
salt, pepper, herbs, and spices (bouquet garni)	add and sauté (or sweat)
principle ingredient (asparagus, carrot, cauliflower, sorrel, etc.)	add and sauté (or sweat)
starch (flour, potato, or rice)	add and blend thoroughly
liquid (stock or water)	add, blend thoroughly, and simmer; purée and return to the fire
butter and/or cream	add and blend ("finish with . . .")
	adjust seasoning and viscosity
garnish (if included)	add

The difference between sauté and sweat is that a sweat is a sauté covered. Sauté means literally "to jump," and will allow one to brown the ingredients that are being sautéed if color is desired. When covered, however, the moisture in the ingredients being sautéed comes out and stays within the environs of the covered pot, inhibiting browning while in the process of releasing food flavors and aromas.

As for the puréeing step, there are several methods. In a production kitchen, the most efficient way is by using a vertical blender, a long, portable, rod that screws into a jack on one end of the motor, and is placed blade end down into the brew. It has two speeds, and one simply moves it around in the soup while the whirling blade purées all. It is easy to clean and transport, and comes in a variety of sizes. This is one of the most efficient ways to perform the puréeing step. On a smaller scale, a blender can be used, though one must exercise *extreme caution*, since hot whirling liquid poses a serious hazard. The blender should only be filled half full, and the top should he held firmly in place with a thick clean (and dry) towel held at arm's length. A food processor is also effective, but must also be filled only half full, since there is no gasket to prevent liquid from seeping out through the edge of the stationary canister and the lid as it whirls around in the canister. Again, a thick, clean towel should be used to keep the processor securely in place. And finally, there is a large, industrial-size food processor—a large cast aluminum or stainless steel bowl on legs with wheels, equipped with a large hinged lid that clamps into place, sometimes with a horizontal wheel that further screws the top on securely. (The top should not be opened until at least 30 seconds have passed after puréeing, since it requires a few seconds before the spinning blade comes to a halt.)

GENERAL NOTES ON THE PREPARATION OF THICKENED SOUPS

There are no absolutes in the culinary universe. What this means in soup preparation is that when a soup calls for a little milk at the end (see following note), or a garnish of unspecified vegetables, or a game stock of unspecified content, one is free to innovate within one's style and the essential content of a specific soup. A perfect example is Cauliflower Soup, referred to variously as Cauliflower Soup Dubarry, Potage du Barry, Purée à la duBarry, and so on. Recipes for this soup vary broadly—from meatless purées to creamed veloutés to potato and cauliflower purées in chicken stock. Hence, when one prepares this soup today, as long as its core is cauliflower, the stock, thickening agent, and garnish can all be chosen according to one's audience and personal preference.

Soups that are finished with milk and then held for service in a hot bain marie risk curdling from exposure to the prolonged heat. In such a case, we suggest substituting a small amount of half-and-half or heavy cream that will hold up to the heat. (See Appendix for information on Culinary Cream, a recently developed cream-based product that contains less fat than ordinary heavy cream.)

Butter and cream are a frequent presence in classical cookery, but there are times when a clientele insists on minimal use of fat. In such cases, there are ways of seasoning that do not sacrifice the experience of fine dining. Fat can be eliminated in the sautéing step by simply adding the vegetables and other ingredients that are typically sautéed, directly to the hot stock.

A bouquet garni is a collection of aromatics, herbs, and spices that are simmered in a stock or soup to add flavor and character, and there are as many variations as there are culinary practitioners. When a puréed soup includes mirepoix vegetables (celery, carrots, and onions) and herbs in the body of the soup, a bouquet garni is not necessary. In other cases, though, a stock is simmered with its thickening agent (barley, beans, rice, etc.) without the addition of aromatic vegetables—here a bouquet garni can be added. An assertive approach is to take two or three long, dark-green, well-rinsed leek leaves and tie them securely with cotton cord, along with a long carrot stick, a split celery stalk, a couple of bay leaves, a few peppercorns (sprinkled into the fold of one of the leeks), 2 sprigs of thyme, and a bunch of parsley stems (additional herbs or aromatics can be included). This flavor enhancer is removed before puréeing.

When a dish is "flat," it lacks a certain acidity that allows the taste buds to fully absorb the flavors of the ingredients of the soup. Adding salt is the most direct manner of bringing up a flat dish, but it is not always enough. The addition of butter (sometimes called "mellowed with butter," similar to "monter au beurre," beating plain or compound butter into a finished sauce in order to "lift the taste") is another technique commonly found in classical cookery that resolves this problem, but there are times when one must be careful with a free-handed use of fat because of the dietary prerequisites of a certain clientele. In such cases, meat glaze (glace de viande)—something that every good potager will have on hand—is an important tool that can be used to augment flavor as needed. Another way to heighten the flavor of a flat soup is to add a little lemon juice—though it is not recommended for creamed soups (it can curdle the cream).

Game soups are almost always prepared as brown soups because their strong and often gamey flavor calls for the strength of a darker soup prepared from a base of brown game stock. This applies to heavier varieties of game, as well as winged game—partridge, pheasant, quail, squab, and so on.

Brown soups require brown roux for thickening and an excellent way of preparing a brown roux is by toasting flour in a roasting pan for about 1½ hours (or longer) at 400°F (205°C). The flour should be stirred with a fork every 15 minutes (the flour will cake up, and the fork easily breaks it up). When it is a dark tan color, remove it from the oven, allow to cool, sift, and combine with fat (clarified butter, duck fat, chicken fat, and so on). Since it has been toasted, it immediately yields a very dark brown roux and can then be applied where needed.

For the use of macaroni as a garnish, the choice of variety is open. Small ditalini—a small cylindrical noodle about an eighth of an inch (3 mm) in length—is a commonly used variety. Though pasta nomenclature varies considerably, depending on where it is produced, there are hundreds of other varieties to choose from, among them conchigliette (very small shells), coralini (very small ditalini), farfallini (small bows), pennette (a small penne, an imitation of a pen quill), puntette (in the shape of rice, also called *riso*), stellette (miniature stars), and mezze tubetti (small elbow).

About stocks: In many classical soup descriptions, a specific stock is not designated. In the soups that follow, chicken is suggested because it is the most common white stock and is a flavorful but fairly neutral presence when combined with other ingredients. White veal and, on rare occasions, white beef are also acceptable, though their aroma is more pronounced. A meatless (vegetable) stock is also an option, particularly if one's audience prefers it.

In the case of puréed game soups, game stock is called for, augmented with the primary flavoring ingredient of each soup. Game is an excellent raw product to work with, but given its limited availability and high cost, it is important to fully utilize such raw materials. For example, in a soup based on pheasant, if one has limited pheasant to work with, it may be necessary to prepare a brown stock utilizing a mixture of different game bones—such as venison, partridge, and quail—and then complete the soup with diced pheasant meat or pheasant quenelles. Sometimes it will be necessary to prepare a brown veal or beef stock and simmer it with pheasant bones in order to be able to produce the pheasant-based soup. This practice will allow you to operate a cost-effective kitchen, while maintaining a level of gastronomic excellence.

BASIC RECIPES

Because soup preparation is unique to the preparer, even when following a time-honored recipe, the following recipes offer basic proportions of starch ingredient to liquid, followed by a sample recipe. These are key recipes from which one can approach all the classical soup descriptions that follow. Remember that the level of starch in these food items will vary based on a number of variables, so subsequent proportions can be modified by slightly increasing the thickening element or by adding additional stock.

For a soup thickened with barley: 1 part barley to 12 parts stock or liquid. A sample recipe follows.

MARIE LOUISE SOUP
(Potage Marie Louise)

2 quarts (1.9L) chicken stock
½ cup (120 mL) barley
1 bouquet garni
4 tablespoons (60 mL)
  beurre manié

1 cup (240 mL) heavy cream
salt and white pepper to
  taste
1½ cups (360 mL) cooked
  small macaroni

- Simmer the stock, barley, and bouquet garni for 1 hour, or until the barley is very soft. Add the beurre manié, blend thoroughly, and simmer for another 10 minutes.

- Remove the bouquet garni and purée the soup. Return to the fire, add the cream, adjust seasoning, and add the macaroni just before service.

For a soup thickened with dried beans (black, garbanzo, kidney, or navy beans): 1 part dry beans to 4 parts stock or liquid. A sample recipe follows.

BRIDES STYLE SOUP
(Potage à la Petite Mariée)

¼ cup (60 mL) olive oil
1 stalk of celery, peeled and
  finely chopped
1 small carrot, peeled, top
  removed, and finely
  chopped

1 small onion, peeled and
  finely chopped
1 bay leaf
1 cup (240 mL) white navy
  beans, soaked overnight in
  water

1 quart (960 mL) chicken
stock
1½ cups (360 mL) ¼-inch
(6-mm) diced vegetables
(cook's choice)

salt and white pepper to
taste

- Sweat the vegetables and bay leaf in the olive oil for 10 minutes. Add the beans and chicken stock, and simmer covered for 1½ hours, or until the beans are very soft.
- Cook the diced vegetables in lightly salted boiling water until al dente.
- Remove the bay leaf, purée the soup, return to the fire, adjust seasoning, and add the diced vegetables just before service.

For a soup thickened with dried beans (lentils, or split peas): 1 part dry beans to 3 parts stock or liquid. A sample recipe follows.

𝓡UMFORD SOUP

(Potage Rumford)

¾ cup (180 mL) slab bacon
cut into ¼-inch (6-mm)
dice
1 medium Spanish onion,
peeled and roughly
chopped
1 small carrot, peeled, top
trimmed, and roughly
chopped
1 stalk celery, peeled,
trimmed, and roughly
chopped
2 cups (480 mL) yellow split
peas

1 bay leaf
1 small ham hock, cut into
thirds
1½ quarts (1.4 L) chicken
stock
salt and white pepper to
taste
¾ cup (180 mL) cooked
barley
¾ cup (180 mL) potatoes cut
into ¼-inch (6-mm) dice,
and cooked al dente

- Render the bacon in a heavy-gauge pot over medium heat, until the bacon is well browned. Remove with a slotted spoon and set aside.
- Sweat the onion, carrot, and celery for 10 minutes. Add the beans, bay leaf, and ham hock, and coat in the fat. Add the chicken stock, stir thoroughly, and simmer for 1 hour.
- Remove the ham hocks, pull off the meat, cut into ¼-inch (6-mm) pieces, and set aside.

- Purée the soup, return to the pot, and adjust seasoning with salt and pepper. Bring to a boil, and add the browned bacon, barley, and potatoes.

For a soup thickened with green peas: Equal parts green peas and stock or liquid. A sample recipe follows.

ST. GERMAIN SOUP
(Potage St. Germain)

2 quarts (1.9 L) chicken
   stock
2 quarts (1.9 L) green peas
1 bouquet garni
salt and white pepper to
   taste

¼ cup (60 mL) sour cream
2 tablespoons (30 mL)
   chopped chervil

- Simmer the chicken stock, peas, bouquet garni, and a little salt and pepper for 20 minutes, or until the peas are very tender. Remove the bouquet garni, purée, return to fire, and adjust seasoning. Garnish with a dollop of sour cream and a little chervil at service.

For a soup thickened with potatoes (or sweet potatoes): Equal parts peeled and diced potatoes, and stock or liquid. A sample recipe follows.

SAVOYARD SOUP
(Potage Savoyarde)

2 quarts (1.9 L) rich brown
   beef tail stock
6½ cups (1.5 L) peeled
   potatoes, roughly chopped
1 bouquet garni
4 tablespoons (60 mL) dark
   brown roux

salt and pepper to taste
8 baguette slices, buttered,
   sprinkled with grated
   cheese and gratinéed

- Simmer the stock, potatoes, and bouquet garni for 30 minutes or until the potatoes are soft. Remove the bouquet garni, add the roux, and blend thoroughly. Simmer another 15 minutes and purée.

- Return to the fire, adjust seasoning, and garnish with the croutons at service.

For a soup thickened with potatoes and vegetables: 1 part peeled and diced potatoes and 1 part vegetables (exclusive of garnish) to 2 parts stock or liquid. A sample recipe follows.

ALGERIAN STYLE ARTICHOKE SOUP
(Potage d'artichauts à l'Algérienne)

10 artichoke bottoms
3 medium (or 2 large) sweet
  potatoes
2 tablespoons (30 mL)
  unsalted butter
1 shallot, minced
1 cup (240 mL) finely
  chopped toasted filberts

1 quart (960 mL) chicken
  stock
salt and white pepper to
  taste
1 cup (240 mL) small diced
  croutons

- Cut the artichokes carefully into ¼-inch (6-mm) dice, and set aside, reserving the trimmed portion (about half of the artichoke should be rendered into dice, and the other half into rough trim).
- Peel the sweet potatoes, cut carefully into ¼-inch (6-mm) dice, and set aside, reserving the trimmed portion (about half of the potatoes should be rendered into dice, and the other half into rough trim).
- Sweat the shallot, and artichoke and potato trim, in the butter for 5 minutes. Add the filberts and chicken stock, season lightly with salt and pepper, and simmer for 30 minutes or until the potatoes are very soft.
- Simmer the diced sweet potato in lightly salted boiling water until tender but still firm. Drain and set aside.
- Purée the soup, return to the pot, and add the diced potatoes and artichokes. Adjust seasoning with salt and pepper, and serve garnished with the croutons.

For a soup thickened with rice: 1 part rice to 6 parts stock or liquid. A sample recipe follows.

*M*ARQUISE STYLE SOUP
(Potage à la Marquise)

2 quarts (1.9 L) chicken
  stock
1½ cups (360 mL) uncooked
  rice
1 bouquet garni
salt and white pepper to
  taste

1 cup (240 mL) heavy cream
1 cup (240 mL) lettuce
  chiffonade
1 cup (240 mL) green peas,
  blanched al dente

- Simmer the stock, rice, bouquet garni, and a little salt and pepper for 45 minutes. Remove the bouquet garni, purée, return to fire, add the cream, and adjust seasoning. Add the lettuce and peas at service.

For a soup thickened with rice and vegetables: 4 parts vegetables and 1 part rice to 12 parts stock or liquid. A sample recipe follows.

*C*ARROT SOUP
(Potage Crécy)

3 tablespoons (45 mL)
  unsalted butter
1 medium Spanish onion,
  finely chopped
1 pound (450 g) carrots,
  peeled, tops removed, and
  sliced thin

1½ quarts (1.4 L) chicken
  stock
½ cup (120 mL) rice
diced croutons (fried in
  butter)
salt and pepper to taste

- Sweat the onion and carrot in butter until tender, without coloring. Add the rice and blend, then add the chicken stock and season with salt and pepper. Simmer for 30 minutes, or until the rice is very soft, then purée. Return to the fire, beat in the butter, adjust seasoning, and serve garnished with the croutons

For a soup thickened with roux or beurre manié: (for the roux or beurre manie: 3 parts flour to 1 part fat): 1 part roux to 6 parts liquid. A sample recipe follows.

ARGENTEUIL SOUP

(Potage Argenteuil)

1 pound (450 g) fat
    asparagus
5 tablespoons (75 mL)
    unsalted butter
3 shallots, minced
1 bay leaf
1 cup (240 mL) flour

6 cups (1.4 L) chicken stock
salt and white pepper to
    taste
1 cup (240 mL) heavy cream
2 tablespoons (30 mL)
    chopped chervil

- Trim the asparagus to 6-inch (152 mm) lengths and discard the woody portion. Peel the stalk, reserving the peels, and cut the stalks in half. Finely chop the bottom halves, combine with the peelings, and set aside. Cut the top halves into ¼-inch (6-mm) pieces and set aside.

- Blanch the ¼-inch (6-mm) asparagus pieces in a small amount of lightly salted boiling water until al dente. Strain, reserving the water.

- Sweat the asparagus peelings and pieces, and shallot in the butter for 5 minutes. Add the bay leaf and flour, blend, and cook another 5 minutes. Add the chicken stock and reserved asparagus water, blend thoroughly, and simmer 15 minutes, stirring occasionally.

- Purée the soup, return to the pot, add the cream, and adjust seasoning with salt and pepper. Serve garnished with the diced asparagus and chopped chervil.

For a soup thickened with winter squash (pumpkin, butternut, or acorn squash): Equal parts peeled and diced winter squash to stock or liquid. A sample recipe follows.

BRESSE STYLE SOUP

(Potage à la Bressane)

1 medium pumpkin (about 6
    pounds, or 2.7 kg)
2 tablespoons (30 mL)
    unsalted butter
1 stalk celery, peeled and
    finely chopped

½ medium carrot, peeled,
    top trimmed, and finely
    chopped
1 small Spanish onion,
    peeled and finely chopped
6 tablespoons (90 mL) flour

½ teaspoon (2.5 mL) grated ginger root
2 quarts (1.9 L) chicken stock
1 cup (240 mL) heavy cream

salt and white pepper to taste
2 tablespoons (30 mL) unsalted butter, soft
¼ cup (60 mL) basil pesto

- Cut the pumpkin in half, scoop out the seeds and webbing, and place on a roasting pan cut side up. Fill the cavity with a few tablespoons of water, and place in a preheated 350°F (176°C) oven for 30 to 40 minutes, or until the flesh is tender. Remove from the oven, allow to cool, then scoop out the flesh with a spoon and set aside. (There should be approximately 5 cups, or 1.2 L, of pumpkin flesh.

- Sweat the celery, carrot, and onion in the butter over medium heat for 10 minutes. Add the flour and blend. Add the pumpkin, ginger, and chicken stock, season lightly with salt and pepper, blend thoroughly, and simmer for 15 minutes.

- Purée the soup, return to the pot, add the cream, and adjust seasoning with salt and pepper. Bring to a boil, beat in the butter, and remove from the fire. Drizzle a little pesto over the top of the soup at service.

For a soup thickened with summer squash (zucchini, yellow crookneck, or patty pan): Equal parts squash to stock or liquid. A sample recipe follows.

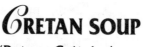

CRETAN SOUP
(Potage Crétoise)

2 quarts (1.9 L) chicken stock
2 quarts (1.9 L) zucchini, roughly chopped
1 cup (240 mL) tomato purée

1 bouquet garni
salt and white pepper to taste
1 cup (240 mL) diced croutons

- Simmer the stock, zucchini, tomato, and bouquet garni for about 30 minutes or until the zucchini is very soft. Remove the bouquet garni, purée the soup, return to the pot, adjust seasoning, and serve garnished with the croutons.

For a soup thickened with tapioca: 1 part quick-cooking tapioca to 8 parts stock or liquid. A sample recipe follows.

$\mathscr{B}$ARCELONA STYLE SOUP
(Potage à la Barcelonnaise)

2 quarts (1.9 L) chicken
    stock
1 cup (240 mL) tomato
    purée
½ cup (120 mL) quick-
    cooking tapioca

1 bouquet garni
salt and white pepper to
    taste
1½ cups (360 mL) ham, cut
    into ¼-inch (6-mm) dice

- Simmer the stock, tomato, tapioca, and bouquet garni for about 10 minutes or until the tapioca has expanded. Remove the bouquet garni, purée the soup, return to the pot, adjust seasoning, and serve garnished with the ham.

PURÉED SOUPS
(POTAGES PURÉE)

Puréed Soups with Generic Nomenclature

Just as there are consommés named for individuals and locales, there are also puréed and creamed soups so named. But when a simple designation is preferred, they are simply named for their primary ingredient. A partial list follows:

Potage Purée de Chayotte (Purée of Chayotte Soup)
Potage Purée de Haricots (Purée of Bean Soup)
Potage Purée de Marrons (Purée of Chestnut Soup)
Potage Purée de Navets (Purée of Turnip Soup)
Potage Purée d'artichauts (Purée of Artichoke Soup)
Potage Purée de Potiron (Purée of Pumpkin Soup)
Potage Purée de Tomates (Purée of Tomato Soup)

Puréed Soups Based on Chicken Stock

African Style Soup
(Potage à l'Africain)

Chicken stock flavored with curry, simmered with rice, puréed, garnished with diced artichoke bottoms and eggplant.

Albert Soup
(Potage Albert)

Chicken stock simmered with potatoes and leeks, puréed, garnished with julienned root vegetables.

Alexandra Soup
(Potage Alexandra)

Chicken stock simmered with tapioca, puréed, garnished with julienned chicken breast and lettuce chiffonade.

Algerian Style Artichoke Soup
(Potage d'artichauts à l'Algérienne)

Chicken stock flavored with filberts, simmered with artichokes and sweet potatoes, puréed, garnished with diced artichoke bottoms and croutons.

Ambassador Style Soup
(Potage purée à l'Ambassadeur)

Chicken stock simmered with green peas, thickened with a little roux, puréed, garnished with rice and lettuce chiffonade.

Balvais Soup
(Potage Balvais [also known as Potage Jubilé])

Chicken stock simmered with green peas, thickened with a little roux, puréed, garnished with diced vegetables.

Barcelona Style Soup
(Potage à la Barcelonnaise)

Chicken stock simmered with tomatoes, thickened with tapioca, garnished with diced ham.

Bean Soup, Turkish Style
(Potage de haricots à la Turque)

Chicken stock flavored with garlic, simmered with white beans, fried onions, and rice, puréed, garnished with some of the whole white beans.

Beaulieu Soup
(Potage Beaulieu)

Chicken stock simmered with assorted vegetables, thickened with tapioca, puréed, garnished with diced root vegetables.

Brides Style Soup
(Potage à la Petite Mariée)

Chicken stock simmered with white beans, puréed, garnished with diced vegetables.

Brie Style Soup
(Potage à la Briarde)

Chicken stock simmered with carrots and potatoes, puréed, garnished with croutons and chervil.

Calabrian Style Soup
(Potage à la Calabraise)

Chicken stock simmered with white beans and sorrel, puréed, garnished with rice.

Carrot Soup
(Potage Crécy)

Chicken stock simmered with carrots sweated in butter and rice, and puréed.

Dishes designated with the term Crécy designate puréed carrots, one of the many varieties of produce grown in either Crécy-la-Chappelle in the Seine-et-Marne region, or Crécy-en-Ponthieu in Somme (there is disagreement over the exact origin of the dish). The Battle of Crécy was a bloody insurrection that took place in 1346 not far from Somme, and Charles Pierre Monselet (1825–1888) wrote a sonnet entitled *La Purée Crécy*, which concludes that the only remaining record of the battles of Crécy is vegetables cut into pieces.

Carrot Soup, Ancient Style
(Potage Crécy à l'Ancienne)

Chicken stock simmered with carrots sweated in butter and potatoes, and puréed.

The carrot is native to Afghanistan, and was considered a medicinal essence by the ancient Greeks and Romans; only from the sixteenth century on has it been cultivated as a food. There are many different varieties of carrot and our familiar orange variety, high in alpha-beta-gamma carotene, was developed in seventeenth-century Holland. In addition to beta carotene, which is transformed into vitamin A (1 pound/460 g yields $4\frac{1}{2}$ times the minimum daily requirement), carrots contain vitamins B, C, E, and carbohydrates. Varieties include Goldinhart, Nantes Half-Long, Danvers Half-Long, Gold Pak, Burpee's Oxheart, Royal Chantenay, and Little Finger.

Champagne Style Soup
(Potage à la Champenoise)

Chicken stock simmered with potatoes and celery, puréed, strained, garnished with diced carrots, celery, and potatoes.

Charlotte Soup
(Potage Charlotte)

Chicken (or vegetable) stock simmered with leeks, potatoes and watercress, puréed, garnished with diced leeks and potatoes, and chopped chervil.

Chatillon Soup
(Potage Chatillon)

Chicken stock simmered with tomatoes, puréed, garnished with vermicelli and sorrel chiffonade.

Clamart is the name of an area in the Hauts-de-Seine district known for its production of green peas. A typical Clamart garnish consists of artichoke bottoms, tartlets, or scooped-out tomatoes filled with buttered and seasoned peas.

Clamart Style Soup
(Potage à la Clamart)

Chicken stock simmered with green peas, puréed, and garnished with green peas and croutons.

Clermont refers to the French region of Auvergne known for its production of excellent cabbage and chestnuts. Typical Clermont garnishes are cabbage paupiettes, and onions stuffed with chestnut purée; and there is a Bavarian cream flavored with rum and chestnut purée.

Clermont Style Soup
(Potage à la Clermont)

Chicken stock simmered with chestnuts, celery, and onions, thickened with roux, puréed, finished with milk, garnished with breaded and deep-fried onions rings and basil pesto.

Compiègne Style Soup
(Potage à la Compiègne)

Chicken stock simmered with white beans, puréed, finished with hot milk, garnished with sorrel chiffonade and chopped chervil.

Conaught Soup
(Potage Conaught)

Chicken stock simmered with lentils, puréed, garnished with diced chicken breast and croutons.

Condé Soup
(Potage Condé)

Chicken stock flavored with red wine, simmered with red beans, puréed, garnished with croutons.

———————————— • ————————————

Condé is a royal French military family, originating with Louis I de Bourbon, prince de condé (1530–1569), who commanded the Huguenots against the house of Guise, and was slain at the battle of Jarnac. His great grandson Louis II (1621–1686) won major victories in the Thirty Years' War; turned against the government in the Fronde (1648–1653); and was later pardoned by Louis XIV, for whom he fought successfully in the Dutch Wars. His great grandson, Louis Joseph (1736–1818) formed an emigré "army of Condé" that fought in alliance with France's enemies against French Revolutionary forces.

——————— • ———————

The Princesse de Conti was daughter of the Duc de Guise, a lady-in-waiting to Marie de Medici, and wife of Henri IV. She created—with the aid of Saupiquet, master-cook of the Baron de la Vieuville and the creator of pâte feuilletée (puff pastry)— Carré de mouton à la Conti.

Conti Soup
(Potage Conti)

Chicken stock simmered with lentils, puréed, garnished with fried croutons and chervil.

Coquelin Soup
(Potage Coquelin)

Chicken stock simmered with green peas, puréed, garnished with julienned chicken breast and leeks.

Coquelin was a popular comedic actor who once challenged the Savoy Hotel manager César Ritz (later the founder of the Ritz-Carlton Hotel) to do something about the English laws that prevented restaurants from being open after 11:00 P.M. or on Sundays. Ritz "lobbied" Savoy customers such as Henry Labouchere (journalist), Mrs. Langtry, and Lord Randolph Churchill, and the British Parliament soon afterward passed legislation that permitted restaurants to remain open until half-past midnight. As a result, dining out became more fashionable than previously, and though Ritz was accused of breaking up home life, he actually promoted it—gentlemen who had dined at men-only clubs now took their wives out to dinner or supper at the Savoy.

Cormeilles Soup
(Potage Cormeilles)

Chicken stock simmered with green beans and potatoes, puréed, mellowed with milk, garnished with green beans cut into small diamonds (losange).

Count's Style Soup
(Potage du Comte)

Chicken stock simmered with lentils and an assortment of vegetables, puréed, garnished with julienned root vegetables.

Creole Style Soup
(Potage à la Creole)

Chicken stock simmered with okra, thickened with roux, puréed, strained, garnished with diced tomatoes and julienned red pepper.

Cretan Soup
(Potage Crétoise)

Chicken (or vegetable) stock simmered with available squash (such as zucchini, yellow crookneck, and patty pan) and tomatoes, puréed, garnished with croutons.

Darblay Soup
(Potage Darblay)

Chicken (or vegetable) stock simmered with potatoes, puréed, garnished with julienned root vegetables.

Egyptian Style Soup
(Potage à l'Égyptienne)

Chicken stock simmered with rice, leeks, and onions, and puréed.

Esau Soup
(Potage Ésaü)

Chicken stock simmered with lentils, puréed, and garnished with rice.

Estérel Soup
(Potage Estérel)

Chicken stock simmered with white beans and pumpkin, puréed, garnished with vermicelli.

Farmer's Style Soup
(Potage à la Paysanne)

Chicken (or vegetable) stock simmered with assorted vegetables, puréed, garnished with croutons and chervil.

Faubonne Soup
(Potage Faubonne)

Chicken stock simmered with white beans, puréed, garnished with julienned vegetables and chervil.

Freneuse Soup
(Potage Freneuse)

Chicken (or vegetable) stock simmered with potatoes and turnips, and finished with a little milk.

Ésaü is the name of a biblical character (Genesis 25:25), son of Isaac and Rebecca, who traded his birthright to his younger twin brother Jacob, for a bowl of thick vegetable soup (pottage). Several soups and a poached egg dish that are named Ésaü include puréed lentils.

Génin Soup
(Potage Génin)

Chicken stock simmered with carrots, leeks, mushrooms, tomatoes, and rice, puréed, garnished with sorrel chiffonade and chervil.

Goatherder's Style Soup
(Potage à la Chevrière)

Chicken (or vegetable) stock simmered with herbs, leeks, lettuce, potatoes, and sorrel, puréed, beaten with fine herb butter, garnished with diced sautéed potatoes.

Gosford Soup
(Potage Gosford)

Chicken (or vegetable) stock simmered with tapioca and abundant asparagus peels and bottoms, puréed, thickened with a little roux, garnished with diced asparagus and asparagus tips.

Gounod Soup
(Potage Gounod)

Chicken stock simmered with green peas, puréed, garnished with diced chicken breast, croutons, and chervil.

Grandmother's Style Soup
(Potage à la Grand-mère)

Chicken stock simmered with potatoes, puréed, garnished with julienned leeks and cabbage, lettuce chiffonade, and small macaroni.

Holstein Soup
(Potage Holstein)

Chicken stock simmered with tomatoes, thickened with roux, puréed, garnished with asparagus tips, lobster quenelles, and cauliflower flowerettes.

Housewife's Style Soup
(Potage à la Bonne Femme)

Chicken stock simmered with potatoes, leeks, lettuce, and cucumber, finished with milk, garnished with croutons.

———— • ————

Peeling asparagus, though a bit tedious, raises a tasty green vegetable to its innate aristocratic status. It is also a cost-effective way of stretching its use—serving the peeled spears as a vegetable or garnish for a larger dish, while using the peels and fibrous bottom portion in the preparation of a puréed soup.

———— • ————

Charles François Gounod (1818–1893) was a French composer and creator of the romantic operas *Faust* (1859) and *Romeo and Juliet* (1867).

Flageolets are small, flat, light-green beans similar to lima beans, and are typically served with roast lamb and mutton.

Jackson Soup
(Potage Jackson)

Chicken stock simmered with potatoes and flageolets, thickened with tapioca, garnished with julienned leeks.

Janin Soup
(Potage Janin)

Chicken stock simmered with white beans, carrots, and leeks, puréed, garnished with croutons.

Kempinski Soup
(Potage Kempinski)

Chicken stock simmered with green peas and carrots, puréed, finished with cream, garnished with rice.

Lamballe Soup
(Potage Lamballe)

Chicken stock simmered with green peas, puréed, garnished with tapioca.

Languedoc Style Soup
(Potage à la Languedocienne)

Chicken stock simmered with green peas, puréed, garnished with small slices of vegetables and chopped chervil.

Lentil Soup, Bavarian Style
(Potage de lentilles, à la Bavarois)

Chicken stock simmered with lentils sautéed in bacon first, puréed, garnished with sliced smoked sausage.

Lentil Soup, Russian Style
(Potage de lentilles, à la Russe)

Chicken stock simmered with lentils, celery root, leeks, and onions, puréed, garnished with diced root vegetables and small slices of sturgeon.

Lithuania Style Soup
(Potage à la Lithuanienne)

Chicken stock simmered with potatoes, puréed, garnished with diced celery root, sorrel chiffonade, and sliced sausage; sour cream, and small hard-cooked eggs cut in half, breaded (flour, egg, bread crumbs) and deep fried, served separately.

Longchamps Soup
(Potage Longchamps)

Chicken stock simmered with green peas, puréed, garnished with sorrel chiffonade, vermicelli, and chopped chervil.

Malakoff Soup
(Potage Malakoff)

Chicken stock simmered with potatoes and tomatoes, puréed, garnished with chopped spinach.

Mancele Soup
(Potage Mancele)

Chicken (or game) stock simmered with celery and chestnuts, thickened with roux and puréed game meat, garnished with julienned partridge.

Market-gardener's Style Soup
(Potage à la Maraichère)

Chicken stock simmered with green peas and onions, puréed, garnished with egg noodles and pearl onions.

Mistinguette Soup
(Potage Mistinguette)

Chicken stock simmered with green peas and tapioca, and puréed.

Mongolian Style Soup
(Potage à la Mongole)

Chicken stock simmered with green or yellow split peas, blended with tomato soup, puréed, garnished with julienned root vegetables.

Mozart Soup
(Potage Mozart)

Chicken stock simmered with white beans and tomatoes, puréed, garnished with croutons.

---•---

Wolfgang Amadeus Mozart (1756–1791) was an Austrian musical prodigy who was composing by the age of five and by the age of thirteen had written concertos, sonatas, symphonies, and operettas. Among his more than 600 musical composition are *Don Giovanni* (1787), considered one of the most brilliant operas ever written. Incredibly, he died in poverty at the age of thirty-five, and was buried in a pauper's grave.

Navarin Soup
(Potage Navarin)

Chicken (or fish) stock simmered with green peas, puréed, garnished with crayfish tails, green peas, and chopped parsley.

Nivernais Style Soup
(Potage à la Nivernaise)

Chicken (or vegetable) stock simmered with carrots and turnips, puréed, garnished with diced root vegetables.

Palestinian Style Soup
(Potage à la Palestine)

Chicken stock simmered with Jerusalem artichokes, thickened with a little roux, finished with milk, garnished with croutons.

Paquita Soup
(Potage Paquita)

Chicken stock simmered with green peas, puréed, garnished with sago and diced tomatoes.

Parmentier Soup
(Potage Parmentier)

Chicken stock simmered with leeks and potatoes, puréed, garnished with croutons and chervil.

---•---

Auguste Parmentier (1737–1817) was captured by the Hanoverian army during the Seven Years' War, and spent 1761 as a prisoner of war. During his year in prison, he subsisted solely on potatoes, and on his return to Paris was determined to popularize potatoes as a nutritional food. After winning an award for the discovery of a plant that could be useful in the event of famine, and writing a treatise on the tuber, he won the support of many, including Louis XVI. His clever ploy of presenting a bouquet of purple potato flowers to the king at a Versailles birthday reception for him on August 25, 1785, further popularized his cause—Marie-Antoinette pinned the flowers onto her corsage, the king placed one flower into his buttonhole, and held out a third flower to Parmentier. The next morning everyone at court sported a potato flower in their buttonholes. The last prejudices regarding potatoes vanished following a dinner Parmentier hosted in honor of Benjamin Franklin, with a menu composed of twenty different potato dishes. For some years after, the potato was actually known as a "parmentier."

Portuguese Style Soup
(Potage à la Portugaise)

Chicken stock simmered with tomatoes, thickened with roux, puréed, garnished with rice.

Rigoletto Soup
(Potage Rigoletto)

Chicken stock simmered with green peas, puréed, garnished with spinach chiffonade and diablotins.

---•---

Rigoletto was the tragic hunchbacked figure of Giuseppe Verdi's opera of the same name. As court jester to the Duke of Mantua, he fails in his attempts to protect his gorgeous daughter Gilda from the philandering duke and his libertine colleagues. After she is kidnapped and then seduced by the duke, Rigoletto hires an assassin to avenge the transgression. Gilda, believing she is in love with the duke, learns of the plot (she is unaware that her father is behind it), dresses up as the duke, and takes his place. The opera ends with Rigoletto rowing out to the middle of a lake to dispose of what he thinks is the duke's body, only to discover his daughter inside the sack. The closing father-daughter duet, ending with Gilda's death, is one of the great tragic scenes in modern opera.

Royan Soup
(Potage Royan)

Chicken stock simmered with cauliflower, thickened with a little roux, puréed, garnished with tapioca.

Rumford Soup
(Potage Rumford)

Chicken stock simmered with yellow split peas, puréed, garnished with pearl barley, diced potatoes, and diced fried bacon.

Rustic Style Soup
(Potage à la Campagnarde)

Chicken stock simmered with vegetables, white beans, and leeks, puréed, garnished with diced green beans, carrots, and green peas.

Two variations of this soup are Potage purée de pois à la menthe—same as St. Germain but made with stock flavored with mint, and the addition of a garnish of mint chiffonade; Potage purée de pois à la polonaise (Polish style)—same as St. Germain, but with a garnish of julienned beets, celery root, leeks, and onions.

Saint Cyr Soup
(Potage Saint Cyr)

Chicken stock simmered with potatoes, turnips, and cauliflower, puréed, garnished with cauliflower flowerettes and green beans cut in diamond shape (losange).

St. Germain Style Soup
(Potage à la St. Germain)

Chicken stock simmered with green peas, puréed, garnished with green peas, chervil, and a dollop of sour cream (or crème fraîche) at service.

Saint Marceau Soup
(Potage Saint Marceau)

Chicken stock simmered with green peas and leeks, puréed, garnished with julienned leeks and lettuce chiffonade.

Saint Martin Soup
(Potage Saint Martin)

Chicken stock simmered with lentils and potatoes, puréed, garnished with croutons.

Saint Sebastian Soup
(Potage Saint Sebastian)

Chicken stock simmered with tomatoes, thickened with roux, puréed, garnished with julienned green peppers and truffle.

———————————— • ————————————

The word *truffle* is related to the Spanish *trufa* and the Italian *truffere*, both meaning "deceit," in reference to the fact that this member of the fungi family grows just underneath the surface of the ground, making it difficult to locate. Since humans lack the keen olfactory sense required to find them, we seek help: in Sardinia, goats are employed; in Russia, bear cubs; in Europe, pigs and specially trained dogs. Pigs are the real experts though, as determined by German researchers' recent discovery of a musky chemical in the truffle that is also secreted in a male pig's saliva and that prompts mating behavior. When they detect the presence of the tuber—both dogs and pigs can detect the scent from as far away as 50 yards—it sends them into a lustful frenzy.

Sicilian Style Soup I
(Potage à la Sicilienne I)

Chicken stock simmered with tomatoes and tapioca, puréed, garnished with croutons.

Sicilian Style Soup II
(Potage à la Sicilienne II)

Chicken stock simmered with leeks, mushrooms, onions, and potatoes, puréed, finished with milk, garnished with sautéed sliced mushrooms and sautéed small-diced potatoes.

Silver Soup
(Potage Argenté)

Chicken stock simmered with leeks and potatoes, puréed, garnished with tapioca.

Split Pea Soup
(Potage de Pois Cassés)

Chicken stock simmered with green split peas, a ham bone, and mirepoix vegetables, puréed, garnished with diced root vegetables, and ham taken from the ham bone.

Sportman's Style Soup
(Potage à la Sportif)

Chicken stock simmered with potatoes, puréed, blended with butter, garnished with sorrel chiffonade, vermicelli, and chervil.

Stamboul Soup
(Potage Stamboul)

Chicken stock simmered with rice and tomatoes, puréed, blended with butter, garnished with croutons in the shape of crescents (half moons).

Tegetthoff Soup
(Potage Tegetthoff)

Chicken stock simmered with green peas, thickened with a little roux, puréed, garnished with white asparagus tips.

Tomato Soup, Chicago Style
(Potage de Tomate à la Chicago)

Chicken stock simmered with tomatoes, thickened with roux, puréed, garnished with sago, tarragon, and croutons.

Turenne Soup
(Potage Turenne)

Chicken stock simmered with leeks and potatoes, puréed, garnished with diced well-browned bacon, croutons, and chervil.

Tyrolese Style Soup
(Potage à la Tyrolienne)

Chicken stock simmered with cucumber, lettuce, green peas, and sorrel, puréed, garnished with brown bread croutons.

Van Duzer Soup
(Potage Van Duzer)

Chicken stock simmered with tomatoes, thickened with roux, puréed, garnished with pearl barley.

Village Style Soup
(Potage à la Villageoise)

Chicken stock simmered with leeks and potatoes, puréed, finished with milk, garnished with spaghetti.

Villars Soup
(Potage Villars)

Chicken stock simmered with artichokes, flageolets, and onions, puréed, garnished with croutons.

Vintager's Style Soup
(Potage à la Vigneronne)

Chicken stock simmered with white beans, leeks, and pumpkin, flavored with red wine, puréed, garnished with brown bread croutons.

Waldèze Soup
(Potage Waldèze)

Chicken stock simmered with tomatoes and tapioca, puréed, garnished with diced tomatoes; grated Swiss and Parmesan cheese (mixed) served separately.

Windham Soup
(Potage Windham)

Chicken stock simmered with whole kernel corn and tapioca, puréed, garnished with rice.

Puréed Soups Based on Duck Stock

Courland Soup
(Potage Courlandaise)

Duck stock simmered with cabbage, carrots, celery root, onions, potatoes, and turnips, puréed, garnished with sliced duck breast.

Danish Style Duck Soup
(Potage de Canard à la Danoise)

Duck stock flavored with Madeira, simmered with artichokes, thickened with roux and puréed duck meat, garnished with duck quenelles.

Puréed Soups Based on Beef (Oxtail) Stock

Oxtail Soup
(Potage de Queues de Boeuf)

Brown stock prepared from sliced oxtail (beef tail), flavored with Madeira, thickened with brown roux, garnished with the diced meat from the tail bones.

Savoyard Soup
(Potage Savoyarde)

Brown oxtail (beef tail) stock simmered with potatoes, thickened with a little brown roux, puréed, garnished with buttered baguette slices sprinkled with grated cheese and gratinéed.

Puréed Soups Based on Lamb (or Mutton) Stock

Bolivian Style Soup
(Potage à la Bolivienne)

White lamb (or chicken) stock simmered with tomatoes, thickened with roux, puréed, garnished with diced lamb and tomatoes, and julienned ham.

Botzari Soup
(Potage Botzari)

White lamb or mutton stock simmered with green peas, thickened with roux, puréed, garnished with diced lean mutton, root vegetables, and rice.

Meissonier Soup
(Potage Meissonier)

White mutton stock simmered with onions, thickened with roux, puréed, garnished with diced mutton and croutons.

Puréed Soups Based on Game Stock

Capri Style Soup
(Potage de Capri)

Brown game stock flavored with quail, thickened with brown roux, garnished with julienned quail breast and cock's combs.

———————————— • ————————————

A cock's comb is a fleshy appendage at the top of a cock's head (similar to a human fingernail) that is found frequently in classical French cookery. They should be pricked with a pin, and washed well to remove any blood. They are poached in salted water until the outer skin begins to detach, then rubbed with salt and a clean cloth to remove the skin. They are then blanched in stock or court bouillon for 30 minutes or so, and used as a garnish in various dishes, including barquettes, croustades, soups, tartlets, and grilled meats.

Castle Style Soup
(Potage à la Castellane)

Brown game stock flavored with woodcock, thickened with brown roux, garnished with julienned woodcock, and lentil royale made with chopped hard-cooked egg yolks.

Condorcet Soup
(Potage Condorcet)

Brown game stock thickened with brown roux, garnished with julienned game meat and game quenelles.

Marie Jean Antoine Nicolas Caritat, Marquis de Condorcet (1743–1794), was a French mathematician, philosopher, and political leader. As an author, he is known for a notable work on the theory of probability (1785) and for *Sketch for a Historical Picture of the Progress of the Human Mind* (1795), which followed human development through nine "epochs" up to the French Revolution, and predicted [erroneously] that in the tenth epoch the human race would reach ultimate perfection.

Cussy Soup
(Potage Cussy)

Game stock thickened with roux, garnished with chestnut royale and julienned partridge meat and truffle.

Danish Style Game Soup
(Potage de Gibier à la Danoise)

Brown game stock flavored with Madeira, simmered with lentils, puréed, garnished with julienned game and truffle.

Fieldfare Soup
(Potage Litorne)

Fieldfare is a large variety of thrush, whose flavor is not quite as delicate as the smaller thrush varieties (song thrush, missal, and redwing). Considered a rare delicacy, they are usually served roasted on croutons fried in the roasting fat.

Brown game bird stock flavored with fieldfare and brandy, thickened with brown roux, garnished with croutons.

Jacobine Soup
(Potage Jacobine)

Brown game stock thickened with brown roux, garnished with game quenelles and Madeira wine royale.

Julius Caesar Soup
(Potage Jules César)

Brown game stock flavored with hazel-hen, thickened with brown roux and puréed hazel-hen meat, garnished with julienned hazel-hen breast, mushrooms, and truffles.

Julius Caius Caesar (102–44 B.C.), Roman statesman and general, was a gifted military strategist and charismatic leader. Whether he was an ambitious demagogue or a champion of the rights of Roman citizens is still debated (he was probably a bit of both), but his accomplishments were significant. He explored and conquered Britain, and established his military greatness in the Gallic Wars by bringing Gaul (what is today France) under Roman control; he was responsible for developing (with the help of Sosigenes) the Julian calendar that is still in use today; and he reformed agrarian and housing laws that improved living conditions for the Roman populace. He was stabbed to death on the senate floor by his close friend Marcus Brutus, who was aided by three other friends. His seven-volume commentary on the Gallic Wars and three volumes on the civil war are considered both literary masterpieces and classic military documents.

Liége Style Soup
(Potage à la Liége)

Brown game stock flavored with fieldfare, simmered with rice and (stale) brown bread, puréed, garnished with julienned fieldfare.

Magellan Soup
(Potage Magellan)

Brown game stock flavored with partridge and Madeira, thickened with brown roux, garnished with croutons.

Médici Soup
(Potage Médici)

Brown game stock flavored with tomato purée, thickened with brown roux, garnished with game quenelles and macaroni; grated cheese served separately.

Metternich Soup
(Potage Metternich)

Brown game stock flavored with pheasant, thickened with brown roux and puréed pheasant meat, garnished with julienned pheasant meat and diced artichoke royale.

Clemens Wenzel Nepomuk Lothar, Fürst von Metternich (1773–1859), became Austrian foreign minister in 1809, and later was the driving force behind the Congress of Vienna, which restructured Europe following the fall of Napoléon I. The years 1815 to 1848 have been called the Age of Metternich, though his goal of maintaining a balance of power in Europe was achieved through censorship, espionage, and suppression of revolutionary and nationalistic movements.

A plover is a migratory bird found in marshlands and water-meadows in Western Europe, and whose name stems from the Latin *pluvia*, meaning "rain-bird." Dating to the sixteenth century, gastronomes have preferred them prepared undrawn; they are nevertheless tender enough to be prepared in the same way as other small winged game—that is, roasted.

Valois is the royal house that ruled France from 1328 to 1589, succeeding the Capetians when Philip VI became king. The direct line ended in 1498 with Charles VIII, but was continued by Louis XII (Valois-Orléans) and Francis I (Valois-Angoulême). With the death of Henry III (1589), Henry IV of the house of Bourbon succeeded to the theme.

Nesselrode Soup
(Potage Nesselrode)

Brown game stock flavored with woodcock, simmered with chopped chestnuts, garnished with woodcock quenelles and croutons.

Quirinal Soup
(Potage Quirinal)

Brown game stock simmered with pheasant, flavored with sherry, thickened with brown roux and puréed pheasant meat, garnished with julienned pheasant and truffles.

Rohan Soup
(Potage rohan)

Brown game stock flavored with plover, thickened with brown roux, garnished with plover's eggs and croutons.

Steward Style Soup
(Potage à la Steward)

Brown game stock simmered with lentils, ham, partridge, and herbs, thickened with brown roux, puréed, garnished with partridge quenelles.

Valois Soup
(Potage Valois)

Brown game stock simmered with pheasant, thickened with brown roux and puréed pheasant, garnished with green peas and pheasant quenelles.

CREAMED SOUPS (POTAGES À LA CRÈME)

Creamed Soups with Generic Nomenclature

Potage Crème d'Artichauts (Cream of Artichoke Soup)

Potage Crème d'Asperges (Cream of Asparagus Soup)

Potage Crème de Céleri (Cream of Celery Soup)

Potage Crème de Champignons (Cream of Mushroom Soup)

Potage Crème de Chicorée (Cream of Curly Endive Soup)

Potage Crème de Choux de Bruxelles (Cream of Brussels Sprouts Soup)

Potage Crème de Courgettes (Cream of Zucchini Soup)

Potage Crème de Cresson (Cream of Watercress Soup)

Potage Crème d'Endive (Cream of Endive Soup)

Potage Crème d'Épinards (Cream of Spinach Soup)

Potage Crème de Gibier (Cream of Game Soup)

Potage Crème de Haricots (Cream of Bean Soup)

Potage Crème de Laitue (Cream of Lettuce Soup)

Potage Crème de Marrons (Cream of Chestnut Soup)

Potage Crème d'Orge (Cream of Barley Soup)

Potage Crème de Poireaux (Cream of Leek Soup)

Potage Crème de Riz (Cream of Rice Soup)

Potage Crème de Volaille (Cream of Chicken Soup)

Note: All soups marked with * were originally intended to fall under the category of Velvet Soups (Veloutés), which means the inclusion of a final liaison of cream and egg yolks. See note on this change under Shifting Classical Soups to Meet Modern Styles, page 117.)

Creamed Soups Based on Fish Stock

Dishes so named are dedicated to the Princess Bagration and were created by Antoine Carême, who worked as chef for the Princess following his return from a stint as chef for the Russian Czar.

Bagration Soup II* (Potage Bagration au Maigre)

Fish stock flavored with mushrooms, thickened with roux, finished with cream, puréed, garnished with julienned sole fillets, fish quenelles, and crayfish tails.

Boatman's Style Soup (Potage à la Batelière)

Fish stock flavored with shrimp, thickened with roux, strained, finished with cream, garnished with shrimp, mussels, and croutons.

Borely Soup*
(Potage Borely)

Fish stock flavored with whiting, thickened with roux, finished with cream, garnished with small mussels and whiting quenelles.

Breton Style Lobster Soup
(Potage de Homard à la Bretonne)

Fish stock simmered with lobster shells, thickened with roux, strained, finished with cream, garnished with diced lobster and lobster quenelles.

Cambacérès Soup
(Potage Cambacérès)

Fish stock flavored with crayfish and pigeon, thickened with roux, finished with cream, garnished with crayfish and pigeon quenelles.

Cambell Soup*
(Potage Cambell)

Fish stock flavored with curry powder, thickened with roux, finished with cream, garnished with strips (large julienne) of sole fillet.

Canoness Soup*
(Potage Chanoinesse)

Fish stock thickened with roux, finished with cream, beaten with crayfish butter, garnished with sliced soft fish roe.

Cardinal's Style Soup
(Potage à la Cardinal)

Fish stock flavored with lobster shells, thickened with roux, strained, finished with cream, garnished with diced lobster meat and lobster royale cut in the shape of a cross.

Catherine Soup*
(Potage Catherine)

Fish stock thickened with roux, finished with cream, garnished with shrimp and green peas.

For Crayfish Soup, Lucullus Style,* add crayfish heads stuffed with a fish farce garnished with truffle; for Crayfish Soup, Oriental Style* (à l'orientale), omit the mushroom and truffle garnish and add rice.

Crayfish Soup, Joinville Style*
(Potage d'Écrevisses, à la Joinville)

Fish stock flavored with crayfish shells, thickened with roux, strained, finished with cream, garnished with diced crayfish tails, mushrooms, and truffles.

D'Estaing Soup*
(Potage Estaing)

Fish stock simmered with crab shells, thickened with roux, finished with cream, strained, garnished with strips of white fish fillet (such as halibut, sole, whiting, etc.) and crab quenelles.

Divette Soup
(Potage Divette)

Fish stock simmered with smelts and crayfish shells, thickened with roux, finished with cream, garnished with diced crayfish tails, fish quenelles, and truffle pearls (or finely diced truffles).

George Sand Soup*
(Potage George Sand)

Fish stock simmered with crayfish shells, thickened with roux, strained, finished with cream, garnished with crayfish tails and lettuce chiffonade.

Jacqueline Soup*
(Potage Jacqueline)

Fish stock thickened with roux, finished with cream, garnished with asparagus tips, carrot pearls, green peas, and rice.

Jean Bart Soup*
(Potage Jean Bart)

Fish stock thickened with roux, finished with cream, garnished with diced tomatoes, brill quenelles, julienned leek, and macaroni.

Malmsbury Style Soup*
(Potage à la Malmsbury)

Fish stock thickened with roux, finished with cream, garnished with mussels, and diced pike and lobster.

Pike is a fresh-water fish, the fastest under water, in fact, due to powerful rear dorsal fins that can propel it like a torpedo towards its prey, up to thirty feet at a lunge. It was nicknamed *grand loup d'eau*—great water wolf—during the Middle Ages, and Grimod de la Reynière called it "the Attilla of ponds and rivers" because of its ferocious nature, razor-sharp teeth on its lower jaw that face backward (making escape impossible), and approximately 700 smaller teeth in bands around its tongue and palate. Gastronomically speaking, unless cooked within hours of being caught, it is not a particularly great-tasting fish, since it can taste muddy if it came from relatively still waters. It is also filled with a multitude of fine, forked bones. For these reasons, it is best prepared deep-fried or as a quenelle (*Quenelles de brochet* is considered a high gastronomic treat), accompanied by a classic beurre blanc or lobster sauce.

Mathurine Soup*
(Potage Mathurine)

Fish stock thickened with roux, finished with cream, garnished with salmon quenelles.

Mignon Soup
(Potage Mignon)

Fish stock thickened with roux, finished with cream, blended with puréed shrimp, garnished with diced shrimp, fish quenelles, and truffle pearls.

Miller's Style Soup*
(Potage à la Meunière)

Fish stock thickened with roux, finished with cream, garnished with strips of white fish fillet (such as sole or halibut) and croutons.

Nelson Soup
(Potage Nelson)

Fish stock flavored with smelts, thickened with roux, puréed, finished with cream, blended with lobster butter, garnished with rice and lobster quenelles.

Nîmese Style Soup*
(Potage à la Nîmoise)

Fish stock simmered with tomato purée, thickened with roux, finished with cream, garnished with croutons.

Normandy Style Shrimp Soup*
(Potage de Crevettes à la Normande)

Fish stock thickened with roux, finished with cream and puréed shrimp, garnished with diced shrimp and oysters.

Oyster Soup, Cancal Style*
(Potage aux Huîtres à la Cancalaise)

Fish stock flavored with oyster liquor (the juice from fresh oysters) and white wine, thickened with roux, finished with cream, garnished with poached diced oysters and fish quenelles.

Saint John Soup
(Potage Saint John)

Fish stock thickened with roux, finished with cream, garnished with fried fish quenelles.

Saint Malo Soup*
(Potage Saint Malo)

Fish stock thickened with roux, puréed, finished with cream, garnished with shrimp and fish quenelles.

Snail Soup*
(Potage d'Escargots)

Fish stock simmered with snails cooked in white wine, flavored with horseradish, thickened with roux, puréed, finished with cream, garnished with diced snails, fish quenelles, and chopped fine herbs.

Trouville Style Soup*
(Potage à la Trouvillaise)

Fish stock thickened with roux, finished with cream, blended with shrimp butter, garnished with diced shrimp.

Victoria Soup*
(Potage Victoria)

Fish stock simmered with lobster meat, rice, and tomato, puréed, finished with cream, garnished with croutons.

---•---

Dishes so titled are named after Victoria Alexandrina (1819–1901), Queen of England (1837–1901). A number of dishes are named for her, including barquettes, bouchées, salads, scallop and lobster gratinées, garnishes for roasts, and an ice cream bombe—all of which include very rich ingredients. A Victoria sandwich made with sponge cake filled with various jams is still popular today and is often served at traditional afternoon tea.

White Friar's Style Soup
(Potage à la Carmelite)

Fish stock thickened with roux, finished with cream, garnished with whiting quenelles and strips (large julienne) of sole fillet.

Yvette Soup
(Potage Yvette)

Fish stock thickened with roux and puréed lobster, finished with cream, garnished with fish quenelles, and diced lobster and truffles.

Creamed Soups Based on Chicken Stock

Agnes Sorel Soup
(Potage Agnès Sorel)

Chicken stock strongly flavored with mushrooms, thickened with roux, finished with cream, and garnished with julienned chicken breast, mushrooms, and beef tongue.

Agnès Sorel, mistress of French king Charles VII (1403–1461) and a celebrated cook, applied Mamam Poisson's theory, "Sex and food—that's the way to hold a man," to attract and hold on to the French king. Jacques Coeur, Charles's chief adviser, was arrested on a concocted charge (1451) of having poisoned Sorel, but he escaped to Rome (1454), and died fighting against the Turks.

Algerian Style Soup
(Potage à l'Algérienne)

Chicken stock flavored with filberts, thickened with roux and sweet potatoes, puréed, finished with cream, beaten with filbert butter.

Alice Soup
(Potage Alice)

Chicken stock thickened with potatoes and turnips, puréed, finished with cream, garnished with croutons.

Amazonian Style Soup
(Potage à l'Amazone)

Chicken stock thickened with rice, puréed, finished with cream, garnished with croutons.

Andalusian Style Soup
(Potage à l'Andalouse)

Chicken stock simmered with tomatoes, onions, and rice, puréed, finished with cream, garnished with diced tomatoes and julienned green peppers.

Antoine Carême Soup*
(Potage Antoine Carême)

Chicken stock thickened with artichoke bottoms and mushrooms, puréed, finished with cream, and garnished with julienned truffle.

Argenteuil Soup
(Potage Argenteuil)

Chicken stock simmered with asparagus peels and bottoms, thickened with roux, puréed, finished with cream, garnished with asparagus tips and chervil.

———————————— • ————————————

Asparagus soup can also be prepared with white asparagus, which is created by piling up soil around the spears towards the end of its cultivation, preventing exposure to sunlight and consequently the development of green chlorophyll. The soup is ideally prepared from the peels and trimmings, while the more tender top portion can be prepared gratinéed or simply cooked in butter.

Arras Soup*
(Potage Arras)

Chicken stock thickened with white beans, garnished with tapioca.

Aurora Soup
(Potage Aurore)

Chicken stock simmered with tomatoes, thickened with roux, puréed, finished with cream, garnished with chicken quenelles.

Balzac Soup
(Potage Balzac)

Chicken stock thickened with pearl barley and celery root, puréed, finished with cream, garnished with julienned leek and celery.

Bean Soup, Hungarian Style
(Potage de Haricots Blancs, à la Hongroise)

Chicken stock and rendered bacon seasoned with paprika, simmered with white beans, puréed, finished with sour cream.

———— • ————

Honoré de Balzac (1799–1850) was a French writer, who, half-starved, began his career writing sensational novels under a pseudonym. His greatest work, *The Human Comedy*, written over a period of twenty years, is a collection of novels and stories that recreates in vivid detail French society of his time.

Bean Soup, Victoria Style
(Potage de Haricots Blancs, à la Victoria)

Chicken stock simmered with white beans, puréed, finished with sour cream, garnished with julienned chicken breast and chicken quenelles.

Beaucaire Soup
(Potage Beaucaire)

Chicken stock thickened with roux and pearl barley, puréed, finished with cream, garnished with julienned celery root, leeks, and chicken breast.

Beauharnais Soup
(Potage Beauharnais)

Chicken stock thickened with roux and pearl barley, puréed, finished with cream, beaten with crayfish butter, garnished with veal quenelles and crayfish tails.

Belgian Style Soup
(Potage à la Belgique)

Chicken stock simmered with Brussels sprouts, thickened with roux, puréed, finished with cream, garnished with fried croutons.

Belle Otéro Soup*
(Potage Belle Otéro)

Chicken stock simmered with sweet potatoes, thickened with roux, puréed, finished with cream, garnished with sliced beef marrow.

Bercy Style Soup
(Potage à la Bercy)

Chicken stock simmered with turnips and potatoes, puréed, finished with cream, garnished with fried croutons.

Bloum Soup
(Potage Bloum)

Chicken stock simmered with celery root, leeks, potatoes, turnips, puréed, finished with cream, garnished with croutons and chervil.

Boïldieu Soup*
(Potage Boïldieu)

Chicken stock thickened with roux, finished with cream, garnished with chicken, foie gras, and truffle quenelles.

---• ---

François-Adrien Boïeldieu (1775–1834) was a French composer known for developing farcical comic opera into a more serious form of romantic opera. He directed the Russian opera at St. Petersburg from 1804 to 1810, became director of music to Louis XVIII in 1817, and was appointed a professor of composition at the conservatory in 1820. His operas include *Jean de Paris* (1812) and *Le Petit Chaperon rouge* (1818; "Little Red Riding Hood").

Bonvalet Soup*
(Potage Bonvalet)

Chicken stock simmered with leeks, potatoes, and turnips, thickened with roux, finished with a little cream, garnished with green beans cut in small diamond shapes (losange) and carrot royale.

Bourdalou Soup*
(Potage Bourdalou)

Chicken stock simmered with rice, puréed, finished with cream, garnished with four different varieties (colors) of royale; grated cheese served separately.

---• ---

Louis Bourdaloue (1632–1704), nicknamed "the king of preachers and preacher of kings," was a French Jesuit with a gift for powerful oratory. Though he disliked flattering

funeral orations for famous personalities, his oration for
Prince Condé moved the Prince's son and successor Henri
Jules to call it "the finest and most Christian panegyric that
has ever been pronounced." He never flattered congregations,
but his beautiful voice and magnetic personality kept them
spellbound.

Brahms Soup*
(Potage Brahms)

Chicken stock flavored with caraway, thickened with roux, finished with cream, garnished with carrot, turnip, and potato
pearls.

Bresse Style Soup
(Potage à la Bressane)

Chicken stock simmered with peeled and chopped pumpkin,
thickened with roux, puréed, finished with cream, beaten with
butter, garnished with basil pesto.

Breton Style Soup
(Potage de Bretonne)

Chicken stock simmered with white beans, leeks, and onions,
puréed, finished with cream, garnished with julienned leeks and
mushrooms.

Brillat-Savarin Soup*
(Potage Brillat-Savarin)

Chicken stock flavored with rabbit and Madeira, thickened with
roux, finished with cream, garnished with julienned carrots,
mushrooms, and truffles.

Switzerland, then Holland, and then New York City. He initially supported himself by offering French language lessons and playing violin on the street, eventually joining the orchestra of the John Street Theater. His treatise on gastronomy—*Le Physioligie du Goût* (The Physiology of Taste)—which would make him a legend (it is still in print today), appeared in bookstores in December 1825, two months before he died.

Bristol Style Soup
(Potage à la Bristol)

Chicken stock simmered with green peas, thickened with a little roux, puréed, finished with cream, garnished with julienned root vegetables, and chopped tarragon and chervil.

Brussels Style Soup
(Potage à la Bruxelloise)

Chicken stock simmered with Brussels sprouts, thickened with a little roux, puréed, finished with cream, garnished with croutons.

Camelia Soup
(Potage Camelia)

Chicken stock simmered with peas, thickened with tapioca, puréed, finished with cream, garnished with julienned chicken breast and leeks.

Capuchin Soup*
(Potage Capuchin)

Chicken stock with mushrooms, thickened with roux, puréed, finished with cream, garnished with profiteroles stuffed with chicken purée.

Carmen Soup*
(Potage Carmen)

Chicken stock flavored with tomato, simmered with a little rice, thickened with a little roux, finished with cream, garnished with diced tomatoes and finely julienned red peppers.

Caroline Soup*
(Potage Caroline)

Chicken stock simmered with a little rice, thickened with a little roux, finished with cream, garnished with rice and almond royale.

Cauliflower Soup
(Potage du Barry)

Chicken (or vegetable) stock simmered with cauliflower and potatoes, puréed, mellowed with milk, garnished with cauliflower flowerettes and chopped chervil.

Cavalier Soup
(Potage Chevalière)

Chicken stock thickened with roux, finished with cream, garnished with julienned truffle and beef tongue.

Celestian Soup
(Potage Céléstine)

Chicken stock simmered with artichokes, puréed, strained, finished with cream, garnished with croutons.

Chabrillan Soup
(Potage Chabrillan)

Chicken stock simmered with tomatoes, puréed, strained, finished with a little cream, garnished with vermicelli (short pieces) and chicken quenelles flavored with tarragon.

Chantilly Style Soup
(Potage à la Chantilly)

Chicken stock simmered with lentils, puréed, finished with a little cream, garnished with quenelles (type of quenelle is cook's choice).

Charterhouse Soup
(Potage Chartreuse)

Chicken stock simmered with a little tapioca, thickened with roux, finished with cream, garnished with ravioli stuffed with foie gras and spinach.

Dishes with the du Barry connotation are named for Marie Jeanne Bécu, the Comtesse du Barry (1746–1783), a French courtesan and last mistress of Louis XV, and always consist of, or include, cauliflower.

Châtelaine Soup
(Potage Châtelaine)

Chicken stock simmered with green peas, puréed, finished with cream, garnished with quenelles and chervil.

Chevreuse Soup
(Potage Chevreuse)

Chicken stock simmered with semolina, puréed, finished with cream, garnished with julienned chicken breast and truffles.

Cream of Chicken Soup, Medici Style
(Potage Crème de Volaille, à la Medici)

Chicken stock thickened with roux, finished with cream, blended with lobster purée, garnished with chicken quenelles.

Cream of Chicken Soup, Viennese Style
(Potage Crème de Volaille, à la Viennoise)

Chicken stock thickened with roux, finished with cream, blended with lobster purée, garnished with sliced chicken breast and diced vegetables.

Choisy Style Soup
(Potage à la Choisy)

Chicken stock simmered with lettuce, thickened with roux, puréed, finished with cream, garnished with croutons and chervil.

Claremont Soup*
(Potage Claremont)

Chicken stock thickened with roux, finished with cream and champagne, garnished with julienned chicken breast, chicken quenelles, and asparagus tips.

Colombine Soup
(Potage Colombine)

Chicken stock flavored with pigeon and anise, thickened with roux, finished with cream, garnished with diced pigeon meat and pigeon quenelles.

Countess Style Soup
(Potage à la Comtesse)

Chicken stock simmered with asparagus peelings and trimmings, thickened with roux, puréed, strained, finished with cream, garnished with asparagus tips, lettuce chiffonade, and chervil.

———————— • ————————

Along with leeks and onions, asparagus is a member of the lily family and is related to grass. Called *sparrow grass* in England until the eighteenth century, cultivated asparagus is derived from a wild form still commonly found in sandy places, woods, and along river banks in south-central Europe, western and central Asia, and in northern Africa. Its use in Europe during the Dark Ages diminished, while it remained popular in Arab countries; its use was revived in Europe during the reign of Louis XIV (the Sun King). Today, its commercial names are derived from the origin of its cultivation: Argenteuil (considered to be the finest), purple Holland, German, Bassano del Grappa, purple Genoa, and Mary Washington (U.S.). Asparagus is unique in having no leaves in the usual sense, but instead phylloclades, which are clustered at the tip. It is expensive today because the shoots grow at different rates and must be harvested by hand.

Croatian Style Soup
(Potage à la Croate)

Chicken stock simmered with whole kernel corn, thickened with roux, puréed, finished with cream, garnished with corn.

Dartois Soup*
(Potage d'Artois)

Chicken stock simmered with white beans, thickened with a little roux, puréed, finished with cream, garnished with julienned vegetables and chervil sprigs.

Delicious Style Soup
(Potage de Délicieuse)

Chicken stock thickened with roux, blended with foie gras purée, garnished (on top, at service) with whipped cream flavored with paprika; small bouchées filled with puréed chicken served separately.

Derby Soup*
(Potage Derby)

Chicken stock flavored with curry and sautéed onions, simmered with rice, puréed, garnished with chicken and foie gras quenelles, rice, and truffle pearls.

Diplomat Style Soup*
(Potage à la Diplomate)

Chicken stock simmered with rice, puréed, garnished with tapioca, truffle rings, and chicken quenelles.

Dolguruki Soup*
(Potage Dolguruki)

Chicken stock flavored with onions and ham, thickened with roux, finished with cream, garnished with julienned chicken breast.

Doyen Soup
(Potage Doyen)

Chicken stock simmered with green peas, puréed, thickened with a little roux, finished with cream, garnished with chicken quenelles and green peas.

Dubarry Soup
(Potage Dubarry)

Chicken stock simmered with chopped cauliflower, thickened with a little roux, puréed, finished with cream, garnished with cauliflower flowerettes and croutons.

Dubelley Soup
(Potage Dubelley)

Chicken stock simmered with chopped lettuce and tapioca, puréed, thickened with a little roux, finished with cream, garnished with lettuce chiffonade.

Duchess Louise Soup
(Potage Duchesse Louise)

Chicken stock simmered with chopped mushrooms, thickened with roux, puréed, finished with cream, garnished with lettuce chiffonade and julienned chicken breast and mushrooms.

Duchess Style Soup
(Potage à la Duchesse)

Chicken stock thickened with roux, finished with cream, garnished with asparagus tips and julienned truffles.

Dunkirk Style Soup*
(Potage à la Dunkerque)

Chicken stock simmered with cauliflower, leeks, and potatoes, puréed, finished with cream, garnished with croutons.

Durham Soup
(Potage Durham)

Chicken stock thickened with roux, finished with cream, garnished with chicken, lobster, and spinach quenelles.

Elisabeth Soup*
(Potage Elisabeth)

Chicken stock simmered with rice, puréed, finished with cream, garnished with croutons.

Eliza Soup*
(Potage Elisa)

Chicken stock thickened with roux, finished with cream, garnished with sorrel chiffonade and chopped chervil.

Erica Soup
(Potage Erica)

Chicken stock simmered with red peppers, puréed, thickened with roux, finished with cream, garnished with a dollop of unsweetened whipped cream at service.

Esmeralda Soup
(Potage Esmeralda)

Chicken stock simmered with celery and morels, puréed, thickened with roux, finished with cream; profiteroles filled with puréed foie gras served separately.

Eveline Soup
(Potage Eveline)

Chicken stock thickened with roux, finished with cream, garnished with a ring of thick tomato sauce at service.

———————————— • ————————————

This is one of a handful of soups that present an opportunity for extravagant presentation. Thick tomato sauce (or tomato paste thinned with stock) is placed in a plastic squeeze bottle, and a spiral line of it is arranged on top of the soup. A toothpick can then be run through it radially from the center out (4 times) and from the outer edge in (4 times). (See Figure 4.1, page 206.)

Excelsior Soup*
(Potage Excelsior)

Chicken stock simmered with asparagus peelings and bottoms, thickened with roux, finished with cream, garnished with pearl barley.

Fanchette Soup*
(Potage Fanchette)

Chicken stock thickened with roux, finished with cream, garnished with asparagus tips, green peas, and large squares of cabbage.

Flemish Style Soup
(Potage à la Flamande)

Chicken stock simmered with Brussels sprouts and potatoes, puréed, finished with cream, garnished with small Brussels sprouts.

Fleury Soup*
(Potage Fleury)

Chicken stock simmered with pearl barley, puréed, finished with cream, garnished with diced root vegetables and cauliflower flowerettes.

Florence Style Soup
(Potage à la Florentine)

Chicken stock simmered with spinach, puréed, finished with cream, seasoned with nutmeg, garnished with croutons.

Fontanges Soup
(Potage Fontanges)

Chicken stock simmered with peas, puréed, finished with cream, garnished with sorrel chiffonade and chopped chervil.

Francis Joseph Soup
(Potage François Joseph)

Chicken stock simmered with celery, chestnuts, and tomatoes, puréed, finished with cream, garnished with vermicelli.

Gascon Style Soup*
(Potage à la Gasconne)

Chicken stock simmered with onion and tomato, thickened with roux, puréed, finished with cream, garnished with diced goose confit.

———— • ————

This soup was name for Mademoiselle de Fontanges, a mistress of Louis XIV (1638–1715).

———— • ————

Dishes so titled are named for Francis Joseph (1830–1916), emperor of Austrian and king of Hungary.

A confit is a piece of meat or poultry cooked in its own fat, cooled, and stored in an earthenware pot known as a *toupin*. It is one of the oldest forms of food preservation, typically a specialty of south-western France, and different regions have their own style of preservation and consumption. It is eaten variously hot or cold, accompanied by cooked vegetables, wild mushrooms, fried potatoes, or in the case of cassoulet—of which it is an essential ingredient— with white beans. Goose is most commonly made into confit because it is often too tough to roast, though other meats preserved in this fashion include chicken, duck, pork, rabbit, turkey, and woodcock.

Gastronomer's Style Soup
(Potage à la Gastronome)

Chicken stock simmered with chestnuts, thickened with roux, puréed, finished with cream, garnished with morels, cock's combs, and julienned truffles.

Gaulish Style Soup
(Potage à la Gauloise)

Chicken stock simmered with celery root, chestnuts, and tomatoes, thickened with roux, puréed, finished with cream, garnished with croutons.

Germinal Soup*
(Potage Germinal)

Chicken stock simmered with tarragon (stems), thickened with roux, strained, finished with cream, garnished with asparagus tips and chervil.

Gervaise Soup
(Potage Gervaise)

Chicken stock simmered with pearl barley, thickened with roux, puréed, strained, finished with cream, garnished with diced lamb and cock's kidneys.

Granada Style Soup
(Potage à la Granada)

Chicken stock thickened with roux, finished with cream, garnished with diced tomatoes and julienned chicken breast.

Greek Style Soup*
(Potage à la Greque)

Chicken stock simmered with tomatoes and pumpkin, thickened with roux, puréed, finished with cream, garnished with croutons.

Green Herb Soup
(Potage aux Herbes)

Chicken stock simmered with a collection of green herbs and vegetables sweated in butter—such as chervil, dandelion, nettle shoots, leeks, lettuce, parsley, purslane, sorrel, spinach, and so on—thickened with potatoes or roux, puréed, finished with cream, garnished with croutons.

——————————— • ———————————

Any variety of green herbs can be used to prepare this soup, depending on availability. Several of the varieties mentioned here, however, are not commonly available, though all three of the following are high in iron and water-soluble vitamins, and are excellent braised or used in soups and other dishes. Dandelion (from the French *dent-de-lion*, or "lion's tooth," in reference to its serrated leaves) can be found occasionally in North American markets. The unpopularity of nettle shoots is probably based on its tendency to cause a skin rash when raw, though when cooked it is perfectly safe. There are several varieties of purslane, all of which are spicy and stand in for watercress as a garnish for roasts, tarragon for Béarnaise Sauce, or mint for Paloise Sauce.

Green Meadow Soup
(Potage Vert-pré)

Chicken stock simmered with potatoes and spinach, thickened with roux, puréed, finished with cream, garnished with croutons and chervil.

Hortensia Soup
(Potage Hortense)

Chicken stock thickened with roux, puréed, finished with cream, garnished with asparagus tips, carrot pearls, and chicken quenelles.

Hotel-keeper's Style Soup
(Potage à l'Hôtelière)

Chicken stock simmered with green beans, lentils, and potatoes, puréed, finished with cream, garnished with croutons and chervil.

Ilona Soup
(Potage Ilona)

Chicken stock simmered with green peas, thickened with a little roux, puréed, finished with cream, garnished at service with a dollop of whipped cream sprinkled with paprika.

Another version of this soup consists of chicken consommé thickened with tapioca, and finished with an egg yolk and cream liaison.

Imperial Style Soup*
(Potage à l'Impériale)

Chicken stock simmered with rice, thickened with a little roux, puréed, finished with cream, garnished with diced almond royale.

India Style Soup*
(Potage à l'Indienne)

Chicken stock flavored with curry, thickened with roux, finished with coconut milk and cream, garnished with rice.

Irma Soup*
(Potage Irma)

Chicken stock thickened with roux, finished with cream, garnished with curried chicken quenelles and asparagus tips.

Jenny Lind Soup
(Potage Jenny Lind)

Chicken stock thickened with roux, finished with cream, garnished with sago.

Josephine Soup
(Potage Josephine)

Chicken stock simmered with green peas, thickened with roux and sago, finished with cream, garnished with julienned vegetables.

Juanita Soup*
(Potage Juanita)

Chicken stock simmered with rice, thickened with a little roux, finished with cream, garnished with diced tomatoes, and quenelles flavored with sieved hard-cooked egg yolks.

Jussieu Soup*
(Potage Jussieu)

Chicken stock thickened with roux, finished with cream, garnished with julienned chicken and chicken quenelles.

Knickerbocker Soup
(Potage Knickerbocker)

Chicken stock simmered with white beans, puréed, finished with cream, garnished with tapioca and croutons.

Lady Morgan Soup*
(Potage Dame Morgan)

Chicken stock simmered with rice, thickened with a little roux, puréed, finished with cream, garnished with diced chicken and cockscombs.

Lady Simone Soup
(Potage Dame Simone)

Chicken stock simmered with lettuce, thickened with roux, puréed, finished with cream, garnished with sorrel chiffonade; gratinéed small poached eggs served separately.

Lavallière Soup*
(Potage Lavallière)

Chicken stock simmered with celery, thickened with roux, puréed, finished with cream, garnished with diced celery royale; profiteroles stuffed with puréed chicken served separately.

Ledoyen Soup*
(Potage Ledoyen)

Chicken stock simmered with flageolets, thickened with a little roux, puréed, finished with cream, garnished with croutons.

Dishes so titled are named after Louise de la Vallière, mistress of Louis XIV.

Lejeune Soup
(Potage Crème à la Lejeune)

Chicken stock thickened with roux, finished with cream, garnished with sago.

Lenclos Soup
(Potage Lenclos)

Chicken stock thickened with roux and puréed crayfish, finished with cream, garnished with pearl barley.

Lentil Soup, German Style
(Potage de Lentilles, à l'Allemande)

Chicken stock simmered with lentils, puréed, finished with cream, garnished with diced rendered bacon and sliced Frankfort sausages.

Lisette Soup
(Potage Lisette)

Chicken stock simmered with celery, puréed, finished with cream, garnished with julienned truffles.

Lison Soup
(Potage Lison)

Chicken stock simmered with celery and rice, puréed, finished with cream, garnished with sago (tapioca).

Longueville Style Soup
(Potage à la Longuevillaise)

Chicken stock simmered with green peas, puréed, garnished with sorrel chiffonade and spaghetti.

Louisette Soup
(Potage Louisette)

Chicken stock simmered with green peas, puréed, garnished with sorrel chiffonade and spaghetti.

Lucullus Soup*
(Potage Lucullus)

Chicken stock thickened with roux, finished with cream, garnished with chicken and truffle quenelles, cock's combs, and cock's kidneys.

———————————— • ————————————

Lucius Licinius Lucullus (106–56 B.C.), a Roman general who retired to his country villa after a brilliant victory over Mithridates, lived on a grand scale, entertaining in various dining halls according to the amount of money spent on the meal. Surprised one day by the unexpected arrival of Caesar and Cicero, who insisted that he not change anything on their account, he served them in the Apollo room, where the cost of meals had been fixed at 100,000 sesterces. He is credited with introducing the pheasant, as well as the peach tree and cherry tree into Italy. Dishes prepared in the Lucullus style include game birds (pheasant, ortolans, quails), tournedos, and poached eggs served in various opulent styles with abundant use of cockscombs and cock's kidneys, foie gras, lamb sweetbreads, and truffles.

Lyon Style Soup*
(Potage Lyonese)

Chicken stock thickened with roux, garnished with diced chestnut royale.

MacDonald Soup*
(Potage MacDonald)

Chicken stock simmered with calf's brains, thickened with roux, puréed, finished with cream and sherry, garnished with diced cucumber.

Magdalena Soup
(Potage Madeleine)

Chicken stock simmered artichokes, white beans, and onion, thickened with a little roux, puréed, finished with cream, garnished with sago (tapioca).

Maintenon Soup
(Potage Maintenon)

Chicken stock thickened with roux, finished with cream, garnished with braised diced vegetables.

Majordomo Soup
(Potage Majordome)

Chicken stock simmered with lentils, puréed, finished with cream, garnished with chicken quenelles and chopped chervil.

Marcilly Soup*
(Potage Marcilly)

Chicken stock simmered with green peas, thickened with a little roux, puréed, finished with cream, garnished with chicken quenelles.

Margaret Soup*
(Potage Marguérite)

Chicken stock simmered with pearl barley, thickened with a little roux, puréed, finished with cream, garnished with chicken quenelles and croutons.

Maria Soup
(Potage Maria; also known as Quebec Style Soup [Potage à la Québécoise])

Chicken stock simmered with white beans, puréed, finished with cream, garnished with diced carrots and turnips, and chervil.

Maria Stuart Soup*
(Potage Maria Stuart)

Chicken stock simmered with pearl barley, thickened with a little roux, puréed, finished with cream, garnished with pearl barley and root vegetable pearls.

Marianne Soup
(Potage Marianne)

Chicken stock simmered with potatoes and pumpkin, puréed, finished with cream, garnished with lettuce and sorrel chiffonade, and croutons browned with grated cheese.

Marie Antoinette Soup*
(Potage Marie Antoinette)

Chicken stock simmered with asparagus peelings and stems, puréed, finished with cream, garnished with diced asparagus royale.

Marie Antoinette (1755–1793), the daughter of François I (King of Hungary) and Maria Theresa (Archduchess and Queen of Hungary), became queen of France when she married Louis XVI in 1770. Her insensitive response to the plight of starving French farmers immortalized her. Said she, "Qu'ils mangent de la brioche. Qu'ils ne mangent de la croûte de pâté?" (If they don't have brioche [ordinary bread] to eat, why don't they eat the pastry on pâté?)

Marie Louise (1791–1847) was the second wife of Napoléon I and the mother of Napoléon II.

Marie Louise Soup*
(Potage Marie Louise)

Chicken stock simmered with pearl barley, thickened with a little roux, puréed, finished with cream, garnished with pearl barley and macaroni.

Marquise Soup*
(Potage Marquise)

Chicken stock simmered with rice, puréed, finished with cream, garnished with lettuce chiffonade and green peas.

Marshal's Style Soup
(Potage à la Maréchale)

Chicken stock thickened with roux, finished with cream, garnished with asparagus tips, and diced chicken and truffles.

Martha Soup*
(Potage Martha)

Chicken stock simmered with onions, thickened with roux, puréed, finished with cream, garnished with chicken quenelles mixed with diced vegetables.

Mathilda Soup*
(Potage Mathilda)

Chicken stock simmered with cucumber and rice, puréed, finished with cream, garnished with cucumber pearls.

Memphis Style Soup
(Potage à la Memphis)

Chicken stock simmered with artichokes, thickened with roux, finished with cream, garnished with diced artichoke bottoms and diced artichoke royale.

Mercédès Soup*
(Potage Mercédès)

Chicken stock simmered with artichokes, thickened with roux, finished with cream, garnished with diced chicken and diced artichoke bottoms.

Milan Style Soup
(Potage à la Milanaise)

Chicken stock thickened with roux, blended with tomato purée, finished with cream, garnished with small macaroni, and julienned ham, truffle, and mushrooms; grated cheese served separately.

Miramount Soup
(Potage Miramount)

Chicken stock simmered with potatoes, puréed, finished with cream, garnished with croutons.

Modena Style Soup*
(Potage à la Modena)

Chicken stock simmered with spinach, puréed, finished with cream, garnished with croutons.

Mogador Soup*
(Potage Mogador)

Chicken stock thickened with roux, finished with cream, blended with puréed foie gras, garnished with julienned chicken breast, beef tongue, and truffles.

Molière Soup
(Potage Molière)

Chicken stock simmered with green peas, puréed, finished with cream, garnished with asparagus tips, and diced calf's sweetbreads and cock's combs.

Monte Christo Soup
(Potage Monte Christo)

Chicken stock simmered with young nettle shoots, thickened with roux, puréed, finished with cream, garnished with julienned mushrooms and truffles.

Montepsan Soup*
(Potage Montepsan)

Chicken stock simmered with asparagus peelings and bottoms, thickened with roux, puréed, finished with cream, garnished with tapioca and green peas.

Montesquieu Soup
(Potage Montesquieu)

Chicken stock simmered with cucumber and mushrooms, thickened with roux, puréed, finished with cream, garnished with diced cucumber.

Montglas Soup
(Potage Montglas)

Chicken stock thickened with roux, finished with cream, garnished with diced boletus mushrooms.

——— • ———

Montglas refers to a salpicon, consisting of finely diced pickled beef tongue, mushrooms, foie gras, and truffles, bound with thick Madeira Sauce. It is named after the Marquis de Montglas, an eighteenth-century French diplomat.

Montmorency Soup
(Potage Montmorency)

Chicken stock thickened with roux, finished with cream and grated cheese, garnished with lettuce chiffonade, vermicelli, and stuffed chicken wings.

———————————— • ————————————

Montmorency usually refers to dishes prepared with tart Montmorency cherries, typically a roasted duck with a demi-glaze flavored with cherry brandy and cherries, and a genoise (sponge) cake topped with Montmorency cherries in syrup, then meringue, and garnished with candied cherries. It can also refer to a garnish for roasted or sautéed meats that consists of artichoke bottoms filled with roasted Parisienne potatoes and carrots.

Montorgeuil Soup*
(Potage Montorgeuil)

Chicken stock thickened with roux, finished with cream, garnished with sorrel chiffonade, diced root vegetables, and chopped chervil.

Montpensier Soup
(Potage Montpensier)

Chicken stock simmered with cauliflower and rice, puréed, finished with cream, garnished with croutons.

Montreuil Soup*
(Potage Montreuil)

Chicken stock simmered with cauliflower and rice, puréed, finished with cream, garnished with croutons.

Morlaix Soup
(Potage Morlaisienne)

Chicken stock simmered with artichokes and rice, puréed, finished with cream, garnished with tapioca and fried croutons (variation of Artichoke Soup [Potage crème d'artichauts]).

Musart Soup
(Potage Musart)

Chicken stock simmered with flageolets, puréed, finished with cream, garnished with flageolets.

Nanette Soup
(Potage Nanette)

Chicken stock simmered with flageolets, puréed, finished with cream, garnished with flageolets.

Navarra Style Soup
(Potage à la Navarraise)

Chicken stock simmered with tomatoes, thickened with roux, puréed, finished with cream, garnished with vermicelli; grated cheese served separately.

Nelusko Soup*
(Potage Nelusko)

Chicken stock thickened with roux, finished with cream, blended with filbert butter, garnished with chicken quenelles mixed with ground toasted filberts.

Nemours Soup
(Potage Nemours)

Chicken stock simmered with potatoes and mushrooms, finished with milk, garnished with tapioca and julienned mushrooms.

Normandy Style Soup
(Potage à la Normande)

Chicken stock simmered with white beans, leeks, potatoes, and turnips, puréed, finished with cream, garnished with chervil.

Norwegian Style Soup
(Potage à la Norvegienne)

Chicken stock simmered with cabbage and turnips, thickened with a little roux, puréed, finished with cream, garnished with julienned beets.

Râble de Veau, Prince Orloff (Saddle of Veal) is a celebrated nineteenth-century dish created by Urbain Debois during his stint as private chef to the Russian Prince Orloff. In addition to the saddle and this soup, there is an Orloff garnish for roasts that consists of braised celery (or celery mousse), roasted turned potatoes, and braised lettuce.

Orléans Style Soup
(Potage à l'Orléanaise)

Chicken stock thickened with roux, finished with cream, blended with puréed crayfish, garnished with chicken quenelles flavored with fine herbs.

Orloff Soup
(Potage Orloff)

Chicken (or white veal) stock flavored with cucumber and onion, thickened with roux, puréed, finished with cream, garnished with diablotins and julienned truffle.

Patti Soup*
(Potage Patti)

Chicken stock simmered with artichokes, thickened with roux, puréed, finished with cream, garnished with diced artichoke bottoms.

Pavillion Soup*
(Potage Pavillion)

Chicken stock simmered with watercress, thickened with roux, puréed, finished with cream, garnished with diced celery and carrots.

Pearl Barley Soup, French Style
(Potage d'Orge, à la Française)

Chicken stock thickened with roux and pearl barley, puréed, finished with cream, garnished with pearl barley.

Pearl Barley Soup, Westfalian Style
(Potage d'Orge, à la Westfalienne)

Chicken stock flavored with ham, thickened with roux and pearl barley, puréed, finished with cream, garnished with pearl barley, diced ham, carrots, celery root, and potatoes.

Peter the Great Soup II
(Potage Pierre le Grand II)

Chicken stock simmered with celery root, thickened with roux, puréed, finished with cream, garnished with diced celery root.

Piedmont Style Soup
(Potage à la Piémontaise)

Chicken stock flavored with tomatoes, thickened with roux, finished with cream, garnished with diced chicken and macaroni.

Pompadour Soup
(Potage Pompadour)

Chicken stock simmered with tomatoes, thickened with roux, finished with cream, puréed, garnished with sago and lettuce chiffonade.

Potato Soup, Saxon Style
(Potage de Pommes de Terre à la Saxonne)

Chicken stock simmered with potatoes, puréed, garnished with vermicelli.

Princess Soup
(Potage Princesse)

Chicken stock simmered with asparagus peelings and trimmings, thickened with roux, finished with cream, puréed, garnished with asparagus tips and diced chicken.

Queen's Style Soup
(Potage à la Reine)

Chicken stock simmered with rice (or thickened with roux), finished with cream, puréed (if thickened with rice), garnished with asparagus tips and diced chicken.

Queen Hortense Soup
(Potage à la Reine Hortense)

Chicken stock simmered with asparagus peelings and trimmings, and rice (or thickened with roux), finished with cream, puréed

Potage à la reine was created by François Pierre la Varenne (1618–1678), in honor of Marguerite de Navarre. La Varenne is also the innovator of mushroom duxelle (cooked mushroom paste flavored with a reduction of wine), named for the Marquis d'Uxelles, the governor of Chalon-sur-Saône, whose kitchens he was in charge of.

(if thickened with rice), garnished with tapioca and asparagus tips.

Queen Margo Style Soup
(Potage à la Reine Margo)

Chicken stock simmered with chopped almonds, thickened with roux, finished with cream, garnished with chicken quenelles mixed with chopped pistachios.

Rachel Soup
(Potage Rachel)

Chicken stock simmered with rice, peas, and sorrel, puréed, finished with cream, garnished with rice and croutons.

Regency Soup*
(Potage Régence)

Chicken stock simmered with pearl barley, thickened with roux, finished with cream, blended with crayfish butter, garnished with crayfish quenelles, cock's combs, and pearl barley.

Rich Style Soup
(Potage à la Riche)

Chicken stock flavored with truffle essence, thickened with roux, finished with cream, garnished with truffle pearls and julienned chicken breast.

Romeo Soup
(Potage Romeo)

Chicken stock simmered with onions and potatoes, puréed, finished with cream, garnished with diced ham and hard-cooked egg white, and chervil.

Rossini Soup*
(Potage Rossini)

Chicken stock thickened with roux, finished with cream, blended with truffled foie gras and butter paste, garnished with chicken quenelles flavored with foie gras.

Roumanille Soup
(Potage Roumanille)

Chicken stock simmered with onions, thickened with roux, puréed, finished with cream, garnished with vermicelli; grated cheese served separately.

Rubens Soup
(Potage Rubens)

Chicken stock simmered with rice and onions, puréed, finished with cream, garnished with diced mushrooms; grated cheese served separately.

Saint Cloud Soup
(Potage Saint Cloud)

Chicken stock simmered with green peas and lettuce, puréed, garnished with lettuce chiffonade, croutons, and chervil.

Saint Louis Style Soup
(Potage à la Saint Louis)

Chicken stock simmered with tomatoes, thickened with roux, puréed, finished with cream, garnished with tapioca and chicken quenelles.

Sévigné Soup
(Potage Sévigné)

Chicken stock simmered with lettuce, thickened with roux, puréed, finished with cream, garnished with chicken quenelles and lettuce chiffonade.

Shepherd's Style Soup
(Potage à la Bergère)

Chicken stock simmered with white beans, leeks, onions, and potatoes, puréed, garnished with chopped tarragon and croutons.

Shepherdess's Style Soup
(Potage à la Pastourelle)

Chicken stock simmered with leeks, mushrooms, onions, and potatoes, puréed, finished with milk, garnished with sautéed sliced mushrooms and sautéed small-diced potatoes.

Sigurd Soup
(Potage Sigurd)

Chicken stock simmered with potatoes and tomatoes, puréed, garnished with chicken quenelles and diced green peppers.

Simone Soup
(Potage Simone)

Chicken stock simmered with white beans, puréed, finished with cream, garnished with diced vegetables.

Soisson Style Soup
(Potage à la Soissonaise)

Chicken stock simmered with white beans, puréed, finished with cream, garnished with chervil.

Solferino Soup
(Potage Solferino)

Chicken stock simmered with carrots, leeks, potatoes, and tomatoes, puréed, blended with butter, garnished with potato pearls, green bean diamonds (losange), and chervil.

Sorrel Soup
(Potage d'Oseille)

Chicken stock simmered with sorrel, thickened with roux, puréed, finished with cream, garnished with croutons.

———————————— • ————————————

This soup was first created by Adolphe Dugléré at the Café Anglais in Paris during his reign there as chef in the late 1860s, which is one reason why it is still popular in France.

Sorrel, also known as "sour grass," is native to northern Asia and Europe. Though quite tart in its raw state—due to a high content of oxalic acid—when it is cooked, this tartness is considerably toned down. In North America, sorrel is no longer cultivated on a large scale, which makes it difficult to find. It is, however, easy to grow and is considered an important dish on any fine-dining menu. Sorrel is low in calories, rich in potassium, magnesium, and vitamin C, and can be prepared in the same manner as spinach (creamed, puréed, sautéed). In France, shad is prepared with a stuffing of puréed sorrel, and the oxalic acid reputedly softens the bones of that fish so that they can be easily eaten right along with the flesh. It is also the typical accompaniment to pike and veal breast, used as an omelet filling, and an ingredient in eggs en cocotte.

Spanish Style Soup
(Potage à l'Espagnole)

Chicken stock simmered with onions, rice and tomatoes, puréed, finished with cream, garnished with rice.

Sultana Soup
(Potage Sultane)

Chicken stock simmered with almonds, thickened with roux, puréed, finished with cream, blended with pistachio butter, garnished with chicken quenelles shaped like crescents embellished with a thin-sliced truffle star.

Surette Soup
(Potage Surette)

Chicken stock thickened with roux, finished with cream, garnished with sorrel chiffonade; miniature puff paste patties stuffed with asparagus tips served separately.

Susanne Soup
(Potage Suzanne)

Chicken stock simmered with cucumber and green peas, thickened with roux, puréed, finished with cream, garnished with sieved hard-cooked egg yolks.

Susie Soup
(Potage Suzon)

Chicken stock simmered with green peas, thickened with roux, puréed, finished with cream, garnished at service with a dollop of unsweetened whipped cream topped with a small poached egg.

Suzette Soup*
(Potage Suzette)

Chicken stock simmered with mushrooms and watercress, thickened with roux, puréed, finished with cream, garnished with green bean diamonds (losange).

•

Watercress in several wild forms was known to the ancient Greeks and Romans. Charlemagne ordered it cultivated during the eighth century, and its juice was used as an ingredient in the medieval verjuice (unfermented grape juice). Louis IX (1214–1270), who was once overcome with thirst while hunting on a hot summer day, was handed a bunch of watercress. It revived and refreshed him. As a result, to this day the coat of arms for the city of Veron bears three bunches of watercress. In the fourteenth century, when Taillevent (Guillaume Tirel, 1310–1395) was chef to Charles VI, on a dinner menu in honor of the Compte de la Marche, he served watercress alone as the fourth course, with the following qualifier: "Watercress, served alone, to refresh the mouth." Alexander Dumas considered it "the healthiest of the fine herbs." Though originally brought to North America in cultivated form from Eurasia, it now grows wild in every state, including Hawaii and Alaska. It grows well in damp places and at high altitudes, and in temperate climates it can be found in clear-running streams all year round; it has the longest season of any salad plant.

Theresa Soup
(Potage Thérèse)

Chicken stock simmered with white beans, puréed, finished with cream, garnished with tapioca, julienned chicken breast, and leek.

Tomato Soup, American Style
(Potage de Tomate, à l'Américaine)

Chicken stock simmered with crayfish shells and tomatoes, thickened with roux, puréed, strained, finished with cream, garnished with diced crayfish tails and tapioca.

Toulousian Style Soup*
(Potage à la Toulousaine)

Chicken stock simmered with mushrooms, thickened with roux, puréed, strained, finished with cream, garnished with chicken quenelles, and diced goose liver, cock's combs, cock's kidneys, and truffle.

Tours Style Soup*
(Potage Crème à la Tourangelle)

Chicken stock simmered with green beans and flageolets, thickened with a little roux, puréed, strained, finished with cream, garnished with green bean diamonds and small flageolets.

Véfour Soup
(Potage Véfour)

Chicken stock flavored with tomato purée, thickened with roux, finished with cream, garnished with tapioca and chicken quenelles.

———————————— • ————————————

Café de Chartres was a Parisian restaurant founded by Aubertot in 1784. In 1820 it was taken over by Jean Véfour, renamed Le Grand Véfour, and was frequented by such personalities as Jérôme Bonaparte (Napoléon I's youngest brother), Brillat-Savarin, Joachim Murat, and Grimod de La Reynière. Subsequent proprietors kept the name through some difficult times in the first half of the twentieth century. In 1948 Louis Vaudable, former owner of Maxim's, and Raymond Oliver, a popular television chef, reopened it and restored it to its former glory.

Venetian Style Soup
(Potage à la Vénitienne)

Chicken stock thickened with roux, finished with cream, garnished with small ravioli filled with spinach.

Verneuil Soup
(Potage Verneuil)

Chicken stock simmered with pearl barley and green peas, puréed, finished with cream, garnished with plain royale, and diced carrots and mushrooms.

Vivian Soup
(Potage Viviane)

Chicken stock thickened with roux, finished with cream, garnished with diced artichoke bottoms, truffles, and carrots.

Voisin Soup
(Potage Voisin)

Chicken stock thickened with roux, finished with cream, garnished with diced spring vegetables, green beans, and green peas.

Voisin was a celebrated Parisian restaurant between the years 1850 and 1930. A man by the name of Bellenger, who was the first manager and also the maître d', was once approached by César Ritz, then in his late teens. Ritz boasted of his experience and quadrilingual ability, but Bellenger was unimpressed. When Ritz said, "I am willing to start at the beginning and learn if you will teach me," Bellenger engaged him as an assistant waiter. Over the years there, he would serve Sarah Bernhardt, Edmond de Goncourt, George Sand, and Alexander Dumas. During the Seige of Paris in 1870–71, while France was at war with Prussia, meat was particularly difficult to come by. Incredible as it may seem, animals from the Paris zoo were sold off and some of the dishes subsequently prepared became legendary: antelope terrine with truffles; elephant trunk, sauce chasseur; elephant blood pudding; civet of kangaroo; wolf haunch, roebuck sauce.

Vuillemot Soup
(Potage Vuillemot)

Chicken stock simmered with white beans, puréed, finished with cream, garnished with rice and sorrel chiffonade.

Washington Soup
(Potage Washington)

Chicken stock simmered with whole kernel corn, thickened with roux (and/or potatoes), puréed, finished with cream, whiskey, and Port, garnished with whole kernel corn.

Watercress Soup*
(Potage Cressonière)

Chicken stock simmered with watercress and potatoes, thickened with a little roux, puréed, finished with cream, garnished with chervil.

Wellington Soup
(Potage Wellington)

Chicken stock simmered with celery root, thickened with roux, puréed, finished with cream, garnished with rice.

White Lady Style Soup*
(Potage à la Dame Blanche)

Chicken stock simmered with crushed almonds, thickened with roux, puréed, finished with cream, garnished with diced chicken breast and chicken quenelles.

Wholesome Style Soup
(Potage de Santé)

Chicken stock simmered with potatoes and sorrel, puréed, finished with cream, garnished with sorrel chiffonade and chervil.

Wilhelmina Soup
(Potage Wilhelmine)

Chicken stock simmered with rice, puréed, finished with cream, garnished with asparagus tips, and julienned carrots and truffles.

Claire Fontaine Soup* is a variation on watercress soup, garnished with diced potatoes and chopped watercress.

Woronzow Soup
(Potage Woronzow)

Chicken stock flavored with Madeira, thickened with roux, finished with cream, blended with puréed foie gras, garnished with julienned carrot and celery, and raviolis stuffed with foie gras purée.

Xavier Soup
(Potage Xavier)

Chicken stock simmered with rice, thickened with roux, puréed, finished with cream, garnished with diced chicken breast and plain royale.

Creamed Soups Based on Duck Stock

Duck Soup, Rouenese Style
(Potage de Canard à la Rouennaise)

Brown duck stock flavored with red wine, thickened with brown roux, puréed, finished with a paste made with duck liver and cream, garnished with julienned duck meat and croutons.

Rouenese Style Soup
(Potage à la Rouennaise)

Brown duck stock simmered with lentils, thickened with brown roux, puréed, finished with cream, garnished with croutons.

Creamed Soups Based on Beef or Veal Stock

Bagration Soup I*
(Potage Bagration au Gras)

White veal stock thickened with roux, finished with cream, strained, garnished with small macaroni; grated cheese served separately.

Balmoral Soup*
(Potage Balmoral)

White veal stock made with calf's feet, flavored with turtle herbs, thickened with roux, finished with cream, strained, garnished with strips of calf's foot and veal quenelles.

Bismarck Soup*
(Potage Bismarck)

White veal stock prepared with calf's head, thickened with roux, finished with cream, garnished with shrimp purée.

Bread Soup, French Style
(Potage de Pain, à la Française)

White beef stock flavored with chopped onions fried in butter without coloring, simmered with diced bread, puréed, strained, finished with cream, garnished with poached eggs.

Cheese Soup, Dutch Style
(Potage au Fromage, à la Hollandaise)

White beef stock thickened with a little roux, finished with cream, grated Gouda cheese added, beaten with butter.

Chervil Soup
(Potage Cerfeuil)

White veal stock simmered with a copious amount of chervil, thickened with roux, puréed, strained, finished with cream, garnished with croutons.

Frog's Leg Soup
(Potage de Cuisse de Grenouilles)

White veal stock simmered with frog's legs, thickened with roux, meat removed from the bones and returned to the soup (bones discarded), puréed, finished with cream; sautéed frog's legs on toast served separately.

Frog's Leg Soup, Sicilian Style*
(Potage de Cuisse de Grenouilles, à la Sicilienne)

Half white veal stock and half fish stock simmered with frog's legs, thickened with roux, garnished with frog's legs, strips of white fish fillet, and chopped pistachios.

Jeanette Soup*
(Potage Jeanette)

Veal stock simmered with salsify, thickened with a little roux, puréed, finished with cream, garnished with diced chicken breast and rice.

———————————— • ————————————

Salsify is also known as oyster plant or vegetable oyster, because of its reputed oyster aroma and slimy texture. There is little agreement on any aspect of this vegetable which is commonly prepared in Europe, whether as to aroma, texture, or which of the two varieties are superior: true salsify, a thick white root; or black salsify, long and tapered. It is prepared in much the same way as other root vegetables: peeled, boiled, then sautéed in butter or gratinéed; as part of a salad or with mayonnaise; or puréed, shaped into small cylinders, breaded, and deep fried (fritter).

Londonderry Soup*
(Potage Londonderry)

White veal stock simmered with rice and mushrooms, flavored with white wine, puréed, finished with cream, garnished with diced turtle meat.

Mac-Mahon Soup*
(Potage Mac-Mahon)

White veal stock simmered with calf's brains, thickened with roux, puréed, finished with cream and sherry, garnished with diced cucumber and diced calf's brain.

Onion Soup*
(Potage Soubise)

White veal stock simmered with onions, puréed, finished with cream, garnished with croutons.

Parisian Style Soup
(Potage à la Parisienne)

White veal stock simmered with leeks and potatoes, puréed, finished with cream, garnished with croutons.

Peruvian Style Soup
(Potage à la Péruvienne)

Brown beef tail stock thickened with brown roux, finished with cream, garnished with croutons.

Windsor Soup
(Potage Windsor)

White veal stock (white) simmered with rice, flavored with turtle herbs (basil, chervil, fennel, marjoram, savory), puréed, finished with cream, garnished with julienned calf's feet and chicken quenelles blended with hard-cooked egg yolks.

Creamed Soups Based on Game Stock

Ardennes Style Soup*
(Potage à l'Ardennaise)

Pheasant stock flavored with Port, thickened with red beans, puréed, finished with cream, garnished with julienned pheasant breast and croutons.

Banker's Style Soup
(Potage à la Financière)

Brown game stock flavored with woodcock, thickened with brown roux, puréed, finished with cream, beaten with foie gras mashed into a paste, garnished with croutons.

Beaufort Soup
(Potage Beaufort)

Rabbit stock thickened with roux, finished with cream, garnished with rabbit and small sliced sausages.

Berchoux Soup
(Potage Berchoux)

Brown game stock simmered with lentils, thickened with brown roux, puréed, finished with cream, garnished with croutons.

Cherville Style Soup*
(Potage de Chervillaise)

Brown game stock flavored with rabbit and Madeira, thickened with brown roux, finished with cream, garnished with julienned rabbit meat, morels, and truffles.

———————————— • ————————————

Morels (along with mushrooms and truffles) are related to molds and yeasts, and are among the most primitive of foods. They are *saprophytic*, which means that they are unable to photosynthesize sugars and must live on the decaying remains of other organisms. The rich flavor of morels (and other fungi) is due to a high content of glutamic acid, which makes them a natural version of monosodium glutamate. (MSG intensifies the flavor of foods by opening the pores of the tongue.)

While the honeycomb-patterned "fruiting body" is identified with the entire mushroom, found only in their wild state, it actually represents only a fleeting stage in the plant's life cycle. The darker their color, the tastier their flavor. They must be washed repeatedly with water and/or cleaned with a soft brush to remove any earth, sand, or insects remaining inside the honeycombs. One of the best ways of enjoying *Morchella deliciosa* (from Latin *Maurus*, meaning "Moor") is for it to be sautéed in butter, deglazed with Madeira, and simmered with cream.

Chestnut Soup
(Potage de Marrons)

Brown game stock simmered with chestnuts, thickened with brown roux, puréed, finished with cream, garnished with croutons.

Chief Hunter's Style Soup
(Potage à la Grand-veneur)

Brown game stock flavored with pheasant, cayenne pepper, and sherry, thickened with brown roux, finished with cream, garnished with diced pheasant meat and truffles.

Choiseul Soup
(Potage Choiseul)

Brown game stock simmered with lentils, puréed, finished with cream, garnished with rice and sorrel chiffonade.

Diana Soup*
(Potage Diana)

Brown game (partridge) stock thickened with brown roux, finished with cream, garnished with julienned partridge meat and truffle.

Grand-duke Style Soup
(Potage à la Grand-duc)

Brown game stock flavored with partridge, thickened with brown roux, finished with cream, garnished with chicken quenelles and diced mushrooms.

Imperator Soup
(Potage Imperator)

Brown pheasant stock flavored with morels, thickened with brown roux, puréed, finished with cream, garnished with pheasant and foie gras quenelles, julienned truffle, and diced plain royale.

Little Duke Style Soup
(Potage à la Petit-duc)

Brown game stock flavored with woodcock meat and Cognac, foie gras added, puréed, finished with cream, garnished with julienned woodcock meat and woodcock royale.

Masséna Soup
(Potage Masséna)

Brown game stock flavored with pheasant, thickened with brown roux and puréed pheasant meat, puréed, finished with cream, garnished with chestnut royale.

Nobleman's Style Soup
(Potage à la Gentilhomme)

Game stock flavored with partridge and Madeira, simmered with lentils, puréed, garnished with partridge quenelles and truffle pearls.

Peter the Great Soup I
(Potage Pierre le Grand I)

Brown game stock simmered with hazel-hen and mushrooms, thickened with brown roux and puréed hazel-hen meat, finished with cream, garnished with julienned carrots and celery root.

Pheasant Soup, Lucullus
(Potage de Faison, Lucullus)

Brown game stock simmered with pheasant, flavored with Port, thickened with brown roux, blended with foie gras, finished with cream, garnished with pheasant quenelles and truffle pearls; small puff pastry shells (bouchées) filled with pheasant purée served separately.

Pomeranian Style Soup
(Potage à la Poméranienne)

Goose stock flavored with chervil, marjoram, and parsley, simmered with white beans, puréed, finished with cream, garnished with diced goose meat.

Récamier Soup
(Potage Récamier)

Brown game stock flavored with pigeon, thickened with roux, finished with cream, garnished with asparagus tips.

Saint Georges Soup*
(Potage Saint Georges)

Brown game stock simmered with rabbit, flavored with mushrooms and red wine, thickened with brown roux, finished with a little cream, garnished with julienned rabbit, mushrooms, and truffles.

Saint Hubert Soup
(Potage Saint Hubert)

Brown game stock simmered with venison, chestnuts, and lentils, puréed, finished with cream and a little gooseberry jelly, garnished with julienned truffle.

Schönbrunn Soup*
(Potage Schönbrunn)

Brown game stock simmered with pheasant, flavored with sherry, lemon juice, and cayenne pepper, thickened with brown roux and puréed pheasant, finished with cream.

Tsar Style Soup
(Potage du Tsar)

Brown game stock simmered with hazel-hen and truffle peelings, thickened with brown roux, puréed, blended with puréed foie gras, garnished with julienned truffle simmered in Madeira.

Tsarina Style Soup*
(Potage à la Czarine)

Brown game stock simmered with hazel-hen and celery, thickened with brown roux and puréed hazel-hen, finished with cream, garnished with julienned celery root cooked in butter and white wine.

BISQUES

Back in the early days of NET (National Educational Television), the precursor of today's PBS, there were a number of educational programs offered, including one on cooking. Once a week Julia Child offered dishes from her tome, *Mastering the Art of French Cooking*, and I can honestly say that her program had at least a modicum of influence on my future choice of careers. Needless to say, she has since become something of a legend in the field of American cookery.

One Saturday afternoon, lying on the floor in front of an ancient black-and-white, two-knob television, hovering over a sheet of light-blue-lined, three-hole, loose-leaf paper with pencil in hand, I listened to Julia Child's pronunciation of the classical lobster dish she was about to demonstrate. But, given her high-pitched voice and my rudimentary grasp of conversational French, I had difficulty understanding her. So, in my best

"Franglais" I wrote, "Lobster au something or other," and proceeded to carefully copy her instructions on preparing the dish. Fifteen years later, I rediscovered the same dish during a stint as an apprentice, and realized that what I had witnessed those many years earlier was none other than *Lobster à l'Américaine* (Lobster, American Style). The method I learned as an apprentice was virtually identical to the method that I had seen fifteen years earlier, but there was something else. From the chef under whom I trained, I learned an *approach*, one that could be applied to all varieties of shellfish, and depending on the manner in which it was served, could also be used as an approach to preparing numerous shellfish-based dishes. The approach then, remains constant, even though there may be variations in the type of shellfish, aromatics, and thickening agent. Nomenclature simply depends on the nature of the dish served: *Lobster à l'Américaine* is an appetizer when served alone; becomes a main course when served with appropriate accompaniments (same name, larger portion, along with starch and vegetable); and in a soup plate garnished with diced lobster and topped with a crouton spread with sour cream or crème fraîche, becomes *Bisque de homard* (Lobster Bisque). With the substitution of crab, crayfish, or shrimp for lobster, one could create an entire family of bisques or variations on the *plat américaine*. Shrimp shells, by the way, taken from raw shrimp intended for other dishes, are often discarded for lack of knowledge about how to use them; yet they make a very fine shrimp bisque (or can augment lobster shells for a lobster bisque) and are an excellent way to utilize an expensive item that would ordinarily be discarded. (Roasting them briefly, without coloring, before they are employed in the dish helps to extract their flavor.)

It has been suggested that Lobster à l'Américaine is a misnamed Lobster à l'Amoricaine, which originated in Brittany and was named for the Armorican massif, a mountain mass in the northwesternmost region of France. Brittany is well known for many lobster dishes, which is understandable given its proximity to the North Atlantic. The conflict with this theory is that Brittany is not known for tomatoes, and until the nineteenth century tomatoes were scarcely known outside of the Mediterranean region. All versions of this dish, however, do include tomatoes, garlic, and olive oil, giving credence to Jules Gouffé's name for this dish—Lobster à la Provençale—as seen in his *Le Livre de Cuisine*, published in 1867. Provence, a region of considerable gastronomic esteem on the French Mediterranean coast, is known for an abundant use of tomato, garlic, and olive oil.

In 1854, Pierre Fraisse opened a restaurant on the Passage des Princes in Paris, after having lived in the United States for a period. Originally named Peter's, and later renamed Noël Peter's after Fraisse took on a partner, Noël Peter's was a celebrated dining establishment frequented by many notable writers and journalists. Fraisse introduced dishes from the United States that were unknown in France then, such as turtle soup, and roast beef sliced at the table to the customer's specifications. He also pioneered the marketing concept of offering a plat du jour, a daily special for each day of the week. About 1860, Monsieur Reculet, the chef at Noël Peter's, supposedly created a dish entitled Homard à l'Américaine (Lobster American) for a distinguished American diner at that establishment. Auguste Escoffier, however, contended that an unnamed cook created Langouste de la Mediterranée at Le Restaurant Français in Nice, then exported the Provence-style dish to the United States when he opened a restaurant there by the same name. It was then re-imported to France with the new name Lobster à l'Américaine.

Though a bisque is typically a seasoned, creamed shellfish soup thickened with roux or rice (or with puréed shellfish and re-duced cream), in contemporary cookery bisque is used to denote a number of shellfish-, tomato-, or vegetable-based creamed and thickened soups. This stretches the use of the word, but its origin is believed to be the Spanish province of Biscay, and early bisques were spicy soups based on meat and game garnished with cray-fish. By the seventeenth century these bisques had evolved into primarily puréed and creamed crayfish-based soups.

The following recipe for Lobster Bisque can be used as a basic guide for all shellfish bisques, as well as Lobster à l'Américaine.

.... *B*ASIC RECIPE FOR LOBSTER BISQUE

2 1½ to 2 pound (6.8 to 9 kg) live lobsters
1 shallot, minced
3 tablespoons (45 mL) olive oil
½ cup (120 mL) brandy
½ cup (120 mL) white wine

1 cup (240 mL) mirepoix (celery, carrots, and onions), finely chopped
1 clove garlic, crushed
6 parsley sprigs
1 sprig tarragon, chopped
1 bay leaf

1 cup (240 mL) crushed
   tomatoes (or tomato
   purée)
1½ quarts (1.4 L) chicken or
   fish stock
¾ cup (180 mL) flour
   kneaded together with ¼
   cup (60 mL) unsalted
   butter
salt and white pepper to
   taste

2 tablespoons (30 mL)
   unsalted butter
½ cup (120 mL) cream
8 ¼ inch (6 mm) thick
   baguette slices, toasted
4 tablespoons (60 mL) sour
   cream
2 tablespoons (30 mL)
   minced chives

- Stun the lobsters by piercing them through the head with a knife, at the center point just about a half-inch behind the eyes. Cut the lobsters up as follows: each claw cut in half; arms split; body quartered; tail split in half. (When cutting, place a pan underneath the cutting board, so that any juices that run out of the lobster can be added to the vegetables during the sweating.)

- Sauté the shallot and the lobster pieces in the oil, sprinkled lightly with salt and pepper, until the shells are bright red (about 6 minutes). Add the brandy, stand back from the stove, and carefully ignite. Allow to cook a minute or so, then extinguish with the white wine. Remove the lobster with a slotted spoon, and set aside to cool.

- Crack the shells, carefully remove the meat, and cut into ¼-inch (6-mm) pieces. Crack all of the lobster shells into 1-inch (25-mm) pieces, place in a food processor, and pulse into even smaller pieces. Set the meat and shells aside.

- Add the mirepoix, garlic, parsley, and bay leaf to the pan, and sweat over medium heat for about 10 minutes. Add the chopped shells, tomatoes, stock, salt, and pepper, and simmer very slowly for 30 minutes.

- Place some of the hot liquid in a bowl, and beat in the butter and flour paste. Return this paste to the simmering ingredients, and blend thoroughly. Simmer another 15 minutes.

- Strain the bisque through a medium-holed strainer, using the ladle to pound the solids, extracting every last bit of liquid. Return to the pan, add the cream, and adjust seasoning. Add the diced lobster meat, and serve garnished with the baguette slices spread with sour cream and sprinkling with chives.

---•---

Rice can be used in place of the beurre manié as the thickening agent. Substitute 1¼ cups (300 mL) of rice, adding it to the mirepoix just before adding the stock, and purée the soup before straining.

Be **very careful** when igniting the brandy. Always stand back and away from the pan, tipping it up using the cooking fire to ignite. If using an electric range, hold a match carefully just over the edge of the pan.

Variations

American Bisque
(Bisques Américain)

Half cream of lobster and half cream of tomato soup, garnished with diced lobster and tapioca.

Chicago Style Bisque
(Bisque de Homard, à la Chicago)

Lobster bisque heavily flavored with tomato, garnished with diced tomatoes and diced lobster.

Crayfish Bisque, Princess Style
(Bisque d'Écrevisses, à la Princesse)

Crayfish bisque garnished with asparagus tips and crayfish quenelles flavored with crayfish butter.

---•---

Two variations of this soup are: Crayfish Bisque with Truffle (Bisque d'Écrevisses, à la Périgourdine), Crayfish Bisque garnished with crayfish quenelles and tails, and truffle pearls; and Vintimille Style Soup (Potage à la Vintimille), Crayfish Bisque garnished with crayfish tails and tapioca.

Crayfish are a freshwater crustacean found throughout the United States, Scandinavia, Europe, Australia, and New Zealand. The Mississippi Delta variety, the most celebrated North American variety in modern times, is also one of the smallest, averaging 3 inches in length. A Tasmanian variety has been recorded at 16 inches in length and weighing 8 pounds, although the average length is 3 to 6 inches. In the United States they are also variously dubbed bay crabs, crawdads, crawfish, and freshwater lobsters—and in Louisiana, creekcrabs, mudbugs, and yabbies. Sadly, water pollution as well as overconsumption has seriously depleted what was once an abundant source of seafood. The town of Breaux Bridge, Louisiana (population 5,000) was designated "The Crawfish Capital of the World" by the state legislature, though the most classic crayfish dishes are qualified by "Nantua," the French town most identified with the crustacean.

Southern Bisque

Diced carrots, celery, leeks, and onions sweated in butter; bay leaf, cloves, garlic, and peppercorns added; sprinkled with flour, blended with white stock; ham bone and tomato paste added and simmered for 2 hours; strained, seasoned with salt and pepper, and garnished with whole kernel corn and diced green peppers.

𝒯OMATO BISQUE
(Bisque de Tomate)

3 tablespoons (45 mL) unsalted butter
1 shallot, minced
1 cup (240 mL) mirepoix (celery, carrots, and onions), finely chopped
2 cloves garlic, crushed
6 basil leaves, roughly chopped
6 mint leaves, roughly chopped
6 parsley sprigs
1 bay leaf
salt and white pepper to taste
6 tablespoons (90 mL) flour

3 cups (720 mL) crushed tomatoes (or tomato purée)
1 cup (240 mL) diced tomatoes
1 quart (960 mL) chicken stock
2 tablespoons (30 mL) unsalted butter
½ cup (120 mL) dry sherry
8 ¼ inch (6 mm) thick baguette slices, toasted
4 tablespoons (60 mL) sour cream
4 sprigs of mint

• Sweat the shallot, mirepoix, garlic, herbs, seasoned with salt and pepper, in the butter over medium heat for 10 minutes.

Add the flour, blend thoroughly, and cook several minutes. Add the tomatoes and stock, blend thoroughly, and simmer for 30 minutes.

- Place in a food processor and purée, then strain through a large-holed strainer.
- Beat in the butter, adjust seasoning, and finish with the sherry. Garnish with the croutons spread with sour cream and topped with a sprig of mint. (See Figure 4.1.)

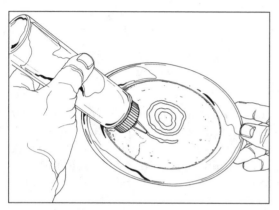

Certain puréed soups lend themselves to decorative painting on their surface. Here, three concentric circles of sour cream are piped out onto Tomato Bisque.

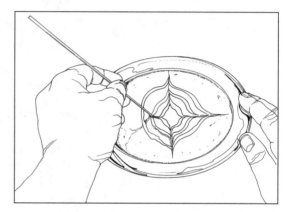

A bamboo pick is run four times outward . . .

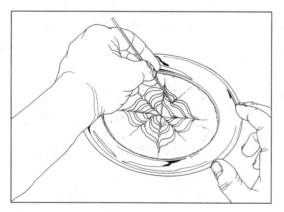

. . . and four times inward.

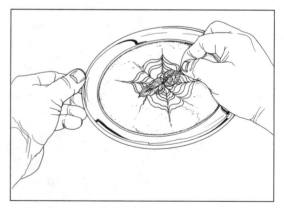

A small sprig of basil is placed in the center. Note: Thinned tomato paste can be piped onto light-colored soups that have some element of tomato in the recipe, such as Eveline Soup, page 169. And, while a sprig of basil is an appropriate garnish for Tomato Bisque, for other soups, flat-leaf parsley is an acceptable all-purpose garnish.)

Figure 4.1

CHAPTER 5

CHILLED SOUPS

Cold soups are greatly appreciated on hot summer days. The stock for these soups must be made of first class ingredients, well skimmed and degreased. Consommés should contain just enough natural gelatinous matter to gel when chilled, making it unnecessary to fortify with powdered gelatin; too much gelatin is not pleasing to the palate. Thick soup should always be well seasoned, otherwise they will taste insipid when chilled; they ought to have the consistency of rich but not thick cream. (Adapted from Hering's Dictionary of Classical and Modern Cookery, 1972)

———————————— • ————————————

Richard Hering, chef de cuisine at Vienna's Hotel Metropole in the late nineteenth century, was the original author of a "Lexikon der Küche," a modest book containing less than 1000 abbreviated recipes. The late Walter Bickel, also a chef of some note, kept Hering's "chef's reminder" up to date over the years of his career, and introduced a number of improvements, including sections on mixology (bar-drinks) and a five-language vocabulary; the repertory now contains in excess of 16,000 entries. (Bickel's accomplishments include four years as chef at the German Embassy in Paris; directeur de cuisine of the German Pavillon during the World Exhibition in 1937; chef at the court of Roumania; and catering director for Ashinger and Kempinski.)

————————————————————————

*C*old soups are not much appreciated in our culture. This may be due in part to not being properly introduced to fine chilled soups—perhaps because in our high-speed culture we are unaccustomed to slowing down and savoring such a first course on a hot summer day. In a first-year production kitchen at my alma mater, I recall, there was a chilled cherry soup on one evening's menu—essentially canned cherry juice thickened with cornstarch, sweetened, and garnished with canned cherries and canned Mandarin orange segments. Hardly an auspicious introduction to the genre. I still remember our collective distaste for that horrendous concoction, even though we were just first-year students.

As a commis at Mory's, a venerable private Yale University club in New Haven, Connecticut, I had the good fortune to work under Arthur Melke, septuagenarian chef de cuisine, irascible big-hearted tough guy, who had run Mory's kitchen for nearly 40 years (his only venture outside of Connecticut was a stint in the Navy during World War I). Among my duties was setting up the cold soup station: two stainless steel inserts (bain maries), one filled with Vichyssoise, the other with Consommé Madrilène, accompanied by a stack of soup cups, a small dish of minced chives, and serving utensils. Unfamiliar with chilled consommé, my initial visual identification of the Madrilène was with cherry Jell-O, but the flavor of clear beef and tomato consommé was unlike anything I had ever tasted before. I was familiar enough with hot consommé, so it was simply a matter of allowing the palate to adjust to the shift in temperature. For a culture weaned on sweet, artificially colored Jell-O™, it takes a little practice, but once the shift is made, the sweet version will never be the same.

CHILLED CONSOMMÉS

A properly prepared consommé (crystal clear with strong flavor) will generally contain sufficient gelatin to be served chilled. It should not be overly firm, but instead slightly gelled, enough to sit well in a spoon. One way to determine whether a consommé hot off the fire is sufficiently gelatinous is to fill a small container with the hot (and degreased) consommé, and place it in a wet ice bath. When it has fully set and appears to have too little gelatin, the consommé can be reduced further; if it is too gelatinous, it can be thinned with wine, Port, brandy, or a little water.

Typical consommés served chilled are as follows:

Celery Consommé
(Consommé Froid à l'Essence de Celeri)

Beef consommé prepared with an abundance of finely chopped celery and served chilled.

Gold Leaf Consommé
(Consommé aux Pailletes d'Or)

Chicken consommé garnished with flecks of gold leaf and served chilled.

Love Apple Consommé
(Consommé en Gelée aux Pommes d'Amour)

Beef consommé flavored with tomato and cayenne pepper and served chilled.

The use of gold in cooking dates back to the Middle Ages, when certain pâtés and roasted birds were wrapped in gold leaf. In addition to this consommé, chocolate confections are also decorated with gold, and tiny pieces are contained in a liqueur (Danzinger Goldwasser).

Tomatoes were brought to the European continent from South America in the sixteenth century by the Spanish Moors, who ruled the kingdoms of Naples and Sicily from 1500 to 1700. *Pomi dei moor* (Moor's apples), as they were then called, were introduced into Paris in the late eighteenth century, though to a Frenchman's ears "pomi dei moro" sounded like *pomme d'amour*, thus the colloquial name "love apple."

Portuguese Style Consommé (Consommé de Portugaise en Gelée) is tomato-flavored beef consommé without the diced peppers.

Madrid Style Consommé
(Consommé Madrilène en Gelée)

Beef or chicken consommé strongly flavored with tomato, garnished with diced red peppers, and served chilled.

Morel Consommé
(Consommé Froid à l'Essence de Morilles)

Beef consommé flavored with morel mushrooms (mostly stems) and served chilled.

Other game-bird-flavored consommés can be prepared in the same fashion, using pheasant, quail, squab, and so on.

Mushroom Consommé
(Consommé Froid à l'Essence de Champignons)

Beef consommé flavored with an abundance of mushrooms and served chilled.

Other beverages used to flavor consommés include Armagnac (Consommé Froid à l'Armagnac), Madeira (au Vin de Madère), Malvasier (au Vin de Malvoisie), Marsala (au Vin de Marsala), and sherry (au Xérès).

Partridge Consommé
(Consommé Froid à l'Essence de Perdreau)

Beef consommé flavored with roasted partridge bones and carcasses, and served chilled.

Port Consommé
(Consommé Froid au Porto)

Beef consommé finished with Port wine and served chilled.

Tarragon Consommé
(Consommé Froid à l'Essence d'Estragon)

Chilled beef consommé flavored with tarragon and served chilled.

Truffle Consommé
(Consommé Froid à l'Essence de Truffe)

Beef consommé flavored with truffle peelings, garnished with minced truffle, and served chilled.

---•---

Other herbs, herb combinations, as well as spices can be used to flavor consommé, including Fine Herbs (Consommé aux fines herbes; traditionally chervil, chives, parsley, and tarragon); basil (au basilic); fennel (au fenouil); rosemary (au romarin); thyme (au thym); anise (au anis); saffron (au safron).

CHILLED CREAMED AND PURÉED SOUPS

Most chilled creamed soups are thickened with roux (or beurre manié), simmered to expand the flour, then strained, creamed, and chilled. Inevitably, the flour will continue to expand as it cools down and will often yield a considerably thicker soup than expected the day after it has been prepared. Additional cream or a little warmed stock can be added to thin it out if necessary, though it is a good idea to experiment, allowing a chilled soup to sit overnight in order to see how much more thickened it has become. Suggested proportions of thickener to liquid are 5 tablespoons (75 mL) roux (or beurre manié) per quart (960 mL) of stock with ½ cup (120 mL) of heavy cream to finish.

It is also recommended that creamed soups that will be served chilled be carefully seasoned. This means preparing the soup initially with plenty of herbs, using a good stock-flavored bouillon or stock, and seasoning sufficiently with salt and pepper.

Chilled Cream of Chicken (Potage Froid au Crème de Volaille)

Strong chicken bouillon lightly thickened with roux, flavored with salt, pepper, and herbs, strained, finished with cream, and chilled.

———————————— • ————————————

Variations on this soup include Chilled Cream of Chicken with Port (Potage froid au crème de volaille au porto), same soup finished with white Port; Chilled Cream of Chicken Sultan (Potage froid au crème de volaille à la sultane), flavored with ground toasted hazelnuts and pistachios; Chilled Duquinha Soup (Potage froid au crème Duquinha), flavored with puréed tomatoes and red pepper and later strained; Chilled Margot Soup (Potage froid au crème Margot), flavored with ground almonds; Cream of Chicken, Portuguese (Potage froid au crème à la portugaise), tomato purée beaten in when soup is chilling down; and Chilled Cream of Duck (Potage froid au crème de caneton), same as Cream of Chicken but prepared with duck stock.

Chilled Cream of Crayfish (Potage Froid au Crème d'Écrevisses)

Prepared in the same manner as Lobster Bisque (Bisque de Homard), but served chilled.

Chilled Cream of Lettuce (Potage Froid au Crème de Laitue)

———— • ————

This is an excellent soup for utilizing the outside leaves of lettuce that would ordinarily be discarded; and it can be served either hot or cold.

Strong chicken bouillon simmered with lettuce, lightly thickened with roux, flavored with salt, pepper, and herbs, puréed, strained, finished with cream, chilled, and served garnished with lettuce chiffonade.

Chilled Cream of Mushroom (Potage Froid au Crème de Champignons)

Strong chicken bouillon simmered with mushroom trimmings, lightly thickened with roux, flavored with salt, pepper, and herbs, puréed, strained, finished with cream, chilled, and served garnished with lettuce chiffonade.

Chilled Cream of Tomato (Potage Froid au Crème de Tomate)

White stock heavily flavored with tomatoes, thickened with roux, seasoned, strained, finished with heavy cream.

GAZPACHO, DUTCHESS VALLEY STYLE

2 cups vine-ripened tomatoes, peeled, cored, seeded, and coarsely chopped

½ cup (120 mL) green pepper, seeded and coarsely chopped

½ cup (120 mL) cucumber, peeled, seeded, and coarsely chopped

½ cup (120 mL) onion, peeled and coarsely chopped

2 stalks celery, peeled and coarsely chopped

4 garlic cloves, coarsely chopped

½ cup (120 mL) tomato purée

¼ (60 mL) cup tarragon vinegar

½ cup (120 mL) rich beef stock or consommé

2 tablespoons (30 mL) olive oil

½ cup (120 mL) tomato juice

salt and white pepper to taste

¼ cup (60 mL) each, finely diced red bell pepper, green bell pepper, avocado, and cucumber

¼ cup (60 mL) small, plain white bread croutons

2 tablespoons (30 mL) minced chives

This soup was created by Peter Van Erp during his tenure as chef at The Dutchess Valley Club in Pawling, New York.

- Place all the ingredients except the garnish, croutons, and chives in a blender or food processor, and purée. Season to taste with salt and pepper. Marinate at least 12 hours.

- Serve in individual chilled bowls, garnished with the vegetables, croutons, and chives.

$\mathcal{V}$ICHYSSOISE

3 tablespoons (45 mL) unsalted butter

2 cups leeks (480 mL), white part only, roughly chopped

3 cups (720 mL) Red Bliss potatoes, peeled and roughly chopped

1 bouquet garni (1 sprig of thyme, 3 bay leaves, and 1 bunch parsley stems)

1 quart (960 mL) chicken stock

salt and white pepper to taste

1 cup (240 mL) cream

2 tablespoon (30 mL) chives, minced

- Sweat the leeks in the butter for about 10 minutes over medium heat. Add the potatoes, bouquet garni, and chicken stock; season lightly with salt and pepper; and simmer about thirty minutes or until the potatoes are soft. Add the cream, bring to a boil, and adjust seasoning.

- Transfer the soup to a blender or food processor and purée. Allow to chill, adjust seasoning, and serve sprinkled with the chives.

———————————— • ————————————

Vichyssoise was created by Louis Diat during his reign as chef at The Ritz-Carlton Hotel in New York City. The late Albert Stockli, a native of Switzerland, former chef at The Four Seasons (also in New York City), and later chef-proprietor of The Stonehenge Inn, Ridgefield, Connecticut, innovated several variations of Vichyssoise. These can be prepared by substituting one-third to one-half of the potatoes with one of the following: peeled, cored, and chopped apple or pear (added towards the end of the cooking); carrots; celery root; or white turnips. The rest of the soup remains the same, though additional garnish can be included as fits these variations: diced apple or pear; diced or julienned carrot; diced or julienned celery root. A sixth variation adds fresh watercress leaves during the puréeing step, substituting chives with chopped watercress leaves.

CHILLED FRUIT AND WINE SOUPS

Many of these soups are of German origin, and are popular during hot summer months. Though they are unlikely to ever become popular in North America, they are included here to give the reader a glimpse into the genre.

Chilled Almond Soup
(Mandel-Kaltschale)

Skinned, toasted, and ground almonds heated with milk and sugar, puréed, finished with egg yolks, chilled, and garnished with crushed macaroons.

Chilled Apple Soup
(Apfel-Kaltschale)

Peeled, cored, and chopped apples sweetened with sugar, simmered in water and white wine, puréed, chilled, and garnished with diced apples and sultanas (golden raisins) cooked in sugar syrup.

Variations include Pfirsich-Kaltschale (substitute peaches); Melonen-Kaltschale (substitute melon).

Chilled Apricot Soup
(Aprikosen-Kaltschale)

Chopped apricots sweetened with sugar, simmered in water and wine, puréed, garnished with peeled and thin-sliced apricots cooked in sugar syrup.

Chilled Elder-Blossom Soup
(Flieder-Kaltschale)

Milk heated with elder blossoms, cinnamon, sugar, and vanilla, finished with egg yolks, strained, chilled, sprinkled with crushed sweet biscuits or cookies.

Chilled Pineapple Soup
(Ananas-Kaltschale)

Chopped fresh pineapple, sweetened with sugar, simmered with white wine, puréed, chilled, and garnished with diced pineapple macerated in sugar and lemon juice.

Variations include Himbeer-Kaltschale (substitute raspberries); Johannisbeer-Kaltschale (substitute red currants); Kirschen-Kaltschale (substitute pitted cherries).

Chilled Strawberry Soup
(Erdbeer-Kaltschale)

Wild strawberries sweetened with sugar, simmered briefly with white wine, puréed, rubbed through a sieve, chilled, garnished with wild strawberries dipped in sugar.

Chilled Wine Soup
(Wein-Kaltschale)

White wine, water, finely ground almonds, cinnamon stick, lemon peel, and sugar simmered, finished with egg yolks, and served chilled.

CHAPTER 6

REGIONAL AND NATIONAL SOUPS

AUSTRIAN Barley Soup
(Ulmer Gerstlsuppe)

Rich beef bouillon garnished with pearl barley, finished with beaten egg yolks and milk.

Beef Bouillon with Stuffed Cabbage
(Preßkohlsuppe)

Blanched cabbage leaves wrapped around small balls of ground pork mixed with bread soaked in milk, eggs, chopped chives, salt, pepper, and nutmeg, and served in strong clear beef bouillon.

Beef Broth with Profiteroles
(Brandkrapferlsuppe)

Strong clear brown beef bouillon garnished with fried profiteroles the size of large green peas.

Beef Soup I
(Fleckerlsuppe)

Rich beef bouillon garnished with small square noodles.

Beef Soup II
(Fridattensuppe)

Rich beef bouillon garnished with very finely julienned crepes, sprinkled with chopped chives.

Biscuit Soup
(Biskuitschöberl-Suppe)

Strong clear brown beef bouillon garnished with biscuits cut into diamond shapes (losange).

Brain Soup
(Hirnschöberlsuppe)

Calf's brain (boiled, drained, and chilled) mashed with butter, egg yolks, bread crumbs, and beaten egg whites, and seasoned with salt, pepper, and nutmeg; baked in a greased pan, cut into diamond shapes (losange), and served with rich beef bouillon.

Dumpling Soup I
(Butternockerlsuppe)

Rich beef bouillon garnished with dumplings made with creamed butter, egg yolks, flour, sour cream, and beaten egg whites, poached in salted water.

Dumpling Soup II
(Wiener Knödelsuppe)

Rich beef bouillon garnished with dumplings made with half bread crumbs and half toasted bread crumbs, mixed with flour, eggs, and milk, seasoned with salt and nutmeg, poached in salted water.

Goose Soup
(Ganslsuppe)

The necks, wings, feet, and giblets of goose simmered in white stock; strained and thickened with white roux, seasoned with salt and pepper, garnished with cauliflower flowerettes, marrow dumplings, and finely diced giblets.

Liver Soup
(Lebersuppe)

Sliced carrots, onions, and shallots, and bay leaf and thyme sweated in rendered diced fatback; sliced calf's liver added, deglazed with white wine, moistened with brown stock, thickened with brown roux, and simmered; the liver puréed, rubbed through a sieve, and returned to the soup; seasoned with salt and pepper, and garnished with croutons.

Tyrolese Dumpling Soup
(Tiroler Knödlsuppe)

Rich beef bouillon garnished with dumplings (made with diced bread soaked in milk, mixed with flour, eggs, chopped onions fried in rendered fatback, and poached in boiling salted water).

BELGIAN Flemish Hotpot Soup
(Hochepot Flamande)

Pig's feet and ears, fatback, beef brisket, mutton shoulder, and small pork sausages simmered in stock with coarsely cut cabbage, carrots, leeks, onions, and potatoes, and seasoned with salt and pepper; broth and a few vegetables served separately from the meat and remaining vegetables.

BRITISH ISLES
English Friar's Chicken Soup

Squabs (pigeons) or young chickens poached in veal stock until tender, strained, thickened with an egg yolk liaison, garnished with the chopped poultry and plenty of chopped parsley.

Giblet Soup

Chicken necks, wings, and gizzards tossed in butter and roasted until golden brown; toasted (brown) flour added, simmered in brown stock with bouquet garni (celery and herbs), strained, seasoned with salt and pepper, strained, garnished with rice, julienned celery, and finely chopped neck and wing meat, gizzards, and giblets.

Hare Soup

Cut up hare browned in butter, dusted with arrowroot (or cornstarch), game stock and turtle herbs (basil, chervil, fennel, marjoram, and savory), simmered until the hare is tender; puréed liver added, garnished with diced meat, and finished with Port wine.

Kale Brose

Beef bouillon simmered with beef jowl and kale, thickened with oatmeal, garnished with sippets (pieces of toasted bread soaked in gravy or jus).

Kidney Soup

Sliced calf's kidneys sautéed in butter, half of them puréed and rubbed through a sieve; brown stock seasoned with cayenne pepper, and thickened with brown roux and the puréed kidneys; garnished with the remaining kidneys and finished with a little Madeira.

Mulligatawny Soup

Diced apple, onions, and ham sweated in butter, seasoned with curry powder, and dusted with flour; chicken stock added, simmered, puréed, finished with cream, and garnished with diced apple, chicken, and vegetables.

Mulligatawny is actually a soup of Indian origin that was adopted by the British. The original version was thickened with rice flour, flavored with coconut milk, and included blanched almonds as a garnish; in Australia, where it is very popular, it generally includes tomatoes and bacon.

Irish Chicken Soup
(Balnamoon Skink)

Rich chicken stock tempered with an egg yolk and milk liaison, garnished with diced celery root, green peas, and lettuce chiffonade.

Scottish

$\mathcal{C}$OCK-A-LEEKIE

1 chicken, about 4 pounds (1.8 kg)

4 pounds (1.8 kg) veal bones, cut into 3-inch lengths

1 bouquet garni (a sprig of thyme, 2 bay leaves, 1 bunch parsley stems, 1 teaspoon/4.9 mL peppercorns, and 6 whole cloves tied up in two leek leaves)

2 medium leeks, trimmed, and cut in half (separating the white part from the dark green part)

2 large carrots, peeled and trimmed

1 cup (240 mL) dried pitted prunes

- Rinse the chicken and veal bones thoroughly in cold water. Place in a stockpot with the bouquet garni, cover with cold water, and bring to a simmer. Skim and discard the fat and albumin from the top of the stock, and continue simmering.

- Cut the white part of the leek and the carrot into julienne, measuring approximately $\frac{1}{4} \times \frac{1}{4} \times 1$ inch ($6 \times 6 \times 25$ mm). Blanch the julienned vegetables in boiling lightly salted water

This version is a more refined approach to a soup that can also be made like a one-pot chicken soup—chicken simmered with rough-cut carrot, leek, onion, and aromatics; the chicken meat is returned to the soup in chunks along with the same vegetables, with prunes added.

until al dente. Set the vegetables aside, and add the cooking water to the stock. Chop up all remaining trim and add it to the simmering stock.

- After the stock has simmered about 2 hours, remove the chicken, and set aside to cool. Remove and discard the skin, and separate the meat from the bones. Return the bones to the stock, and continue simmering for 2 (or more) hours. In the meantime cut about one third of the chicken meat into julienne, saving the remaining meat for another use.

- Pass the stock through a fine strainer, return to the fire, adjust seasoning, and add the julienned leek and carrot. Pour hot water over the prunes, and allow to sit for 15 minutes. Drain, cut into quarters, and add to the soup.

Scotch Broth

Rich mutton bouillon garnished with pearl barley, diced carrots, celery root, leeks, potatoes, turnips, and mutton.

CHINESE

....

Cream stock is a curious dish, and its method breaks an important rule about stock preparation: that is, the vigorous simmering (i.e., boiling). But it is this method that disperses fat and gelatin throughout the hot liquid, giving it a creamlike quality. The use of chicken feet is also important here, since they contain an abundance of gelatin.

*B*EAN SLIVERS IN CREAM STOCK

For the stock:

1 small chicken, roughly cut into 1-inch (25-mm) pieces

1¼ pounds (563 g) duck (about ¼ of the bird), roughly cut into 1-inch (25-mm) pieces

½ pound (227 g) pork rib bones, cut into 1-inch (25-mm) lengths

1 pound (450 g) chicken feet

4 scallions, green tops only (save the white part for another use)

6 very thin slices ginger root

For the slivers:

2 fresh bean curd (tofu) cakes

¼ cup (60 mL) cilantro leaves

To prepare the stock:

- Immerse the meat and bones in cold water, and clean thoroughly by rubbing and massaging them vigorously under the water. Discard this water, place the meat and bones in a stockpot, and cover with cold water, several inches above the highest bone. Bring to a boil and simmer vigorously for 15 minutes. Skim any albumin and fat from the top, and continue simmering.

- Lift the meats out with a slotted spoon, and place into 3 pints of cold water. Massage these ingredients again, dislodging albumen, coagulated blood, and impurities, then return them to the simmering stock. (*Save the cold cleaning water!*) Simmer vigorously for 4 hours, adding the cleaning water as the stock evaporates. Strain and return to the fire again, and simmer until reduced to approximately 3 pints (1.4 L).

- Place the bean curd on a cutting board, and cut into very thin slices (about 1/16 inch/1 mm thick). Stack several of these slices at a time, and cut into long slivers (julienne). Place in a bowl, sprinkle with salt, cover with boiling water, and allow to sit for 30 minutes. Drain carefully, and place the slivers in soup plates or a soup tureen. Pour boiling hot stock over the slivers, and garnish with the cilantro leaves.

CHICKEN SOUP, HUNAN STYLE

1 chicken, about 5 pounds (2.3 kg)
6 thin slices ginger root
1 bunch scallions, sliced
½ cup (120 mL) sake (or dry sherry)
½ teaspoon (2.5 mL) salt
2 cups (480 mL) water
½ cup (120 mL) champagne vinegar
1 shallot, minced
½ cup (120 mL) soy sauce
1 teaspoon (5 mL) ginger root, grated

- Place the chicken into boiling water, bring back to a boil, then drain and rinse thoroughly.

- Rub the chicken inside and out with the ginger, scallions, sake, and salt. Place in a heatproof casserole dish (preferably glass), add the water, and cover with a securely fitting lid. Wrap the entire covered casserole with plastic wrap.

- Set the casserole onto a rack in a pot large enough to accommodate the casserole, fill half full with water, cover, and bring to a boil. Simmer for 3 hours, replacing hot water in the larger pot as needed.

- Combine the vinegar and shallot, and the soy sauce and ginger, and set aside.

- Remove the casserole dish, and pour off the liquid and strain, discarding the ginger and scallions. Serve the hot broth with the warm chicken, pulling off pieces of meat and dipping them into the two dipping sauces.

𝒟UCK SOUP

2 duck carcasses remaining
  from Peking Duck, broken
  up into small pieces
2 quarts (1.9 L) water
3 slices ginger root
1 bunch scallion greens,
  trimmed, and roughly
  chopped

½ teaspoon (2.5 mL) salt
2 pounds (900 g) Chinese
  (Napa) cabbage, cut into
  1-inch (25-mm) pieces
½ teaspoon (2.5 mL) sugar

- Bring the duck, water, ginger, and scallion to a simmer, and cook for 1 hour. Drain, discarding the bones, and return the broth to the pot. Add the remaining ingredients, simmer for 45 minutes, and serve.

Peking Duck is a Chinese specialty in which the duck is poached in sherry, soy sauce, and sugar, then hung up before a fan. The air blowing on the bird dries out the skin and causes it to separate from the flesh. When roasted, the skin turns extremely crispy, and is served as a separate dish along with the roasted flesh, carved scallion flowers, hoisan sauce, and a simple flat pancake that comes out crisp on one side and steamed on the other. In the absence of the carcass for this soup, which is the traditional element of this dish, we suggest substituting the carcasses from 5-spice roasted duck, which is often displayed in the front window of many Asian food markets.

ℰGG DROP SOUP

1 quart (960 mL) rich
  chicken stock
salt and white pepper to
  taste

3 tablespoons (45 mL)
  cornstarch, dissolved in 6
  tablespoons (90 mL) cold
  water
3 large eggs, well beaten

- Bring the stock to a boil, and season with salt and pepper. Add the cornstarch, blend, and bring back to a simmer. Add the eggs, stir, bring to a boil, and serve.

An attempt to prepare Egg Drop Soup, after having sampled it during my first restaurant dining experience at the age of seven, was my first clue as to a profession I might be well suited for. It was not a particularly successful attempt, however. More than a dozen whole eggs were cracked open into boiling water and beaten vigorously in an attempt to imitate the paper-thin ribbons of egg I had witnessed earlier. My mother caught me in the act, and after musing about my valiant effort, sternly introduced me to an innovation that remains a humorous endnote to the experience. It took more than a week's worth of school lunches to work my way through a daily ration of Egg Drop Soup Salad Sandwiches.

*F*ISH BALLS SOUP

2 quarts (1.9 L) chicken stock
2 scallions, cut on a sharp bias into 1-inch (25-mm) pieces
½ pound (227 g) pork spare ribs, cut into 1-inch (25-mm) pieces
½ teaspoon (2.5 mL) salt

½ teaspoon (2.5 mL) sugar
¼ teaspoon (1.23 mL) pepper
½ recipe fish balls (see *Happy Family*)
1 cake bean curd (tofu), cut in half horizontally, then into 9 squares

- Bring the stock, scallions, ribs, and seasoning to a simmer, and cook for 1½ hours, adding additional hot water as it evaporates. Skim and remove the fat and albumin from the top, and adjust seasoning.
- Add the fish balls, and simmer 15 minutes, then add the tofu.

*H*APPY FAMILY

For the Pearly Meat Balls:

½ cup (120 mL) short-grain (glutinous) rice
½ cup (120 mL) ground lean pork
½ cup (120 mL) ground fat pork

2 teaspoons (10 mL) sherry wine
1 teaspoon (5 mL) soy sauce
½ teaspoon (2.5 mL) sugar
1 tablespoon (15 mL) cornstarch
cornstarch as needed

For the fish balls:

1 pound (450 g) white fish fillet (cod, sole, halibut, etc.; a combination is okay)

5 tablespoons (75 mL) ice water

1 teaspoon (5 mL) salt

½ teaspoon (2.5 mL) white pepper

For the soup:

2 quarts (1.9 L) cream stock (see *Bean Slivers in Cream Stock*)

salt and white pepper as needed

½ cup (120 mL) chicken breast, skinless and boneless

½ cup (120 mL) shrimp, peeled, deveined, and medium diced

1 lamb or veal kidney

½ cup (120 mL) cauliflower flowerettes, blanched

1 cup (240 mL) mustard greens, cut into large chiffonade

To prepare the Pearly Meat Balls:

- Cover the rice with 3 cups (720 mL) of water, and allow to sit for 45 minutes. Drain, and season lightly with salt.

- Combine the remaining ingredients (except the last cornstarch) and blend thoroughly. Shape into ¾-inch (18-mm) round balls, dust with cornstarch, and roll in the rice. Place on a lightly oiled plate, and steam for 30 minutes. Remove and set aside.

To prepare the fish balls:

- Place the fish in the freezer for 30 minutes, then transfer to a food processor. Add the ice water, and pulse until puréed. Remove to a clean cutting board, and work in on the board with a Chinese cleaver or large French knife (like mortar on a trowel). As stringy membranes appear, pick out and discard.

- Shape into ½-inch (12-mm) balls, using ice water between the hands when rolling them. Refrigerate until ready to use.

To prepare the chicken:

- Slice the chicken breast in half widthwise, then into thin slices lengthwise (with the grain). Pound these thin by placing them in between two sheets of plastic wrap or wax paper, and smacking them with a Chinese cleaver. Season lightly with salt and pepper, and set aside.

To prepare the kidneys:

- Rinse the kidneys well, and remove any extraneous material or membranes. Cut widthwise into ¼-inch (6-mm) thick slices.
- Score each slice on one side, cutting about ¹⁄₁₆ inch (1 mm) into the meat in parallel cuts about ¹⁄₁₆ inch (1 mm) apart. Repeat across the first scores, leaving a diamond-shaped grid.
- Place the slices in a bowl, sprinkle with a little salt and a little sherry. Allow to sit 5 minutes, then rinse thoroughly by massaging each slice vigorously in the water.
- Pour boiling water over the kidney slices, stir for about 30 seconds, then discard the water. Repeat this process four more times, then set aside.

To assemble the soup:

- Bring the stock to a simmer, add the meat balls and fish balls, and simmer for 15 minutes. Add the chicken and shrimp, and simmer another 5 minutes. Add the kidney, cauliflower, and mustard greens, check seasoning, and serve.

———————————— • ————————————

Classical Chinese gastronomy is a strange realm, indeed, employing in part certain rare ingredients with virtually no flavor of their own, yet heralded both for their texture and difficulty in obtaining, as a gesture of homage from host to guest. Some such ingredients include *bêche-de-mer* (a south Pacific dried sea slug), *bird's nest* (entwined twigs adhered with a swift's secretions), *fish maw* (puffed fish air bladder), and *shark's fin* (mucilaginous gelatin). Of course there is much more to Chinese gastronomy than these unusual oddities, not the least of which is the nomenclature, with honest and self-deprecating titles that reveal a childlike character: Cheap Stock (no meat included), Economy Sauce (hot, tart, salty, sweet), Fried Slices (a pork dish from Szechwan), Chicken 4-4-4-4 (4 pounds chicken; 4 tablespoons each wine, oil, and soy sauce), and so on. As for Happy Family, I have always imagined it to be a reflection of the tone of the family that sat down to share the meal. It is instead a name applied to the ingredients in the dish—fish, meat, vegetables—inferring that they are happily combined gastronomically. Unfortunately, it contains bêche-de-mer, pork kidneys, and fish maw, none of which would make me particularly happy. Thus, in keeping the name and essence of the dish, I have taken culinary license and made some minor changes.

———————————————————————

Sweet Bird's Nest Soup

Soak a 2-ounce (57-g) dry bird's nest in 6 cups (1.5 L) of water, until doubled in volume. Rinse in cold water, picking out the down, and shaking off excess water. Place on a plate or small pan, sprinkle with 6 ounces (170 g) rock candy sugar, and steam for 1 hour. Serve warm or chilled.

CZECHOSLOVAKIAN

Cabbage Soup
(Zelná Polevká)

Beef stock simmered with chopped cabbage, thickened with white roux, seasoned with salt, pepper, and nutmeg, finished with beaten egg yolks and milk.

Czechoslovakian Potato Soup
(Bramborová Polevká)

Brown beef stock seasoned with garlic, marjoram, salt, and pepper; thickened with brown roux, and strained; garnished with diced cabbage, carrots, and celery root, mushrooms, and potatoes, sweated in rendered salt pork.

Fish Soup
(Rybi Polevká)

Cabbage, carrots, cauliflower, celery root, onions, and parsley cooked in fish stock, puréed, finished with beaten milk and egg yolks, garnished with carp's roe poached in fish stock.

GARLIC SOUP
(Cesneková Polevká)

5 cups (1.2 L) beef bouillon
6 garlic cloves, pressed
1 sprig marjoram
2 eggs

2 cups (480 mL) diced black bread
oil as needed

- Simmer the stock, garlic, and marjoram for 15 minutes. Remove the marjoram.
- Sauté the black bread in hot oil until crisp, and place on absorbent paper.
- Beat the eggs, then beat into the bouillon. Bring just up to a simmer, adjust seasoning with salt and pepper, and serve garnished with the croutons.

Kidney Soup
(Ledvinková Polevká)

Sliced onions and peeled potatoes sweated in lard, dusted with flour, blended and briefly cooked, white stock added, seasoned with salt, pepper, paprika, caraway seeds, and garlic, puréed and garnished with sliced sautéed calf's kidneys.

Yellow Split Pea Soup
(Hrachová Polevká)

Beef stock seasoned with garlic, marjoram, onions, and pepper, thickened with white roux, simmered with yellow split peas, puréed, garnished with diced pig's ears, croutons, and chopped parsley.

DUTCH

*D*UTCH STYLE LENTIL SOUP

For the stock:

2 veal shanks
2 pork knuckles
1 carrot, peeled and coarsely chopped
1 stalk celery, coarsely chopped
1 onion, peeled and coarsely chopped
1 large leek, green tops only, well rinsed and coarsely chopped

1 bay leaf
1 teaspoon (5 mL) black peppercorns, crushed
1 bunch parsley stems, rinsed and trimmed
2 sprigs thyme
1 gallon (3.8 L) water

For the soup:

½ cup (120 mL) bacon, medium diced
2 cups (480 mL) green lentils, culled and rinsed
1 medium onion, peeled and cut into medium dice
1 large carrot, peeled and cut into medium dice

2 stalks celery, peeled and cut into medium dice
1 leek, white part only, rinsed, root removed, and cut into medium dice
1 large potato, peeled and cut into medium dice

Soup remaining from its first
service can be reheated,
puréed, and served with
sliced cooked sausage or
croutons for a second service.

- Simmer the stock ingredients 4 to 6 hours, then strain, reserving the stock. Remove the meat from the shanks and knuckles, coarsely chop, and set aside.
- Render the bacon until lightly browned. Add the vegetables and sweat for 5 minutes. Add the lentils, and cook several minutes. Add the stock and simmer about 30 minutes, or until the lentils are fully cooked. Add the diced meat and season to taste with salt and pepper.

Dutch Eel Soup
(Hollandse Palingsoep)

Cut skinned eel into 1-inch (25-mm) pieces, and blanch in boiling salted water. Drain and sweat in butter with chopped leeks, onions, and fish heads and trimmings; season with salt and cayenne pepper, add water and white wine, and simmer about 20 minutes; remove eel and strain stock; thicken with egg yolks and butter; serve over thin croutons, garnished with julienned celery and leeks, and the eel.

FRENCH Albigensian Style Soup
(Soupe à l'Albiegoise)

Calf's foot, diced ham, goose confit, sliced smoked sausage, and lima beans (or any variety of broad bean) simmered in water with bouquet garni; diced carrots, leeks, and cabbage, added and simmered until tender; lettuce chiffonade added at service, and served with thin croutons.

Ardenne Style Soup
(Soupe à l'Ardennaise)

Sliced Belgian endive, leeks, and potatoes sweated in butter, seasoned with salt and pepper, milk added and simmered until potatoes are tender, beaten with butter, and served with thin croutons.

Auvergne Style Pot Soup
(Potée à l'Avergnate)

Stock made with pig's head; a small amount of lentils, and sliced carrot, leek, potato, and turnips added, garnished with the diced meat taken from the pig's head; thin sliced rye bread served separately.

Turnips are a native of Europe, cultivated since prehistory (about 4000 years). Along with cabbage, they are an important food staple in central and northern Europe, possessing 6 or 7 percent carbohydrate content. Their use as food for humans has declined since the acceptance of the potato, and they are now used mainly by the impoverished, and for animal fodder. Varieties are based on root shape: 1. three or more times longer than broad; 2. spindle-shaped, twice as long as broad; 3. round or globe-shaped (Just Right, Purple-top White Globe, Purple-top Yellow Globe, Tokyo Cross, Amber Globe); 4. flat, with roots broader than long (Tokyo Market, Early Purple-top Milan, Flat Milan); 5. a foliage type, with no swollen root, only leaves cooked as greens (Seven-Top, Shogoin).

Bearnese Style Farmer's Soup
(Garbure à la Paysanne)

Sliced carrots, leeks, onions, potatoes, and turnips simmered in white stock until very soft, puréed, reduced as needed, spread on slices of coarse bread cut into triangles, sprinkled with grated cheese, drizzled with stock fat (taken from the top of a stock), and gratinéed; served separately with rich beef bouillon.

Bearnese Style Household Soup
(Garbure à la Béarnaise)

Peeled and thick-sliced potatoes placed in boiling water; add a bouquet garni (thyme and parsley or marjoram), some seasonal vegetables (typically carrots, green beans, leek, potato, pumpkin, turnip), garlic, broad (lima) beans, and season with salt and white pepper; add finely shredded cabbage and a piece of pickled pork (*lou trébuc* is a local variety; if unavailable, a piece of goose confit plus a ham hock, piece of bacon, or smoked sausage is used), and simmer for 30 minutes; add sliced stale whole wheat bread, and serve when it is thick enough for the serving ladle to stand up in it.

Garbure, from the Spanish *garbias* ("stew"), is typical of the cookery of the Béarnais region of France, which borders the Pyrenees. There are numerous varieties, and all are thick—from bread or potatoes, and from puréeing a portion of the soup. A *goudale* is the typical way to finish the dish—a glass of red or white wine poured into the empty soup plate, mixed with any remaining vestige of the soup, and drunk. In Béarn it is considered the ultimate remedy for illness, as per a local saying: "A well-made goudale keeps a coin from the doctor's pocket."

Burgundy Style Pot Soup
(Potée à la Bourguignonne)

White stock, pork knuckle, and bouquet garni simmered, knuckle meat removed; shredded cabbage and diced carrots, leeks, potatoes, and turnips sweated in rendered fat back, combined with the stock and knuckle meat; croutons served separately.

....

———— • ————

Printinière is a reference to baby spring vegetables, the first growth of vegetables following winter. In practice, the name indicates a style, rather than the actual use of spring vegetables—their season is short and they are generally expensive.

————————

CHICKEN BOUILLON, SPRING STYLE
(Bouillon de Volaille, à la Printinière)

For the bouillon:

6 pounds (2.7 kg) fresh chicken bones, backs, necks, and wings

1 whole fresh chicken, cut into 8 pieces

2 gallons (7.7 L) water

1 large onion, peeled, and coarsely chopped

1 large carrot, peeled, top removed, and coarsely chopped

2 celery stalks, coarsely chopped

1 leek, well rinsed and coarsely chopped

2 bay leaves

3 sprigs thyme

1 bunch parsley stems

1 teaspoon (4.9 mL) white peppercorns, crushed

For the garnish:

2 cups (480 mL) assorted vegetables (celery, carrot, leek, zucchini, turnip, sweet potato, etc.), cut into fine julienne

measuring 1″ × ¼″ × ¼″ (25 × 6 × 6 mm), and blanched in lightly salted boiling water.

• Rinse the bones and chicken thoroughly in cold water. Place in a stockpot, and cover with enough water so that it is 4 inches

(100 mm) above the highest bone. Bring the stock up to a boil, drain and discard the liquid, and rinse the bones and chicken again in cold water.

- In a clean stockpot, cover the bones again with cold water, 4 inches (100 mm) above the highest bone, and bring to a simmer. Skim the top of the stock, removing the fat and foam. Add the aromatics and simmer **very gently** for 1 hour, then remove the whole chicken. When cool, remove the meat from the chicken, cover, and refrigerate for another use. Return the bones of the chicken to the stock, and continue simmering another 3 to 5 hours, skimming fat and impurities from the top periodically. Strain, adjust seasoning with salt, white pepper, and if necessary, a little chicken glaze. Serve garnished with the julienned vegetables.

CREAM OF SORREL SOUP
(Potage Germiny)

1 pound (450 g) sorrel, well rinsed, dried, and roughly chopped
3 tablespoons (45 mL) butter
6 tablespoons (90 mL) flour
1 quart (960 mL) rich, clear chicken stock

2 egg yolks
1 cup (240 mL) heavy cream
¼ cup (60 mL) crème fraîche or sour cream
4 baguette croutons
salt and white pepper to taste

- Simmer the sorrel in the stock for 10 minutes. Remove to a blender or food processor and purée. Return to the stove.

- Blend the flour and butter together into a smooth paste, add to the soup, blend thoroughly, and simmer 10 minutes. Season to taste with salt and pepper.

- Beat the yolks and cream thoroughly, then pour the hot soup slowly into this mixture, while beating continuously. When half of the stock has been incorporated, stir this back into the remaining soup. Bring just to a simmer while stirring continuously, then remove from the heat (do not allow to boil).

- Serve the soup in hot bowls, topped with a crouton spread with the crème fraîche or sour cream.

FISH SOUP, MARSEILLE STYLE

(Bouillabaisse)

For the stock:

¼ pound (113 g) unsalted
   butter
5 pounds (2.3 kg) white fish
   bones (sole, flounder,
   halibut), cut into 2-inch
   (50-mm) pieces
2 cups (480 mL) mirepoix,
   finely chopped

1 bay leaf
1 teaspoon (4.9 mL) white
   peppercorns, crushed
2 sprigs thyme
1 bunch parsley stems
2 cups (480 mL) dry white
   wine

For the rouille:

4 garlic cloves, pressed
2 egg yolks
2 tablespoons (30 mL)
   tomato paste
salt and white pepper to
   taste

⅓ cup (80 mL) mashed
   potato
the juice of 1 lemon
1 cup (240 mL) olive oil
16 baguette croutons

For the soup:

½ cup (120 mL) olive oil
1 pound (450 g) each of five
   varieties of fish, as
   available (such as sea bass,
   cod, conger eel, halibut,
   mackerel, red snapper,
   etc.)
1 large onion, medium dice
1 large leek, well rinsed,
   medium dice
4 garlic cloves, crushed
1 small fennel bulb, cut into
   strips

2 pinches saffron
the rind of half an orange
2 cups (480 mL) diced
   tomatoes
1 bay leaf
2 sprigs thyme
1 bunch parsley stems, tied
   together with cotton
   twine
¼ cup (60 mL) chopped
   parsley

- Sweat the fish bones, mirepoix, herbs, and spices in the butter.
  Add the white wine, and enough water to rise above the bones
  by 2 inches (50 mm). Simmer 45 minutes, then strain, reserving the stock.

- Pound the garlic, yolk, tomato, salt, pepper, and potato into a
  smooth paste using a mortar and pestle or a small food processor. Pour in the olive oil in a slow steady stream while blend-

ing (or pulsing), interspersing it with the lemon juice. Set aside.

- Sauté the fish in the olive oil for 5 minutes. Remove with a slotted spoon, and set aside. Add the remaining vegetables, herbs, and spices, and sauté for 5 minutes. Add the fish stock and fish, and boil rapidly for 10 minutes. Adjust seasoning with salt and pepper.

- Ladle the soup into wide soup plates, and top with chopped parsley. Spread the croutons with the rouille, and serve alongside the soup.

———————————— • ————————————

The word Bouillabaisse is derived from the French *bouillir*—to boil, and *abattre*—to lay down. "Boil and settle" (down) is an old Provence colloquial command for the fish to calm down after the dish was boiled. The resulting brew, a specialty of coastal southern France, is intended to be busy (with ingredients) and cloudy (from the boiling), reflective of the passionate nature of Mediterranean-French cookery and the hearty nature of this dish.

Rouille means "rust," in reference to the reddish tint of the thickened and seasoned olive oil that is spread on croutons.

𝓕ISH SOUP, PROVENCE STYLE
(Bourride)

1 leek, white part only, medium dice
2 medium Spanish onions, medium dice
2 medium carrots, peeled, tops removed, medium dice
2 large overripe tomatoes, roughly chopped
4 garlic cloves, crushed
a strip of orange zest
1 pinch of saffron
1 bouquet garni (1 celery stalk, 1 stick of fennel, 1 bunch parsley stems, 1 sprig of thyme, and 2 bay leaves, all tied together with cotton cord)
1 quart (1 L) fish stock
1 quart (1 L) white wine
salt and pepper to taste
2 pounds (900 g) monkfish cut into 1-inch (25-mm) pieces
1 cup (240 mL) aïoli or rouille
1 baguette, sliced and toasted

- Combine all the ingredients except the fish and aïoli (or rouille), and boil for 45 minutes. Strain, pressing all the liquid from the vegetables; return the liquid to the pot and discard the vegetables.
- Add the fish to the stock and simmer fifteen minutes. Remove from the fire, and stir in about 2 cups (480 mL) of the stock into half of the aïoli (or rouille), a little at a time, then blend the aïoli into the remaining broth. Serve the pieces of fish on croutons, with additional aïoli, and the broth separately. Adjust seasoning with salt and pepper.

*F*ISH AND GARLIC SOUP, PROVENCE STYLE

(Aïgo-saou)

3 pounds (1.4 kg) assorted fresh fish fillet, skinless and boneless, cut into 1-inch (25-mm) pieces

2 medium Spanish onions, sliced

3 cups (720 mL) diced tomatoes in juice

8 medium Red Bliss potatoes, trimmed of blemishes and quartered

1 bulb garlic, crushed and peeled

1 bouquet garni (1 celery stalk, 1 stick of fennel, 1 bunch parsley stems, 1 sprig of thyme, a long strip of orange zest, and 2 bay leaves, all tied together with cotton cord)

salt and pepper to taste

1 slightly stale baguette, sliced

olive oil as needed

- Combine all the ingredients except the baguette and oil, cover with enough water to rise several inches above the ingredients, and simmer until the potatoes are tender. Adjust seasoning with salt and pepper.
- Brush the slices of baguette with olive oil, toast in an oven or broiler until golden brown, and set into a tureen (or in individual soup plates). On a separate plate, arrange a bed of the onions, tomatoes, and potatoes, and place the fish on top. Pour the broth over the bread in the tureen and serve.

———————————— • ————————————

Garlic (*Allium sativum*) is native to Central Asia and has been cultivated since the earliest days of agriculture. The Latin genus *Allium* is derived from the Celtic word *all*, meaning "hot" and "burning," in reference to the sensation it produces on the palate. The name *garlic* (from Old English *garleac*, Middle English *garlec* and *garly*) means *spear leek*, in reference to the plant's long spearlike green shoots. The culinary uses of garlic are well known in all cultures, but it is also well known for its health-maintaining properties. In *New England Cookery*, c. 1808, author Lucy Emerson wrote: "*Garlicks though used by the French, are better adapted to medicine than cookery.*" Still used today in the manufacture of pharmaceuticals, in its unaltered state it acts as a purgative, antiseptic, and expectorant. It stimulates digestive organs, thus relieving problems associated with poor digestion. Garlic also regularizes the action of the liver and gallbladder, and is helpful for all intestinal infections. Rumor has it that raw garlic cloves eaten at regular intervals will spare the traveler from encountering "Montezuma's revenge" when traveling in foreign lands where parasite-laden food and drink are difficult to avoid.

𝓕RENCH ONION SOUP
(Soupe à l'Oignon, Gratinée)

4 tablespoons (60 mL) unsalted butter

12 medium onions, halved, core removed, sliced lengthwise ¼-inch (6-mm) thick

2 garlic cloves, pressed

2 tablespoons (30 mL) toasted flour

1 bay leaf

¼ cup (60 mL) sherry

3 pints (1.5 L) brown stock

salt and pepper to taste

4 3-inch (75-mm) round croutons

1 cup (240 mL) Gruyère cheese, grated

- Sauté the onions and the garlic in the butter, stirring frequently, until they are well caramelized (browned) throughout. Add the flour and blend thoroughly. Add the bay leaf and sherry, and deglaze. Add the stock, blend thoroughly, and simmer for 30 minutes, skimming the foam and other impurities off the top. Season to taste with salt and pepper.

- Ladle the soup into oven-proof crocks, and place a crouton on top. Sprinkle with the cheese, and melt under the broiler or in a hot oven.

Flour is toasted by sprinkling it on a baking sheet, placing it in a 375°F (190°C) oven until it turns light brown, then sifting. This adds color, flavor, and body to the soup.

The brown stock is generally made from beef and/or veal bones, though a white veal or chicken stock is also sometimes used.

Gruyère cheese is named after a valley in Switzerland where the cheese is produced, though any number of other cheeses can also be used, including Emmenthal (Swiss), Monterey Jack (California), Fontina (various European origins), and so on.

Frogs' Leg Soup
(Potage aux Grenouilles)

Frog's legs poached in fish stock flavored with white wine, meat removed and diced, added to rich fish consommé finished with Madeira wine.

GARLIC SOUP
(Soupe à l'Ail)

3 garlic bulbs, cloves peeled and cut lengthwise into approximately uniform pieces	salt and pepper to taste
	12 slices baguette
	olive oil as needed
2 quarts (1.7 L) water	6 egg yolks, beaten
1 sprig sage	4 tablespoons (60 mL)
2 bay leaves	unsalted butter (optional)

- Simmer the garlic, water, herbs, salt, and pepper for 30 minutes, or until the garlic is tender. Remove and discard the sage and bay leaves.

- Brush the baguette slices with olive oil, and brown under a broiler or in the oven.

- Temper the hot liquid slowly into the egg yolks, then return to the pot, bring just to a simmer, and remove from the fire. Beat in the butter (if used), until fully emulsified.

- Place the croutons in a soup plate or tureen, ladle the soup over them, and sprinkle with salt and pepper.

The origin of the proverb "Garlic is as good as ten mothers," is unknown, though the properties and characteristics of *Allium sativum* (garlic) have been written about by many, including Aristophanes, Charlemagne, Gandhi, Henry IV, Herodotus, Hippocrates, Mohammed, Pasteur, Pliny, Eleanor Roosevelt, and Virgil. Waverly Root, in his last tome, *Food* (c.1980), wrote: "Garlic has been the vehicle in the United States of a self-reversing snobbery. Before I left America to live in Europe in 1927, you were looked down upon if you ate garlic, a food fit only for ditch diggers; when I returned in 1940, you were looked down upon if you didn't eat it." In France, garlic's presence is more of a regional phenomenon, scorned within the boundaries of *haute cuisine*, and looked on askance by *cuisine bourgeoise*. Generally, garlic reigns decisively south of the river Loire. In the east, it is referred to as "the truffle of Provence," and aïoli, the garlicky mayonnaise from that region, is known as "the butter of Provence." Garlic is also a regional phenomenon in Italy, well known in Piedmont's *bagna cauda* ("hot bath"), but more prevalent in the south. Alexander Dumas wrote that the Greeks disliked garlic, which was erroneous. It was an important vegetable in ancient Greece, and was eaten in its own right, not simply as a seasoning for something else.

*H*OUSEHOLD SOUP, PROVENCE STYLE
(Soupe Aïgo à la Ménagère)

¼ cup (60 mL) olive oil
1 medium Spanish onion, cut into ½-inch (12-mm) dice
1 medium leek, white part only, cut into ½-inch (12-mm) dice
4 garlic cloves, crushed
1 strip orange zest
1 pinch saffron
1½ cups (360 mL) diced tomatoes in juice
1 bouquet garni (1 sprig thyme, 1 bunch rinsed and trimmed parsley stems, 2 bay leaves, ½

teaspoon/2.5 mL peppercorns, wrapped in two leek leaves and tied together with cotton string)
1 sprig fennel
4 Red Bliss potatoes, scrubbed and sliced
salt and pepper to taste
2 quarts (1.9 L) water
4 large eggs
12 thick slices baguette, cut on the bias, and toasted
¼ cup (60 mL) finely chopped parsley

- Sauté the onion and leek in the oil until lightly and evenly browned. Add the garlic, zest, and saffron, and cook several minutes.
- Add the tomatoes, herbs and spices, potatoes, a little salt and pepper, and the water. Simmer for about 20 minutes or until the potatoes are tender. Adjust seasoning with salt and pepper, and remove from the fire.
- Poach the eggs immersed in barely simmering water, slightly acidulated with a little vinegar and salt.
- Arrange the sliced potatoes in the bottom of a large flat bowl, place the eggs on top, and sprinkle with chopped parsley. Place the bread in four soup plates, pour the remaining hot soup the bread, and serve.

ℋOUSEHOLD GARLIC SOUP, PROVENCE STYLE
(Aïgo Bouïdo à la Ménagère)

2 quarts (1.9 L) water
1 cup (240 mL) olive oil
bouquet garni (1 sprig sage,
    1 sprig thyme, 2 bay
    leaves, and 1 bunch rinsed
    and trimmed parsley
    stems, tied together with
    cotton cord)
2 bulbs garlic, cloves crushed
    and peeled

1 tablespoon (15 mL) salt
½ teaspoon (2.5 mL) cracked
    black pepper
12 thick slices stale baguette,
    cut on the bias, and
    toasted
¼ cup (60 mL) finely
    chopped parsley

- Bring the water, olive oil, bouquet garni, garlic, salt, and pepper to a boil, and simmer until the garlic is tender. Remove and discard the bouquet garni, and adjust seasoning with salt and pepper.
- Place the bread in the bottom of a tureen (or divided among four soup plates), sprinkle with parsley, and pour the hot broth and garlic over the bread.

———————— • ————————

This soup is typical of the peasant-style cookery of Provence, and given several variant spellings of *bouïdo* (such as *boulido, bullido*), there are numerous variations to the soup as well, many of which are undoubtedly undocumented. Two known variations are *Aïgo Bouïdo aux Oeufs Pochés* (with the addition of poached eggs); and *Aïgo Ménagère* (sliced onions and leeks sautéed in the olive oil, sage in the bouquet garni replaced with fennel and orange peel, a pinch of saffron, and sliced potatoes cooked in the broth and topped with poached eggs, served separately).

Périgord Wedding Soup (*Bouillon de Noce*)

A French version of the Spanish Olla Podrida (see page 279), with the following exceptions: (1) the meat ingredients consist of veal shank, beef knuckle, a stuffed chicken, and a turkey; (2) the vegetables include Swiss chard; and (3) the addition of sliced onions well-browned in lard.

ᴾ𝐼STOU SOUP
(Soupe au Pistou)

In Provençale dialect, *pistou* means *pesto* (from the Latin *pestare*, meaning "to pound") and refers to the basil, garlic, olive oil paste well known in Italian cuisine.

For the pistou:

2 cups (480 mL) diced tomatoes
8 garlic cloves
¼ cup (60 mL) basil leaves

¾ cup (180 mL) grated Parmesan cheese
½ cup (120 mL) olive oil
salt to taste

For the soup:

¾ cup (180 mL) white beans, culled, rinsed, and soaked overnight in fresh water
¾ cup (180 mL) kidney beans, culled, rinsed, and soaked overnight in fresh water
1 gallon (3.8 L) water
1 bouquet garni
salt and pepper to taste
2 large carrots, peeled, and cut into medium dice

1 large rutabaga, peeled and cut into medium dice
2 medium Red Bliss potatoes, peeled and cut into medium dice
1 cup (240 mL) green string beans, cut into medium dice
2 medium zucchini, cut into medium dice
1 cup vermicelli (240 mL), broken up; into 1-inch (25-mm) pieces

• Place the pistou ingredients in a food processor and purée. Set aside.

- Place the beans, water, bouquet garni, and salt and pepper in a large soup pot, and bring to a boil. Simmer, skimming periodically, for 1½ hours or until the beans are tender but still firm.
- Add the carrot, turnip, and potatoes, and simmer for 15 minutes. Add the string beans and zucchini, and simmer another 10 minutes. Add the vermicelli, and simmer until cooked. Stir in the pistou, adjust seasoning, and serve.

Small Pot Soup
(Petite Marmite)

Beef bouillon simmered with a small piece of beef tail, a small piece of beef rump, a beef rib cut in half, two small marrow bones, and two sets of browned chicken giblets; when the meats are almost tender, add uniform chunks (about 2 inches/50 mm in size) of carrot, white part of a leek, white turnip, pearl onions, a split celery heart, and a quarter of a head of cabbage, and simmer until all ingredients are tender. Remove and discard the giblets; remove the marrow bones, push out the marrow, and spread it on small pieces of toast or croutons; spread other croutons with the fat from the top of the broth, sprinkled with Parmesan cheese and black pepper. Serve in an earthenware bowl or casserole accompanied by the croutons.

GERMAN Apple Soup, Hamburg Style
(Hamburger Apfelsuppe)

Peeled, cored, and chopped apples simmered until soft in water and apple wine with ground almonds, ground rusks (biscotti), cinnamon, lemon peel, sugar, then puréed, beaten with a little butter, and served chilled, garnished with croutons.

Bean Soup, Frankfurt Style
(Frankfurter Bohnensuppe)

Soaked kidney beans cooked in stock with an herb bouquet garni (removed when the beans are tender), beaten with butter, garnished with sliced frankfurters (can also be partially puréed for additional body).

Crayfish Soup, Hamburg Style
(Hamburger Krebssuppe)

Crayfish and chopped mirepoix sautéed in butter, flamed with brandy, tail meat removed, shells pounded, and simmered with fish stock; thickened with white roux (or beurre manié), seasoned with salt and white pepper, strained, and garnished with green peas, small dumplings, and the crayfish meat.

Eel Soup, Hamburg Style
(Hamburger Aalsuppe)

Initially entitled Aolsuppe (meaning "All Soup"), this was a hodge-podge of available ingredients, none of which originally included eel. The name Aalsuppe eventually evolved after someone experimented with eel, which is "aal" in German.

For the stock:

1½ pounds (6.8 kg) eel, skinless, and cut into 1-inch (25-mm) thick slices
2 small ham knuckles or 1 ham hock
1 cup (240 mL) white wine
¼ cup (60 mL) white wine vinegar

the green leaves of 1 large leek, rough chopped and well rinsed (reserve white part)
1 bay leaf
1 bunch parsley stems
2 sprigs thyme

For the fruit:

½ cup (120 mL) pitted prunes, quartered
½ cup (120 mL) dried apricots, quartered
1 cup (240 mL) dry white wine

1 tablespoon (15 mL) sugar
1 medium Granny Smith apple, peeled, cored, and cut into medium dice

For the dumplings:

1 cup (240 mL) water
2 tablespoons (30 mL) unsalted butter
½ teaspoon (2.5 mL) salt

1 cup (240 mL) flour (approximately)
2 large eggs

For the soup:

2 tablespoons (30 mL) unsalted butter
3 ribs celery, trimmed, cut into medium dice
1 large carrot, peeled and cut into medium dice
1 large leek (the white part from above), cut into medium dice and well rinsed

1 medium rutabaga, peeled, cut into medium dice
1 cup (240 mL) broccoli flowerettes
1 cup (240 mL) green peas (frozen)
salt and pepper to taste

To prepare the stock:

- Place the eel, ham, white wine, vinegar, leek, bay leaf, parsley, and thyme in a small stockpot, along with 3 pints (1.5 L) of cold water, bring to a simmer, and allow to cook until the eel is tender (about 20 minutes). Strain, reserving the liquid, and set the ham and eel aside, discarding the remaining ingredients.

To prepare the fruit:

- Cover the dried fruit with boiling water, and allow to sit 15 minutes. Drain, then place the fruit, wine, sugar, apple, and pear in a stainless-steel (or noncorrosive pan), simmer for fifteen minutes, then set aside.

To prepare the dumplings:

- Bring the water, butter, and salt to a boil. Add the flour, and stir until blended, and the mixture balls up (more flour may need to be added). Remove from the fire and allow to cool.
- Add the eggs one at a time, and blend thoroughly.
- Using a tablespoon dipped in water, scoop out spoonfuls of the dough, and drop into boiled salted water. Continue until all the dough is used up. Simmer about 10 minutes, or until fully cooked. Remove with a slotted spoon, and set aside.

To assemble the soup:

- Sauté the celery, carrot, leek, and rutabaga in the butter. Add the stock and ham hock, and bring to a simmer. Add the fruit mixture and season to taste with salt and pepper. Add the broccoli, and simmer for 10 minutes. Add the peas, and bring to a simmer.
- Place a few dumplings and a few pieces of eel in the bottom of a soup bowl. Ladle in the soup, and serve.

Beer soup can also be served cold, though the preparation is slightly different. Beer or ale is seasoned with a little sugar and salt, mixed with dry rye bread crumbs (allow to sit for a period to expand the bread), puréed, and served chilled garnished with currants and peeled slices of lemon.

German Beer Soup
(Bier-Suppe)

3 tablespoons (45 mL)
   unsalted butter
1 garlic clove, crushed
2 thin slices ginger root
3 tablespoons (45 mL) flour
2½ cups (600 mL) beer
2 cups (480 mL) rich chicken
   stock

2 egg yolks
1 teaspoon (4.9 mL) sugar
the zest of half a lemon
¼ teaspoon (1.23 mL) fresh
   grated nutmeg
12 toasted baguette slices

- Sauté the garlic and ginger in the butter for several minutes. Remove the garlic and ginger, and discard.
- Add the flour, blend thoroughly, and cook several minutes, stirring continuously.
- Add 2 cups (480 mL) of the beer, and the stock, and blend well.
- Beat the yolks, ½ cup (120 mL) of beer, and sugar, and temper into the soup. Add the lemon and nutmeg, season to taste with salt and pepper, and serve with the toasted baguette.

Split Pea Soup
(Löfferlerbsen)

Chicken stock simmered with yellow split peas and pig's ears (removed when peas are soft), puréed, garnished with diced pig's ears, diced fried bacon, and croutons.

Westphalian Bean Soup
(Westfälische Bohnensuppe)

Red kidney beans simmered with white stock, puréed, garnished with diced carrots, celery root, leeks, potatoes, and sliced Bologna sausage.

GREEK

....

*E*GG AND LEMON SOUP
(Soúpa Avgolémono)

2 quarts (1.9 L) rich chicken
   bouillon
½ cup (120 mL) long grain
   rice, washed in cold water
the juice of 3 lemons

4 eggs, beaten
6 thin slices of lemon
4 tablespoons chopped
   parsley

- Bring the stock to a boil, and stir in the rice. Simmer about 25 minutes, or until the rice is cooked.
- Beat the eggs vigorously for 2 minutes. Beat in the lemon juice, then about 1 cup (240 mL) of the hot broth, while continuing to stir the eggs. Return the egg mixture to the hot broth, bring just up to a simmer, and remove from the fire. Serve garnished with a slice of lemon and some chopped parsley.

Cabbage Soup
(Laghanosupa)

Thin-sliced onions browned in olive oil, thin-sliced cabbage added and sweated; water, dill, parsley, salt, and pepper added, garnished with toasted croutons, and sliced sausage.

Greek Soup

Chicken stock simmered with tomato and pumpkin, slightly thickened with roux, puréed, finished with cream, garnished with croutons.

———————————— • ————————————

Pumpkin and squash are all of American origin, thriving in the arid climates of the southwestern United States and northern Mexico. Some of the 25 species have been cultivated for 9000 years. Part of the reason for so many varieties is that squash is easily hybridized, resulting in such a wide range of colors and forms that it is difficult to tell the varieties apart. Summer varieties—zucchini, yellow crookneck, golden, pattypan—are eaten when young and soft. Winter varieties—acorn, banana, butternut, Hubbard (Ohio), Sea (Chioggia), and Yokohama squashes (also Chayote); American, Brazilian, and Whale pumpkins—are allowed to mature into hard, starchy fruits that will keep for months. There are also ornamental varieties, such as Turban squash, Scallop and Bottle gourds, and various hybrids.

Green Pea Soup, Greek Style

Mutton stock simmered with green peas, puréed, garnished with diced root vegetables and lean mutton.

Peasant White Bean Soup
(Soúpa Fasolada)

Diced carrot, celery, onion, and garlic sweated in olive oil, water and tomato paste added, seasoned with salt and pepper, garnished with cooked white Navy beans (a portion of the beans can be puréed to add body).

When the cultivation of the olive began is not known with certainty, but it may date to the Minoan civilization (3000–1500 B.C.). In the Bible, Moses spoke of the olive tree on Mt. Ararat, and a dove brought an olive branch to Noah. The Jesuits introduced it to Mexico and California. Prior to the seventeenth century, olive oil was used for religious rites, as a cosmetic, and for lighting. Since then, use of olive oil as a food has increased continuously. Today, 95 to 98 percent of world production comes from the Mediterranean basin, with Spain and Italy competing for the lead. Oil extraction is a complex operation, generally resulting in several grades: extra virgin, virgin, superfine, and fine. Raw olives are extremely bitter and must be processed in order to be made edible. In California they are dipped in a solution of ferrous gluconate, treated with lye, rinsed, and packed in brine. Greek black olives are cured with salt, though their green olives are treated in the traditional method.

HUNGARIAN

Brain Soup
(Velös Leves)

Chopped calf's brain and parsley, and sliced mushrooms sweated in butter, dusted with flour, blended; beef stock added, seasoned with salt, pepper, mace, simmered and strained, blended with puréed calf's brain, and garnished with croutons.

Fish Soup
(Magyar Halleves)

Chopped onions sweated in lard, dusted with flour, fish stock added, seasoned with paprika, blended with sour cream, garnished with small pieces of fish, carp's roe, and cooked torn noodles.

Goulash Soup
(Magyar Gulyás Leves)

Chopped onions and medium diced beef lightly browned in lard; tomatoes added, and seasoned with salt, crushed caraway seeds, marjoram, and paprika; water added and simmered until beef is tender; garnished with julienned red peppers, diced potatoes, and cooked coarsely cut noodles.

ITALIAN Bread Soup
(Mille-Fanti)

Fresh white bread crumbs, grated cheese, eggs, salt, pepper, and nutmeg blended into a paste, beaten into hot beef bouillon, simmered for about 10 minutes, and stirred again at service.

Cheese Soup
(Polpetti)

Beef bouillon beaten with grated Parmesan cheese, and garnished with macaroni.

Egg Soup
(Zuppa Pavese)

Raw eggs placed on toasted croutons, sprinkled generously with grated cheese; rich beef bouillon poured over, then gratinéed in a hot oven.

ᖴARMER'S VEGETABLE SOUP
(Minestrone alla Contadina)

¼ cup (60 mL) fat back (or bacon), finely diced
¼ cup (60 mL) olive oil
2 celery stalks, medium dice
1 large carrot, medium dice
1 medium onion, medium dice
1 medium leek, trimmed and rinsed, and medium dice
1 medium rutabaga, peeled and medium dice
1 cup (240 mL) white cabbage, medium dice
6 garlic cloves, pressed
1½ cups (360 mL) red kidney beans (cooked)

1½ cups (360 mL) chick peas (cooked)
¼ cup (60 mL) tomato purée
1 gallon (3.8 L) chicken stock
1 cup (240 mL) potatoes, medium dice
1 cup (240 mL) fresh spinach leaves, well rinsed and firmly packed
salt and pepper to taste
2 cups (480 mL) small ditalini, cooked al dente
grated cheese as needed

- Render the fatback over medium heat until golden brown. Add the olive oil, vegetables, and garlic, and sweat about 10 minutes over medium heat, stirring frequently. Add the beans and peas, tomato, and stock, blend thoroughly, and simmer about

10 minutes. Add the potatoes, and simmer until al dente. Add the cauliflower, and simmer until tender.

- Combine the eggs and cottage cheese, and temper into the soup. Adjust seasoning with salt and pepper.

Just as *tortelloni* is bigger than *tortelli* and *panettone* is bigger than *pane*, *minestrone* is bigger and richer than *minestra*, which means "to serve, to dish out" (from *minister*). Minestrone offers a very creative window, since it is often made according to availability of local ingredients, and there is no limit to its contents. A suggested approach to preparing any minestrone or minestra involves the following criteria: one ingredient from each of the following categories (with suggestions)—aromatic vegetables (garlic, onion, shallot), legumes (kidney beans, Navy beans, chick peas), fresh vegetables (cabbage, cauliflower, celery root, green peas, green beans, turnip, zucchini), seasoning vegetables (celery, leek, tomato), farinaceous (noodles, rice, potatoes), and meat (beef, bacon, ham, pork).

Fisherman's Soup
(Zuppa dei Pescatore)

A variety of small seafish cut in pieces, seasoned with salt, pepper, and allspice; water and a bouquet garni added (carrots, celery, leek, onion, thyme, and bay leaf), and simmered; fish placed on croutons fried in olive oil, and the strained hot soup poured over; grated Parmesan cheese served separately.

Genoese Fish Soup
(Zuppa Genovese)

Chopped fish, onions, and parsley sweated in butter, seasoned with salt, pepper, and nutmeg; fish stock added, puréed, finished with beaten egg yolks, and garnished with fish dumplings fried in olive oil.

*I*TALIAN FISH SOUP
(Brodetto di Pesce)

3 pounds (13.5 kg) mussels, scrubbed and debearded

1½ cups (360 mL) dry white wine

1½ cups (360 mL) water

1 garlic clove, crushed

1 bay leaf

1 bunch parsley stems, trimmed, rinsed, and tied in a bundle with cotton string

3 tablespoons (45 mL) olive oil

2 large garlic cloves, sliced very thin

1 small hot red chile pepper, stemmed and roughly chopped

1 teaspoon (4.9 mL) orange zest, grated

1 scallion, finely chopped

2 cups (480 mL) diced tomatoes in juice

the leaves of 1 sprig of marjoram

the leaves of 1 sprig of thyme

salt and black pepper to taste

4 to 8 1-inch (25-mm) slices of crusty bread

1 garlic clove mashed in ¼ cup (60 mL) olive oil

1 pound (450 g) raw squid, cleaned, and cut into ¼-inch (6-mm) slices

1 pound (450 g) cod or other whitefish (snapper, sea bass, monkfish, etc.)

- Place mussels, wine, water, garlic, bay leaf, and parsley stems in a pot, and simmer for 10 minutes, or until the mussels are all open. Set aside.
- Brush the bread with olive oil, and broil or bake until golden brown.
- Sauté the garlic, chile pepper, orange zest, and scallion several minutes in the olive oil. Add the tomatoes, marjoram, thyme, and mussel broth, season to taste with salt and pepper, and simmer briefly. Purée carefully (it's hot!) in a blender or food processor, and return to the fire. Add the fish and simmer 3 minutes. Add the mussels until hot. Adjust seasoning, and ladle over the bread in serving bowls.

Palermo Soup
(*Zuppa Palermitana*)

Diced carrots, celery root, leeks, onions, beef, ham, calf's liver, and veal sweated in diced fatback rendered golden brown and butter; seasoned with salt, pepper, bay leaf, and marjoram; water and dry white wine added, simmered, and puréed; garnished with veal quenelles; grated Parmesan cheese served separately.

ROMAN EGG AND CHEESE SOUP
(Stracciatella alla Romana)

4 eggs
⅓ cup (80 mL) fresh white
  bread crumbs
⅓ cup (80 mL) grated
  Parmesan cheese

1 teaspoon (4.9 mL) grated
  lemon zest
6 cups (1.5 L) beef bouillon
salt and pepper to taste

- Combine the eggs, bread crumbs, cheese, and zest, and beat until thoroughly blended.
- Bring the bouillon to a boil, then pour slowly into the egg mixture, stirring continuously. Bring just up to a simmer and season to taste with salt and pepper.

Tomato Soup
(Minestra al Pomodoro)

Chopped onions and sliced garlic sweated in olive oil; diced tomatoes, basil, marjoram, mint, salt, and pepper added; water added and simmered, garnished with rice; grated Parmesan cheese served separately.

Tripe Soup
(Busecca)

Chopped cabbage, carrots, celery, leeks, and onions sweated in olive oil with bacon; soaked kidney beans, julienned tripe, covered with white stock flavored with garlic, sage, and tomatoes, and simmered until tender.

---•---

Tripe is the stomach of ruminants (hooved mammals: cattle, goats, pigs, sheep), the preparation of which dates back to ancient Greece, and around which there is considerable lore. Lacking sufficient taste of its own, and having what Waverly Root calls a "boiling laundry odor," it requires long cooking and highly spiced flavorings to make it palatable. M.F.K. Fisher called it "slippery, ivory-white rubber," though confessed to having been "a happy, if occasionally frustrated tripe eater." Her frustration may have stemmed from the fact that her children were never able to develop an appreciation for it, or from the prolonged cooking it requires. One of the most celebrated dishes in which tripe is featured is *Tripe à la mode de Caens:* tripe, calf's feet, aromatics (including plenty of garlic), apple cider, and Calvados, cooked in a slow oven for 10 hours.

Turinese Soup
(Minestra Turinese)

Diced cabbage, celery root, leeks, tomatoes, and ham sweated in olive oil, white stock flavored with garlic and saffron added, and garnished with rice; grated Parmesan cheese served separately.

Saffron, the world's most expensive spice, is the dried stigmas of a variety of crocus. Its high cost is due to the painstaking labor required to remove the stigmas as well as the number of each required to yield one pound of saffron: roughly 300,000. It was introduced into Eastern Pennsylvania in the eighteenth century by the Schwenkfelder's, a family that had emigrated from Germany and transplanted to American soil what they had been pursuing in their homeland.

Venetian Soup
(Minestra Veneziana)

Diced fatback, cabbage, onions, tomatoes, blanched calf's feet, calf's ears and liver, seasoned with salt, pepper, allspice, bay leaves, and marjoram; boiled in water, garnished with chopped meat from the feet, the calf's ears and liver, and rice. (This soup can also be served puréed, garnished with rice.)

NORTH AMERICAN American Style Soup
(Potage à l'Américaine)

One-part lobster bisque and one-part tomato bisque blended together, garnished with diced lobster.

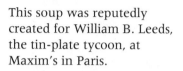

*B*ILLY BI (also BILIBI)

This soup was reputedly created for William B. Leeds, the tin-plate tycoon, at Maxim's in Paris.

2 pounds (900 g) mussels, scrubbed, rinsed, and debearded
2 cups (480 mL) dry white wine
1 medium onion, small dice
2 shallots, finely chopped
1 bunch parsley stems, tied together with cotton twine
¼ teaspoon (1.2 mL) salt

¼ teaspoon (1.2 mL) black pepper
pinch of cayenne pepper
1 bay leaf
2 cups (480 mL) heavy cream
3 egg yolks
4 tablespoons (60 mL) unsalted butter

• Steam the mussels, along with the vegetables, herbs, and spices 8 to 10 minutes, or until all the mussels are open. Remove the mussels and set aside. Strain the liquid, place in a saucepan, and bring to a simmer.

• Beat the cream and egg yolks together, and temper into the soup by pouring about half the hot soup slowly into the cream while continuously beating. Beat this back into the hot soup, bring just to a simmer, and serve over the steamed mussels.

*B*OSTON CLAM CHOWDER

(also known as New England Clam Chowder)

¼ cup (60 mL) finely diced fat back or bacon
1 cup (240 mL) Spanish onion, medium dice
½ cup (120 mL) celery, medium dice
2 level tablespoons (30 mL) flour
1½ quarts (1.5 L) fish or chicken stock
1 bay leaf

salt and white pepper to taste
1 tablespoon (15 mL) white Worcestershire sauce (optional)
2 cups (480 mL) potatoes, peeled and medium dice
2 cups (480 mL) clams, finely chopped
1 cup (240 mL) heavy cream

• Render the fatback or bacon in a heavy-gauge pot over medium heat until golden brown. Add the onions and celery and sweat about five minutes.

• Add the flour and blend, then add the stock and stir to thoroughly blend. Season to taste with salt and pepper, then add the potatoes and simmer until tender. Add the cream, bring to a boil, adjust seasoning.

•

The original clam chowders of New England were more stews than soups: a layer of bread crumbs and crumbled crackers seasoned with pepper, butter, and parsley, followed by a layer of clams, another layer of crackers, moistened with milk and/or water, then covered and baked. Later versions were even simpler, reflecting the ascetic nature of a Puritan society: hot milk, minced clams, a little salt and pepper, a pat of butter, with plain soda crackers served separately. As a result of recent regional food revivals, this soup has tended to go to the other extreme, using ingredients such as bell peppers, leeks, dill, sage, thyme, Worcestershire sauce, and cream. A middle approach is a comfortably seasoned clam broth thickened with white roux, garnished with minced clams, and diced onions and celery (the latter excluded by some purists) cooked in rendered fatback (or bacon), and finished with cream.

Manhattan Clam Chowder seems to be a nearly vanished species, since it is rather bland compared to the New England version, and rarely made with the care required. James Beard once referred to it as ". . . that horrendous soup . . . which resembles a vegetable soup that accidentally had some clams dumped into it."

CHICKEN SOUP, AMERICAN STYLE

1 chicken, 5 to 6 pounds (2.3 to 2.7 kg)
1½ gallons (5.8 mL) chicken stock
1 stalk celery, rinsed, and roughly chopped
1 carrot, peeled and roughly chopped
1 medium Spanish onion, roughly chopped
1 bunch scallion greens, trimmed, rinsed, and roughly chopped

1 bunch parsley stems, trimmed and rinsed
2 sprigs fresh thyme
1 bay leaf
½ teaspoon (2.5 mL) black peppercorns, crushed
2 cups (480 mL) carrots, peeled, and sliced thin
salt and white pepper to taste

- Place the chicken and stock in a stockpot (add water to cover, if necessary), and bring to a simmer. Skim and discard fat and albumin, and add the vegetables, herbs, and peppercorns. Simmer for 2 hours, skimming periodically. Remove the chicken and set aside to cool. Strain the stock, discarding the solids, and return the stock to the pot.

- Remove the meat from the chicken, discarding the skin and bones. Cut the meat into medium slivers, and set aside. Add the carrots to the stock, and simmer until tender. Add the chicken meat, adjust seasoning, and garnish with chopped parsley.

Cioppino

For the rouille:

16 baguette croutons
4 garlic cloves, pressed
2 egg yolks
2 tablespoons (30 mL) tomato paste
¼ teaspoon (1.2 mL) cayenne pepper

1 cup (240 mL) olive oil
salt to taste
⅓ cup (80 mL) mashed potato
the juice of 1 lemon

Though Cioppino is a mid-nineteenth century import from Genoa, it has been a part of Northern California cooking for so many years that it is considered a local specialty of the San Francisco Bay area.

For the Cioppino:

¼ cup (60 mL) olive oil
½ cup (120 mL) onions, cut into julienne
½ cup (120 mL) carrots, cut into julienne
½ cup (120 mL) leeks, cut into julienne
½ cup (120 mL) fennel root, cut into julienne
2 garlic cloves, pressed
2 cups (480 mL) dry champagne
1 cup (240 mL) tomatoes, diced
3 cups (720 mL) good clear fish stock
2 pinches saffron threads

1 zest of half an orange
salt and white pepper as needed
1 fresh raw Dungeness crab, cut up into roughly 1-inch (25-mm) pieces
8 16–20 shrimp, in the shell
12 littleneck or Manila clams, well scrubbed
8 mussels, debearded and well rinsed
½ pound (225 g) squid, cut into ½-inch (12-mm) rings
¼ cup (60 mL) parsley, chopped

- Pound the garlic, yolk, tomato, salt, pepper, and potato into a smooth paste using a mortar and pestle. Pour in the olive oil in a slow steady stream, interspersing it with the lemon juice. Set aside.

- Sauté the vegetables and garlic in the olive oil, covered, over medium heat for 10 minutes, stirring frequently. Add the champagne, tomatoes, stock, saffron, and orange zest, and simmer another 10 minutes. Season to taste with salt and white pepper.

- Add the seafood, and simmer until the clams and mussels open (6 to 8 minutes). Top with the chopped parsley, and serve with the baguette slices spread with the mayonnaise.

Clam Broth Bellevue

Strong chicken bouillon and clam broth (equal parts) garnished at service with a dollop of unsweetened whipped cream.

CORN CHOWDER

4 slices bacon, finely diced
2 tablespoons (30 mL) unsalted butter
1 medium onion, finely diced
1 celery rib, finely diced
2 cups (480 mL) whole kernel corn

1½ cups (360 mL) potatoes, cut into ¼-inch (6-mm) dice
1 quart (960 mL) chicken stock
1 cup (240 mL) heavy cream
salt and white pepper to taste

- Render the bacon until brown and crispy. Pour off excess fat, add the butter, onion, and celery, and sauté for 5 minutes. Add the corn, and blend. Add the potatoes and stock, and simmer until the potatoes are tender. Add the cream and season to taste with salt and pepper. Place a third of the soup in a food processor or blender, purée.

———————————— • ————————————

In England the word *corn* refers to the seed of any grain. In 1324 King Edward II decreed that three grains of barley—barleycorns—placed end to end would equal one inch. He also ruled that the longest human foot was 39 barleycorns, roughly the equivalent to a size 13. This measuring system was formally adopted by the U.S. shoe industry in 1888. Cultivars include Sugar and Gold, Buttercorn, Butter and Sugar, Gold Mine, Sunchief, Golden Cross Bantam, White

Jewel, and Silver Queen. Eastern Sunburst and White Cloud are two varieties grown for popcorn.

Cream of Corn, George Washington

Diced celery, leeks, and onions sweated in butter, dusted with flour, blended with chicken stock, seasoned with salt and white pepper, and simmered; whole kernel corn and diced red peppers (or pimentoes) added, finished with egg yolk and cream liaison.

In her book *Much Depends on Dinner*, Margaret Visser terms corn "the driving wheel of Western civilization." Corn is a native of South America and an essential and sacred part of ancient cultures there. Today there is not a single product in a North American supermarket that has not been touched in some way by corn—whether in the form of starch, sugar, or caramel color. These include fresh meat and poultry, frozen meat and fish, soft drinks, puddings, canned food, all cartons and packaging, margarine, candy, ketchup, ice cream, soft drinks, beer, gin, vodka, baby food, jams, pickles, adhesives, toothpaste, cosmetics, and detergents.

Duck Gumbo

Diced celery, leeks, onion, green pepper, and ham sweated in butter, duck stock flavored with tomato added, thickened with very dark brown roux, and garnished with rice and julienned roasted duck.

The term gumbo is a corruption of *gombo*, which is a corruption of *ngombo*, and a shortened form of *ochinggombo*, an African term—in the Umbundu language—for okra, a mucilaginous botanical fruit. Cultivated by the Egyptians in the twelfth century A.D., it was brought to the United States from Africa during the slave trade in the eighteenth century, and has been cultivated here ever since. In culinary usage it also refers to one of the few dishes in the U.S. in which it appears, the gumbo of southern Louisiana, a stew in which it is used primarily as a thickening agent along with filé (ground sassafras). In a 1974 Department of Agriculture survey, it was rated one of three vegetables least liked by the adults surveyed, though it is quite good pickled, as well as deep-fried (dipped in flour, egg, and corn meal). Gumbo (the dish) can also made with any number of meats, including crab, crayfish, and chicken.

Fish Chowder

There are probably more varieties of chowders than will ever be known or collected in recipe form, since they are typically prepared with ingredients—fish and aromatics—based on availability. The types of vegetables and herbs used will also depend on regional styles, as well as individual preferences. The basic ingredients and approach are similar to those of Boston Clam Chowder, though without the thickener and cream; milk is typical of New England chowders, though rarely seen elsewhere; and fatback (salt pork) is fairly universal (for flavor), as are onion and potatoes. Other possible vegetable ingredients include bell pepper, celery, garlic, leeks, and tomatoes; other seasonings are bay leaf, cayenne pepper, dill, fennel, saffron, and tarragon.

The term chowder dates back to the seventeenth century and is a corruption of *chaudière* (pronounced "show-dee-air"; *chaud* means "hot" in French), a large cast iron pot carried aboard ship by the French emigré fishermen of New England, who stayed out at sea for days at a time before returning with their catch to the New England fish markets. They prepared coarse fish stews similar to Mediterranean *bouillabaisse* and *bourride*, the ingredients of which were based solely on the types of fish caught in their nets.

*F*RIED CHICKEN GUMBO

½ cup (120 mL) vegetable oil

1 4-pound (18-kg) chicken, cut up into 10 pieces

½ cup (120 mL) flour, toasted until golden brown, and sifted

¾ pound (340 g) andouille or chorizo sausage, cut into ½-inch (12-mm) slices

¼ pound (113 g) ham, medium dice

1 large yellow onion, medium dice

1 green bell pepper, seeded and medium dice

3 stalks celery, medium dice

1 bunch scallions, sliced very thin

4 garlic cloves, pressed

⅔ cup (80 mL) chopped parsley

2 sprigs thyme (or 2 teaspoons/10 mL dried)

2 bay leaves

2 quarts (1.9 L) water

salt, black pepper, and cayenne pepper to taste

2 tablespoons (30 mL) filé gumbo powder

3 cups (720 mL) cooked white rice

- Heat three-fourths of the hot oil in a pan and cook the chicken until brown on all sides. Remove the chicken and set aside.
- Add the flour to the pan, and continue cooking until very dark brown. Set aside to cool down.
- Sauté the sausage, ham, onion, pepper, celery, and scallions in a separate pan in the remaining oil for about 10 minutes, and set aside.
- Add the water to the roux, and stir until smooth. Add the chicken, garlic, parsley, thyme, and bay leaf, and simmer covered for 45 minutes. Remove the chicken with a slotted spoon, and when cool enough, pull the meat from the bones, discard the bones, and return the meat to the soup. Return the vegetables to the soup, along with the filé, bring to a boil, cover and allow to sit 10 minutes. Serve in soup bowls over hot rice.

$\mathscr{L}$OBSTER CHOWDER

2 1¼- to 1½-pound (560 to 680 g) lobsters, cooked

1 carrot, peeled and coarsely sliced

1 stalk celery, rinsed and coarsely chopped

1 medium Spanish onion, peeled, and coarsely chopped

a bouquet garni, made with tarragon and parsley

stems, a sprig of thyme, bay leaf, and scallion greens

2 quarts (1.9 L) good clear fish stock

3 tablespoons (45 mL) unsalted butter

2 bunches scallions, cleaned, trimmed, and sliced on the bias very thin

6 medium Red Bliss
potatoes, peeled, and cut
into ½-inch (12-mm) dice
2 cups (480 mL) whole
kernel corn

1 tablespoon (15 mL)
tarragon leaves, minced
2 tablespoons (30 mL)
parsley, minced
salt and black pepper

- Crack the lobster shells, remove the tail and claw meat, cut into ½-inch (12-mm) dice, and set aside.
- Cut up the lobster body, and add to the fish stock along with the tail and claw shells, vegetables, and bouquet garni. Simmer for 30 minutes, then strain and set aside.
- Sauté the scallions in the butter for several minutes. Add the stock and potatoes, season with salt and pepper, and simmer until the potatoes are tender. Add the corn and herbs, and adjust seasoning.

———————— • ————————

Up until the mid-nineteenth century, lobsters were so plentiful that they were often found piled up on the beaches of New England following a storm. Back then the frightful looking crustaceans cost a penny each, and Lobster Chowder was as well known in some parts of New England as Clam Chowder. Purists may adhere to the puritan approach to this dish—hot milk thickened with a paste made with ground soda crackers, butter, tomalley (the liver), salt, and cayenne pepper, then garnished with diced lobster.

Commercial fishing for the 100 million-year-old *Homarus Americanus*—a second cousin to spiders—began in the mid-nineteenth century, when it became a delicacy of robber barons and businessmen on expense accounts. This demand severely depleted the supply, causing sales to drop from an all-time high of 130 million pounds in 1885 to a low of 33 million in 1918. Conservation laws and commercial regulation eventually brought the annual harvest back to between 70 and 80 million pounds; in the 1980s lobster sales averaged 40 million pounds a year. In truth, though, most of the "Maine" lobsters sold in the U.S. actually come from Québec, Newfoundland, and Canada's Maritime Provinces.

MUSSEL CHOWDER

2 pounds (900 g) mussels, scrubbed, rinsed, and debearded
1 cup (240 mL) dry white wine
1 medium onion, small dice
2 garlic cloves, pressed
1 pinch saffron
3 cups (720 mL) tomatoes, diced
2 cups (480 mL) fish stock
1 cup (240 mL) clam juice
3 cups (720 mL) potatoes, cut into ¼-inch (6-mm) dice
salt and pepper to taste
2 tablespoons (30 mL) unsalted butter

- Steam the mussels in the white wine, 8 to 10 minutes, or until all the mussels are open. Remove the mussels and set aside. Add all the remaining ingredients, except the butter, and simmer until the potatoes are tender. Return the mussels to the soup, and garnish with a piece of the butter.

Oyster Chowder

Diced onions, green peppers, and okra sweated in butter, dusted with flour, white stock added and blended, seasoned with salt and cayenne pepper, finished with cream, and garnished with diced poached oysters.

PHILADELPHIA PEPPER POT

For the stock:

2 veal knuckles (with some meat still attached)
1 bouquet garni (1 bunch parsley stems, 1 sprig thyme, 2 bay leaves, 1 teaspoon crushed black peppercorns, wrapped in 2 leek leaves with cotton cord)
2 pounds (900 g) fresh tripe
1½ gallons (5.8 L) water
1 teaspoon (4.9 mL) salt

For the späetzle:

1 cup (240 mL) flour
½ teaspoon (2.5 mL) salt
pinch of nutmeg
1 large egg
6 tablespoons (90 mL) milk
3 tablespoons (45 mL) melted butter
For the soup:
3 tablespoons (45 mL) unsalted butter

½ cup (120 mL) ham, medium dice

½ cup (120 mL) celery root (or celery), medium dice

1 large Spanish onion, medium dice

1 green bell pepper, medium dice

1 small leek, white part only (use green leaves for the bouquet garni), medium dice

2 cups (480 mL) potatoes, peeled and medium dice

3 tablespoons (45 mL) chopped parsley

- Simmer the stock ingredients for 3 hours. Strain, reserving the liquid. Separate the meat from the knuckle and cut into dice, and cut the tripe into julienne strips.
- Blend the späetzle ingredients together until smooth. Place a small-holed colander over boiling salted water and pour the dough into the colander, pressing through the holes with a rubber spatula. Stir the späetzle gently, and when the water returns to a boil, remove with a slotted spoon or wire strainer and set aside.
- Sweat the onion, leek, celery, and pepper in the butter. Add the potatoes, veal, and tripe, and blend. Add the stock and season with salt and pepper. Simmer until the potatoes are tender, skimming foam from the top, and add the späetzle. Serve topped with chopped parsley.

Potato Chowder

Diced celery, leeks, and onions sweated in rendered and lightly browned diced fatback, white stock and diced potatoes added, seasoned with salt and cayenne pepper, finished with cream, and sprinkled chopped parsley.

———————— • ————————

In ancient Greece, celery was made into a crown and placed on the head of a victorious athlete; in Plutarch's time, it was used as a funeral wreath. Its first recorded use as a food was in France in 1623. A member of the carrot family, it consists of a bunch of petioles, or leaf stalks, and is rich in mineral salts, vitamins, and iron. It also has diuretic properties, making it a natural remedy for kidney ailments. A Chinese remedy known to alleviate high blood pressure consists of 4 ounces of raw celery per day. Celeriac, also called German or turnip-rooted celery, possesses a starch-storing root; its leaves develop only minimally. Cultivars include Stuffed White Pascal, Giant Pascal, American Stuffed White, Fordhook, Golden Self Blanching, Verona, and Alabaster.

ℛHODE ISLAND REDS' CLAM CHOWDER

This soup was created in 1975 by Alan R. Gibson, in honor of the Providence Reds, a minor league hockey team.

¼ pound (113 g) unsalted butter
1 medium onion, medium dice
1 celery stalk, medium dice
1 medium carrot, peeled, medium dice
2 garlic cloves, pressed
½ cup (120 mL) fennel root, medium dice
1 teaspoon (4.9 mL) fresh thyme leaves
6 stalks dill, tied together with cotton twine
1 cup (240 mL) tomato, peeled, medium dice
1 cup (240 mL) potatoes, medium dice
1 tablespoons (15 mL) Worcestershire sauce
5 cups (1.2 L) clam juice
2 cups (480 mL) clams, finely chopped
1 tablespoons (15 mL) minced dill
salt and white pepper to taste
4 4-inch (100-mm) round French or Kaiser rolls

- Sweat the vegetables and herbs in the butter for 10 minutes.
- Preheat an oven to 400°F (205°C). Slice and reserve a lid off the tops of the rolls. Scoop out the inside of the rolls, discarding the inside and reserving the scooped-out rolls. Bake for about 10 minutes, or until toasted and golden brown.
- Add the tomatoes, potatoes, Worcestershire, juice, and clams, and simmer until the potatoes are tender. Add the dill, and adjust seasoning with salt and pepper.
- Serve the piping hot soup in the toasted rolls, in a wide soup plate with the lids on.

POLISH
Cold Soups

Cold Beet Soup
(Barszcz zimny czyli zupa)

The juice of pickled beets and cucumbers thickened with semolina, tempered with an egg yolk and sour cream liaison, seasoned with salt and pepper, chilled, and garnished with three slices of hard-cooked eggs.

Cold Polish Soup
(Polski Chotodriece)

Pickled cucumber juice blended with sour milk, garnished with julienned or diced beets, sliced hard-cooked eggs, and crayfish tails, and sprinkled with chopped chives and dill; served over an ice cube in each soup plate.

Herb Soup
(Kolodnik)

Julienned beet tops and diced beets (2 parts to one) simmered in white stock, flavored with chopped chives, dill, and pickled cucumber juice, garnished with diced cucumber (fresh), diced (or quartered) hard-cooked eggs, crayfish tails, sliced lemon, small pieces of poached sturgeon, and sour cream; served with a cube of ice in the soup plate.

Hot Soups
Buckwheat Soup
(Rosol)

Beef and chicken stock thickened with buckwheat groats (kasha), garnished with diced chicken and bacon, chopped parsley and fennel.

Polish Chicken Soup
(Kalia)

Chicken bouillon flavored with the juice of pickled cucumbers, garnished with diced chicken, carrots, and celery root, and chopped parsley.

Polish Duck and Beet Soup
(Borschtsch Polski)

Roasted duck carcasses simmered in beef stock and strained (duck breasts reserved for the soup); garnished with medium julienned beet root and duck breast, and cabbage chiffonade; sour cream served separately.

———————————— • ————————————

Beets are native to the coasts of Western Europe and North Africa, and have been eaten by humans since before recorded history. They contain as much as 10 percent by weight of carbohydrate, mostly in the form of sucrose, and 1.5 to 2 percent protein, iron, and calcium. In the eighteenth century, a white variety was cultivated for sugar production. Beets are classified as having (1) a round root; (2) a flat-roundish root; or (3) a long root (up to 12″ long). Varieties include Crosby's Egyptian, Burpee Red Ball, Early Wonder, Detroit Dark Red, Burpee's Golden, Dark Red Massy, Dark Red Globe Early, and Dark Red Turnip-rooted Egyptian.

Rye Soup
(Polewka)

Water thickened with rye flour, seasoned with salt and pepper, and finished with cream.

Sauerkraut Soup
(Kapustniak)

Sauerkraut, marrow bones, a piece of pork and a piece of bacon, simmered in water until the pork and bacon are nearly tender, and thickened with a little roux; pork sausages, carrots, celery root, onions, and parsley added and simmered until all ingredients are tender; garnished with the diced marrow, pork, bacon, and sausages.

Vegetable and Barley Soup
(Gesinka)

Carrots, celery root, mushrooms, and onions cooked in butter and a little water, drained and puréed, added to beef bouillon, seasoned with salt and lemon juice, bound with a liaison of sour cream and egg yolks, garnished with pearl barley.

RUSSIAN
Cold Soups

Cold Herb Soup
(Botwinja or Batwinja)

Sorrel and young beet tops (leaves) simmered in white stock and kvass, and purèed; seasoned with salt and pepper, and sweetened with a little sugar; garnished with julienned cucumber, and chopped tarragon, dill, and fennel; served with a small ice cube (in each plate); small pieces of poached salmon or sturgeon, and grated horseradish served separately.

Kvass (also *kwas*) is a semi-sparkling Russian beverage made from fermented barley malt and rye flour, or black bread, or fruit. Similar to beer, though with a low alcohol content, it is brown in color and bittersweet in taste. It is sold on the streets of Moscow during the summer, where it is drunk as is; it can also be mixed with stronger spirits or tea, and is commonly used in soup.

Cold Fish Soup
(Okroschka is Riba)

Small pieces of sturgeon fried in oil and chilled; place in a soup plate with diced lobster and crayfish tails seasoned with salt and pepper, filled with kvass, and sprinkled with chopped chervil and tarragon.

Sour Soup
(Okroschka)

Sour cream, sour milk, and kvass blended together, seasoned with mustard, salt, and pepper, garnished with chopped roast veal, hazel-hen breast, beef tongue, ham, crayfish tails, sprinkled with chopped dill, and served over a piece of ice.

Hot Soups

CABBAGE SOUP
(Schtschi)

2 gallons (7.7 L) white stock
3 pounds (1.4 kg) beef brisket
1 bouquet garni (dill and parsley sprigs, bay leaves, and peppercorns tied together in leek leaves with cotton cord)
6 tablespoons (90 mL) rendered fatback (or stock fat)

½ cup (120 mL) celery root (or celery), medium diced
1 large carrot, peeled, and cut into medium dice
1 medium Spanish onion, medium dice
1 leek, white part only, medium dice
1 small head cabbage, medium dice

1 parsnip, peeled and
  medium dice
1 large white turnip, peeled
  and medium dice
2 garlic cloves, pressed
1½ cups (360 mL) dice
  tomatoes in juice

2 cups (480 mL) sauerkraut,
  rinsed and drained
salt and pepper to taste
4 tablespoons (60 mL)
  chopped dill
½ cup (120 mL) sour cream

- Simmer the stock, brisket, and bouquet garni for 2 hours. Discard the bouquet garni, and set the stock and meat aside to cool. When the brisket has cooled down, cut into medium dice.

- Sweat the vegetables in the fat, then add the tomatoes, sauerkraut, and stock, and season to taste with salt and pepper. Serve sprinkled with dill and garnished with sour cream.

———————————— • ————————————

Cabbage soup is an important nutritional mainstay in Russia, in both rich and poor households, and variations abound, including *Schtschi Nikolaijewski*, made with brown pork stock (from roasted pork bones), grated instead of diced vegetables, and tomato paste or purée; *Schtschi i Russki*, made with cabbage, onions, and other available vegetables cooked in lard, simmered in pork stock, and garnished with diced bacon and brisket, with buckwheat groats (kasha) served separately; *Schtschi Soldatski* (Soldier's Soup), made with sauerkraut instead of cabbage; and *Sjeloni* (Green Soup), Schtchi with the addition of sorrel, spinach, and sliced hard-cooked eggs.

Citizen's Soup
(Sup Meschanski)

Beef stock garnished with julienned carrot, celery, and leek; stuffed cabbage balls served separately (blanched cabbage leaves filled with a veal farce, sprinkled with grated cheese, and gratinéed).

Crayfish Soup
(Sup Rakowa)

Strong fish stock garnished with sliced carrots and leeks, and chopped onions and parsnips sweated in butter; crayfish tails and fish dumplings (quenelles); a little crayfish butter melted on top of the soup at service; peeled lemon slices sprinkled with chopped dill served separately.

Fish Soup I
(Soljanka is Riba)

Sliced onions sweated in oil, fish stock flavored with pickled cucumber juice added, garnished with small pieces of sturgeon poached in the fish stock, julienned pickled cucumbers and mushrooms, capers, and peeled sliced lemons, sprinkled with chopped dill; black olives served separately.

———————————— • ————————————

Cucumber is a native of India and tropical Asia, and has been under cultivation for 4000 years. It was introduced to France in the ninth century and to England in the fourteenth; and from the Middle Ages through the eighteenth century cucumbers were considered unhealthful. They were considered "hard of Digestion," because they continue "long in the Stomach" (Dr. Lemery). Samuel Johnson (1709–1784) wrote, "A cucumber should be well-sliced, dressed with pepper and vinegar, and then thrown out." Early cultivars such as Russian and Holland Yellow have disappeared due to agricultural methods geared toward large monoculture. One ancient variety—Paris Green—still exists, and newer varieties include Victory, Ohio MR 17, Sunnybrook, Pioneer, Marketeer, West Indian Gherkin, Straight Eight, Marketmore 70, China (Kyoto), and Mariner.

Fish Soup II
(Ucha is Sterlett)

Rich clear fish stock garnished with pieces of sterlet poached in fish stock, lemon juice, and Madeira, garnished with thin slices of peeled lemon.

Goose Giblet Soup
(Potroka)

Beef bouillon flavored with pickled cucumber juice, garnished with diced goose giblets, sliced pickled cucumbers, bound with sour cream and egg yolks, and sprinkled with chopped dill, fennel, and parsley.

Green Borscht
(Borschtsch Sjeloni)

Meat stock garnished with julienned spinach, sorrel, lettuce, and beets; sour cream served separately.

————————————— • —————————————

Spinach is indigenous to southwestern Asia, or may be of Persian origin. Introduced into Europe by the Moors around 1000 A.D., its widespread cultivation began only after the 18th century, and today it is cultivated the world over. It has been said that the greatness of a chef could be demonstrated by his ability to create great spinach dishes. Spinach is used in dishes as diverse as croquettes, omelettes, pasta, puddings, salads, soufflés, soups, and tarts. It is one of the healthiest foods, containing vitamins A, B, C, E, K, oxalic acid, and some iron (though not quite as much as has been generally believed).

Hare Soup
(Sup Malorussiski)

Stock simmered with hare and barley, puréed, flavored with beet juice, garnished with sour cream and julienned hare.

Lithuanian Soup
(Sup Litowski)

Potatoes simmered in white stock, blended with sour cream, garnished with sorrel chiffonade, julienned celery root and smoked goose breast, small fried pork sausages, and small egg fritters (small hard-cooked eggs dusted with flour, dipped in egg wash, rolled in bread crumbs, and fried in lard).

Moscovite Soup
(Sup Moscowskaia)

Rich beef bouillon; Moscow style dumplings served separately (cottage cheese, butter, flour, egg yolks, sour milk, salt, sugar, grated lemon zest, stiffly beaten egg whites, poached in salted water or stock, sprinkled with grated cheese, and gratinéed.)

Nettle Soup
(Krapiwa)

Young nettle shoots and chopped onions sweated in oil, beef bouillon and a piece of beef brisket added, garnished with the diced brisket and pearl barley.

---•---

Though young nettle shoots are perfectly safe used raw in salads, the stinging hairs on the mature leaves of the perennial large, or common, nettle plant can cause a skin rash. Cooked in green vegetable soups, or handled like spinach and combined with cabbage, leeks, sorrel, and/or watercress, they are a healthful food, containing more iron than spinach and the same amount of vitamins A and C. "... if it be withered or boiled it stingeth not at all" (John Gerard).

Russian Chicken Soup
(Rossolnik)

Chicken bouillon flavored with the juice ogourzi (pickled cucumber), garnished with julienned celery root, ogourzi, and chicken, finished with beaten egg yolks and sour cream.

Russian National Soup
(Borschtschock)

Meat stock garnished with julienned cabbage, root vegetables, and beets; sour cream served separately.

---•---

There is no specific criteria for the stock used in this soup, though it is sometimes beef and sometimes has a ham bone or ham hock added. Two variations of this soup are *Borschtschock skobeleff*, made with rendered diced fatback, and the addition of diced potatoes, small fried sausages, and meat balls, with toasted croutons served separately; and *Borschtschock flotski* (Russian Navy Soup), with the addition of diced vegetables.

SCANDINAVIAN

Finnish

Cold Soup

....

CHILLED VEGETABLE SOUP, FINNISH STYLE
(Kesäkeitto)

1½ quarts (1.4 L) chicken stock
½ cup (120 mL) string beans, cut into ¼-inch (6-mm) dice
½ cup (120 mL) carrots, cut into ¼-inch (6-mm) dice
½ cup (120 mL) cauliflower, cut into small buds
½ cup (120 mL) radishes, cut into ¼-inch (6-mm) dice
¼ cup (120 mL) potatoes, cut into ¼-inch (6-mm) dice

2 cups (480 mL) fresh spinach, cut into 1-inch (25-mm) pieces
3 tablespoons unsalted butter, kneaded together with 4 tablespoons (60 mL) flour
1 cup (240 mL) heavy cream, beaten together with 1 egg yolk
½ pound (225 g) titi shrimp
salt and white pepper to taste
2 tablespoons (30 mL) chopped dill

- Bring the stock to a boil, and blanch the vegetables separately, until each is tender but firm (al dente; the potatoes should be cooked until tender).

- Beat the flour and butter paste into the remaining liquid, and simmer 10 minutes. Strain, and return to the fire. Add the blanched vegetables, radishes, spinach, and shrimp, and simmer briefly.

- Temper the cream and egg yolk liaison into the soup, bring to a boil, and remove from the fire. Adjust seasoning, allow to cool, then refrigerate (or place in an ice bath) until well chilled. Serve garnished with the dill.

Hot Soup

Finnish Soup
(Finnlandskaia)

Rich beef bouillon; croutons topped with a slice of crepe flavored with sour cream, sprinkled with grated cheese and gratinéed, served separately.

Swedish
Cold Soup

.... # *B*UTTERMILK SOUP
(Kænemælkskolskål)

3 egg yolks
½ cup (120 mL) sugar
the juice of 1 lemon
1 quart (960 mL) buttermilk
the zest of 1 orange and 1
   lemon

1 cup (240 mL) fresh white
   bread, cut into ¼-inch (6-
   mm) croutons
2 tablespoons (30 mL) sugar
4 tablespoons (60 mL)
   unsalted butter
4 sprigs fresh mint

- Whip the eggs and sugar until thick and lemon yellow. Beat in the lemon juice, then blend in the buttermilk.

- Blanch the zest briefly in boiling water, drain, then add to the buttermilk. Chill until ready to serve.

- Toss the croutons in the sugar, then sauté in butter until golden brown. Refrigerate until well chilled. Serve in chilled cups, garnished with croutons and mint.

———————————— • ————————————

Some years ago I offered Buttermilk Soup in my first solo kitchen out on the eastern end of Long Island. It rarely sold, however, and several weeks into the season it was brought to my attention that my primary waiter, a gentleman who possessed exceptional skills as a waiter and salesman for my kitchen offerings, had decided that since *he* did not like this dish, he would simply not recommend it. Valuing our friendship as well as his professional ability, I opted to discontinue offering it on the menu—we ran a very fine kitchen that summer, and I preferred to maintain that level of gastronomic offerings rather than try and change the world's palate.

Kænemælkskolskål, pronounced "canneh-mal-**skole**-skal," is translated as follows: *Kæne*—to churn from butter; *mælk*—made from milk; *skol*—cold; *skål*—bowl.

———————————————————

Cold Garlic Soup
(Ajo Blanco)

Garlic and almonds pounded with olive oil into a thick paste, moistened with water, seasoned with salt and pepper, garnished with sliced croutons.

1 medium cucumber, peeled and seeded
1 medium green pepper
1 bunch scallions
2 fresh vine-ripened tomatoes, peeled
¼ cup (60 mL) olive oil
4 garlic cloves
1 quart (960 mL) peeled tomatoes packed in tomato juice
2 tablespoons (30 mL) Worcestershire sauce
¼ teaspoon (1.2 mL) ground cumin

salt and cayenne pepper to taste
1 small, stale, hard roll, finely chopped, and soaked in 1 cup (240 mL) water and ½ cup (120 mL) white wine vinegar
2 egg yolks
1 cup (240 mL) diced crouton, toasted
2 tablespoons (30 mL) chopped parsley

- Cut enough cucumber, green pepper, scallion, and tomatoes into a fine dice to yield ¼ cup (60 mL) each.

- Purée the remaining parts of each vegetable, along with the remaining ingredients (except the croutons and parsley), in a blender or food processor. Add the diced vegetables, adjust seasoning, and garnish with the croutons and chopped parsley.

———————————— • ————————————

The name Gazpacho is of Arabic origin, and means "soaked bread." There are numerous regional variations; it can be served hot in the winter (Cadiz), thickened with cream and corn flour (Cordoba), garnished with raw onion rings (Jerez), made with veal stock and garnished with almonds and grapes (Malaga), and seasoned with basil and cumin (Segovia). In the *Alice B. Toklas Cook Book*, the author shares Chilean writer Marta Brunet's description of this typical meal of the Spanish mule driver: an earthenware vessel rubbed inside with a garlic, oil, and salt paste, then filled with alternating layers of sliced cucumbers and tomatoes spread with bread crumbs, topped with more bread crumbs and drizzled with oil. It is wrapped in a wet cloth and left in the sun; when the cloth is dry, the dish is ready.

Hot Soups

For Madrid Style Chick Pea Soup, substitute beef stock, purée all or part of the cooked beans (adjust thickness with stock), and garnish with croutons.

Bean varieties fall under three basic categories: French (common string beans), Faba (or Broad beans), and Lima beans. The status of beans in the ancient world is perhaps demonstrated by the fact that the names of four prominent Roman families were derived from four varieties of legumes: Fabius (Faba), Lentulus (lentil), Piso (pea), and Cicero (chick).

Andalusian Chick Pea Soup

Chick peas (garbanzos; soaked overnight and drained) cooked with a seasonal herb bouquet, seasoned with salt, cayenne pepper, and saffron, sprinkled with crushed caraway seeds at service.

Andalusian Pot Soup
(Cocido Andaluz)

Soaked chick peas (garbanzos), covered with water and simmered with beef bones, a ham bone, a piece of beef, and a small piece of thick bacon; green beans cut in half, diced potatoes and pumpkin, sliced chorizo and morcilla (Spanish black sausage), puréed garlic, saffron, and large diced green peppers added and simmered until cooked; broth served first, followed by the meat and vegetables.

Bread Soup
(Sopa Victoria Ena)

Diced white bread fried in oil or butter, simmered in beef stock, puréed, mellowed with milk, finished with egg yolks and butter, and garnished with chopped hard-cooked eggs and chopped chervil.

Egg Soup
(Tonnillo)

Water simmered with white bread crumbs, puréed, seasoned with salt, pepper, and thyme, a little olive oil added, finished (tempered) with eggs.

GARLIC SOUP
(Sopa de Ajo)

¼ cup (60 mL) olive oil
1 garlic bulb, cloves peeled
    and split in half
    lengthwise
6 croutons

6 cups (1.5 L) rich chicken
    bouillon, hot
1 teaspoon (4.9 mL) paprika
2 eggs, beaten
4 tablespoons (60 mL)
    chopped parsley

- Sauté the garlic in the olive oil until lightly browned, then re-move to a blender with the chicken bouillon, and purée. Sauté the croutons on both sides in the remaining oil, and set aside.

- Season the bouillon with paprika, salt, and pepper, and ladle into an ovenproof tureen. Place the croutons on top of the broth, and pour the beaten egg on top of the croutons. Place in a broiler until the eggs are lightly browned, and sprinkle with chopped parsley.

Mussel Soup
(Al Cuarto de Hora)

Mussels steamed in a little water until open, then set aside (save the liquid). Diced ham, onions, and rice sweated in butter, moist-ened with water·and the mussel liquor, seasoned with salt, pep-per, and chopped parsley, simmered until the rice is tender, garnished with the mussels and sprinkled with chopped hard-cooked eggs at service.

Mutton Soup, Barcelona Style
(Barcelonessa)

Mutton stock flavored with a little tomato purée, thickened with white bread crumbs browned in butter, garnished with small mutton dumplings, sprinkled with chopped parsley and chervil at service.

Mutton Dumplings:

Blend ground mutton (or lamb) with eggs (about 1 egg per cup/240 mL of meat), chopped parsley, season to taste with salt and pepper, and shape into small ovals; dust with flour, pan-fry in oil, and drain on absorbent paper.

Spanish Fish Soup
(Mallorquina)

Chopped onions and garlic sweated in olive oil, diced tomatoes, fish stock, and white wine added, seasoned with salt, pepper, and chopped parsley, garnished with croutons fried in olive oil.

Spanish Household Soup
(Huevos à la Casera)

Water and olive oil thickened with fresh white bread crumbs, garnished with eggs poached in the soup.

Spanish Liver Soup
(Chanfaina)

Chopped onions sweated in olive oil, seasoned with mint, parsley, caraway, cinnamon, paprika, and saffron; water and diced calf's and pork liver added, simmered until tender; sprinkled with bread crumbs at service.

Spanish National Soup
(Puchero)

Beef, ham, mutton, choriza (garlic sausage), vegetables, and chick peas simmered in water, seasoned, and garnished with fried dumplings (made of ham, bacon, eggs, bread crumbs, and garlic).

Spanish Onion Soup
(Cebolla Española)

White stock simmered with chopped onions sweated in olive oil and dried diced bread, seasoned with salt and pepper, and simmered until slightly thickened.

ᔭPANISH POT SOUP
(Olla Podrida)

1 pound (450 g) beef brisket	1 lamb shank
½ pound (227 g) mutton breast or shoulder	1 ham hock
½ pound (227 g) ham	¼ pound (113 g) salt pork
	1 pig's ear

1 tablespoon (15 mL) salt
¼ pound (113 g) chickpeas (garbanzos), soaked in water overnight
1 small chicken
2 chorizo
4 cloves garlic, peeled
2 bay leaves
1 bunch parsley stems, trimmed, rinsed, and tied together with cotton twine
1 tablespoons (15 mL) black peppercorns, crushed, and tied in cheesecloth

2 leeks (white part only), rinsed and cut into ¼-inch (6-mm) thick slices
1 large carrot, peeled, and cut into ¼-inch (6-mm) thick slices
1 medium onion, peeled, and cut into 1-inch (25 mm) pieces
½ head cabbage, cut into 1-inch (25-mm) pieces
2 Red Bliss potatoes, cut into ¼-inch (6-mm) thick slices

- Place the beef, mutton, ham, ham hock, salt pork, pig's ear, and salt in a large pot, and cover with cold water (4 inches/100 mm above highest ingredient). Simmer for 2 hours, skimming the top throughout.

- Add the chickpeas, chicken, chorizo, garlic, herbs, and peppercorns, and simmer for 2 more hours (continue skimming).

- Add the leeks, carrot, onion, and cabbage, and simmer another 15 minutes. Add the potatoes, and simmer until tender. Season to taste with salt and pepper.

- Remove the meat ingredients and roughly chop. Remove and discard the pepper sachet and parsley stems. Typically served as two dishes: the broth first, followed by all the solid ingredients on a large platter.

Spanish Vegetable Soup
(Boronia)

Eggplant, garlic, pumpkin, and tomato sweated in olive oil, seasoned with salt, allspice, and caraway seeds; water, dried bread crumbs, and a pinch of saffron added, simmered until tender, and puréed.

———————————— • ————————————

Eggplant is a very ancient fruit (botanically speaking), and native to India. It was unknown to the ancient Greeks and Romans, and appeared in Europe via Africa in the fourteenth century. It is virtually never eaten raw, probably due to the high content of solanine, a bitter, poisonous alkaloid once used to treat epilepsy. The cooking process is believed to eliminate the solanine. Four well-known dishes made with eggplant are *Ratatouille* from Provence, *Imam Beyeldi* ("swooping Imam") from Turkey, *Babaganoosh* from Persia; and *Eggplant Parmesan* from Italy. Varieties include Barbentane, Naples Early Purple, Giant New York, Chinese, and Japanese.

Wilfredo Soup
(Sopa Wilfredo)

Diced green peppers, onions, and garlic sweated in olive oil, white stock and tomato purée added, seasoned with salt and cinnamon, finished with eggs, and garnished with croutons and sliced blood sausage.

Other Hispanic Soups

•

Pumpkin, along with avocado, green beans, corn, cucumber, eggplant, okra, olives, pepper, and squash are all botanical fruits, since they are a ripened ovary containing one or more seeds of the plant from which they come.

Cuban Soup
(Ajaco Cubano)

Salt pork (fat back), pickled pork, and fresh pork simmered in water flavored with saffron, salt, and pepper, chick peas (garbanzos; soaked overnight) added, along with garlic, eggplant, kernel corn, and diced potatoes and pumpkin.

Mexican Chicken Soup
(Cancha Mexicana)

Chicken stock garnished with diced onions and tomatoes sweated in fat, diced chicken, cooked rice, and chopped mint.

Mexican Noodle Soup
(Sopa de Fideos)

1 chicken, 5 to 6 pounds (19 to 27 kg)	1 bunch parsley stems, trimmed and rinsed
1½ gallons (5.8 mL) chicken stock	2 sprigs fresh thyme
1 stalk celery, rinsed, and roughly chopped	1 bay leaf
1 carrot, peeled and roughly chopped	2 garlic cloves, crushed
1 bunch scallion greens, trimmed, rinsed, and roughly chopped	½ teaspoon (2.5 mL) white peppercorns, crushed

¼ cup (60 mL) olive oil
¼ pound (113 g) cappellini (fideos) broken into 2-inch (50-mm) pieces
1 large Spanish onion
2 garlic cloves, crushed
pinch of saffron
1 jalapño pepper, stemmed, and roughly chopped

2 cups (480 mL) diced tomatoes, packed in juice
salt and white pepper to taste
¼ cup (60 mL) cilantro leaves, roughly chopped
½ cup (120 mL) ripe avocado, medium diced
½ cup (120 mL) grated cheese

- Place the chicken and stock in a stockpot (add water to cover, if necessary), and bring to a simmer. Skim and discard fat and albumin, and add the vegetables, herbs, garlic, and peppercorns. Simmer for 2 hours, skimming periodically. Remove the chicken and set aside to cool. Strain the stock, discarding the solids.

- Remove the meat from the chicken, discarding the skin and bones. Cut the meat into medium dice and set aside.

- Sauté the cappellini in the olive oil over medium heat, stirring frequently. When the noodles are light brown, remove with a slotted spoon and place on absorbent paper.

- Add the onion to the oil, and sauté several minutes. Add the garlic and continue sautéing. Add the saffron and jalapeño, stir briefly, then add the tomatoes. Simmer several minutes, then transfer to a blender or food processor and purèe)add some of the stock if necessary). Combine the tomato mixture and the stock, bring to a simmer, and season with salt and pepper. Add the noodles and simmer until tender. Skim the top, adjust seasoning, and serve garnished with cilantro, avocado, and grated cheese.

Mexican Pot Soup
(Puchero Mexicana)

A piece of beef, veal, and pickled pork, and goose giblets simmered until tender in water seasoned with salt and hot chile peppers; skimmed; carrots, onions, parsnips, and turnips, and chick peas added; broth and vegetables served separately from the meats.

———————————— • ————————————

The genus *Capsicum*, to which the pepper belongs, is so called because it resembles a box (Latin "capsa"), which encloses its seeds, although it may also stem from the Greek *capto*, meaning "I bite," referring to the acrid and pungent flavor of some varieties. Peppers are native to South America and have been cultivated there for nearly 8000 years. There are at least 300 known varieties, with many different divisions and subdivisions. In the United States, mild peppers are known as sweet, or bell peppers; in England all peppers are chilies, the hotter varieties termed "hot" chilies; and in Latin American mild peppers are called pimentos and hot ones "chilies."

Peppers contain more vitamin C than citrus fruits and as much vitamin A as carrots. The heat in a pepper depends on how much *capsaicin* it contains. Capsaicin is a reddish-brown alkaloid that develops during ripening and is concentrated mostly in the internal connective tissue. Leading cultivars of sweet peppers in the U.S. include Bellringer, Bell Boy, California Wonder, Merrimack Wonder, and Worldbeater; popular fresh hot pepper varieties include habanero, jalapeño, serrano tabasco, and thai.

TURKISH

Cold Soup

Cold Potato Soup
(Abji l'Amid)

Chicken stock simmered with potatoes, seasoned with salt, pepper, and lemon juice, puréed, and served chilled.

Hot Soups

Beef Soup
(Duyne Tchorbassi)

Beef stock flavored with paprika, thickened with brown roux, garnished with diced beef, and drizzled with melted butter at service.

Mutton Soup
(Ekshili Tchorba)

Mutton stock thickened with a paste made with flour, eggs, lemon juice, and water, garnished with diced mutton.

GLOSSARY

al dente: Literally "to the tooth" or "to the bite," this term is used to describe pasta and vegetables cooked until they are tender but not mushy, making them somewhat firm and resilient when bitten into.

bain marie: A vessel full of hot water, used for maintaining the heat of a smaller vessel containing soup, sauce, or some other food item that is placed within the larger vessel full of hot water. May refer to small vessels placed into a steam table. It can also be used for chilling, placing a cold container into a larger one filled with ice and water.

blanch: To place a food item in boiling salted water, stock, or other liquid in order to cook it partially, set its color, or facilitate peeling.

boil: To cook a food in water or another liquid at 212°F (100°C). A full rolling boil is essential for cooking some foods (such as pasta), but undesirable for cooking others (such as stocks).

bouquet garni: A collection of herbs and spices, tied together in a bundle with cotton twine, and added to a stock, soup, sauce, or stew to impart the flavor of those herbs and spices to the dish it is simmered with. A standard bouquet garni consists of parsley stems, bay leaf, thyme, and peppercorns. Variations on this are limitless, depending on an individual's style and the dish in which it is used. Loose herbs and spices can be added by placing them in a tea ball, or they can be tied up in a large leek leaf.

caramelize: To cook sugar or another food in a sauté or sauce pan over direct heat long enough to allow the sugar, or the sugar in the food, to begin to brown. Caramelizing imparts a brown color and a nutty flavor to the finished dish.

chiffonade: A leafy vegetable (such as lettuce, basil leaves, radicchio, etc.) cut into shreds, approximately 1/8-inch (3-mm) wide, and used as a salad base or as a garnish.

china cap (*chinoise*): A cone-shaped strainer with a single handle extending from the wide end of the strainer. China caps come in three basic varieties, defined by the size of their perforations: large (chinoise gros), small (chinoise fin), and very fine (bouillon strainer, or chinoise mousseline).

court bouillon: A liquid medium used for poaching various forms of meat, fish, poultry, quenelles, and vegetables. The ingredients vary depending on the item to be poached, but generally include water, wine, and aromatics (mirepoix, herbs, and spices).

crouton: A small, round piece of toasted or fried bread, sliced from a baguette or cut out of a larger slice of bread and used as a base for canapés or as a garnish for various soups (as a garnish for soups or salads, it can also be in the form of a small square, also toasted or fried). (From Old French *crouste*, and Latin *crusta*, meaning "crust.")

diablotin: A small, round crouton spread with butter (thick, cold Béchamel sauce or mayonnaise is also used), sprinkled with grated cheese, browned, and used as a garnish or accompaniment for soup.

farce (also forcemeat): A finely ground, seasoned paste of meat, game, poultry, fish, or shellfish, raw or cooked, used as a stuffing for a ballotine, gallantine, or roulade, or as the main body of a pâté, terrine, sausage, or quenelle. The French term *farce* (from *farcir*, meaning "to stuff"), which also connotes a prank or practical joke, comes from an earlier practice dating back to ancient Rome, when a host would play a joke on his guests by filling a roasted sow, hen, fish, or some other animal with an unexpected filling.

fine herbes: A mixture of finely minced fresh herbs, traditionally parsley, chervil, tarragon, and chives; though in actual practice it may consist of any assemblage of herbs—parsley plus three others.

flowerettes: Cauliflower or broccoli, cut into ¼- to ½-inch (6- to 12-mm) pieces.

foie gras: Literally "fat liver"; the fattened liver of geese or duck, prepared in various ways.

food mill: A straight-sided or conical container with a perforated bottom and a curved flange attached to a crank, which rests in the center of a perforated plate at the bottom. The crank is manually rotated, pressing a soup or sauce through one of three different sizes of perforated plates. With the advent of food processors, this ingeniously simple device has fallen on hard times, but it can still be a tremendous aid in puréeing soups and sauces.

julienne: A designated rectangularly shaped vegetable cut, generally used for garnishes, measuring from ⅛ × ⅛ × 1 inch (3 × 3 × 25 mm) to ¼ × ¼ × 2 or 3 inches (6 × 6 × 50 or 76 mm), or any food cut into strips. A large julienne is also referred to as bâtonnet (little stick).

large dice (*jardinière*): A designated vegetable cut, measuring approximately ⅓ to ½ inch (8 to 12 mm) square.

losange: Diamond-shaped cut, often used for canapé bases, but also for meat, fish, poultry, game, and vegetables.

medium dice (*macedoine*): A size of vegetable cut, measuring approximately ¼ inch (6 mm) square.

mince: To chop a spice, herb, or vegetable very fine.

mirepoix: A mixture of celery, carrot, and onion, commonly used for flavoring a stock or sauce.

mise-en-place: From the verb *mettre*, meaning "to place." In culinary parlance this phrase is translated to mean *a place for everything, and everything in its place*. It refers to the importance of being well organized and well prepped, so that kitchen production can move smoothly and all problems can be handled in the heat of peak production.

offal: Edible internal organs (and some external parts) of an animal, considered by some to be gastronomically superior to other edible parts, and which figure significantly in classical cookery. They include bone marrow, brains, cockscombs, ears, feet, heart, kidneys, liver, sweetbreads (thymus gland), tongue, and tripe (stomach lining).

Parisienne scoop: Commonly known as a melon baller, this tool creates spherical garnishes from fruits and vegetables.

paupiette: Literally "little package," referring to a rolled fish fillet, bundle of julienned vegetables tied together with scallion greens, and so on.

peasant style (*paysanne*): A common term for both a style of cooking and a method of cutting food ingredients. As a cooking style, it is characterized by a robust and spontaneous approach, based on available ingredients, and/or refashioned leftovers, often including root vegetables (potatoes, carrots, and turnips) and cabbage. As a cutting technique, it refers to mirepoix cut into approximately 1-inch (25 mm) size uneven pieces, then used as an aromatic, as well as an integral ingredient in various dishes.

sachet: A small piece of cheesecloth (muslin) tied into a small bag, containing herbs and/or spices for flavoring a stock or court bouillon.

shallot (*eschallote*): A unique aromatic vegetable, a separate variety of the onion family, and an essential ingredient in finished sauces. The name is derived from Ascalon, an ancient Palestinian port. It is believed that shallots were cultivated as early as the middle of the eighth century. Their flavor is subtler than that of onion, and carries a hint of garlic. Shallots are also served raw in salads, and grilled or roasted as an accompaniment to scores of dishes. Because of their ancient and Middle Eastern origins, they are also found in Vietnamese, Chinese, Indian, and Creole cookery.

small dice (*brunoise*): A designated vegetable cut, measuring approximately 1/8 inch (3 mm) square.

steel: A long, thin, abrasive tool used to maintain a sharp cutting edge on knives—not to be confused with a sharpening stone, which is used to grind a sharp edge. The end of a steel is magnetized to hold any metal burrs removed from a knife's cutting edge.

stockpot (*marmite*): A large pot, taller than it is wide, with straight sides, and two opposing handles near the top edge. In French, a stockpot is call a *fait-tout*, literally "do-all," in reference to its many uses. Some stockpots also come with a spigot attached near the bottom, which can expedite the careful removal of a stock, and particularly a consommé.

temper: To combine two liquids, one hot and the other cold, by slowly blending the hot liquid into the cold one. By gradually raising the temperature of the cold liquid, the two can be combined, without adversely affected either liquid. Applies to the incorporation of final liaisons—such as egg yolks, and egg yolks and cream—crème anglaise, pastry cream, as well as melting chocolate.

turned (*tourné*): A vegetable or potato cut into a seven-sided oval or olive-shaped oval, measuring 1 to 3 inches (50 to 76 mm) long.

turtle herbs: A mixture of herbs—basil, chervil, fennel, marjoram, and savory—used to flavor turtle soup and turtle sauce.

white pepper: Black pepper that has been soaked in water, then rubbed to remove the skin and thin outer pulp. White pepper is preferred over black pepper in some dishes because of its lighter color. Dedicated cooks often keep two pepper mills—one filled with black pepper, the other with white, and each labeled accordingly.

zest: The outermost skin of a citrus fruit, excluding the pith (the underlying white part of the skin). It is shaved off with a zester, a five-holed tool specifically engineered for that purpose, or with a sharp paring knife or vegetable peeler. Zest contains the essential oils of the fruit, and is used as both a flavoring agent and a garnish.

SPECIALTY SUPPLIERS

For information on special food items, tools, and unique related products, contact the following organizations.

Books and Tools: Pro Chef International, 12656 Mengibar Avenue, San Diego, CA 92129; (619) 484 6423. Carries some of the finest and most difficult to find ice and mukimono carving tools, and books. Call or write for current catalog.

J.B. Prince, 36 East 31st Street, New York, NY 10016; (212) 683-3553. Suppliers of unique and difficult to find culinary tools, books, and smallwares. Call or write for current catalog.

Buffet and Dining Tableware: Robert King Associates, 11 Tillman Place, San Francisco, CA 94108; (415) 989-5866. Distributors of several lines of exquisite plateware, table fabrics, and accessories from some of the finest manufacturers in the world. Call or write for current catalog.

Le Creuset of America, Inc., P.O. Box 575, Yemassee, SC 29945; (800) 827-1798. Manufacturers of exceptional, high-quality cast-iron cook and serve ware. Call or write for current catalog.

B.I.A. Cordon Bleu, Inc., 1135 Industrial Road, San Carlos, CA 94070; (415) 595-2400. Northern California distributors of a line of porcelain and ceramic serviceware. Call or write for current catalog.

Towle Silversmiths, P.O. Box 9115, East Boston, MA 02128; (617) 568-1300. Manufacturers, for over 300 years, of classical sterling and silverplated flatware, holloware, and giftware. For information, contact Mr. Robert J. McAniff, Vice President of Sales, or Ms. Sue McCarthy, National Bridal Director.

Centerpieces: Bread Effects Culinart, 5677 Rapid Run Road, Cincinnati, OH 94070; (800) 333-5678; (513) 922-5329. Suppliers of extraordinary tallow and bread sculptures, and sculpting supplies, including a modern tallow sculpting medium. Contact Mr. Dominic Palazzolo, President and contact person.

Dairy Products: For information on "Culinary Cream," an innovative lower-fat form of heavy cream, manufactured by L.J. Minor's, telephone their customer service number: (800) 243-8822.

Laura Chenel's Chevre, 1550 Ridley Avenue, Santa Rosa, CA 95401; (707) 575-8888. Producer of an exceptionally fine line of goat cheeses. Ms. Laura Chenel, contact person.

Wisconsin Milk Marketing Board, 8418 Excelsior Drive, Madison, WI 53717; (800) 373-9662. Primary marketing division of Wisconsin cheese producers. Offers information on cheese, including the *Cheesecyclopedia Study Course*, a comprehensive self-directed study course on how cheese is manufactured. Ms. Linda Funk, National Communications Manager, contact person.

Maytag Dairy Farms, P.O. Box 806, Newton, IA 50208; (800) 247-2458. Producers of one of the first blue-veined cheeses produced in

North America (1941) and descendants of F.L. Maytag, early innovator of the washing machine. Call or write for information.

Duck and Goose Liver (Foie Gras): Sonoma Foie Gras, P.O. Box 2007, Sonoma, CA 95476; (707) 938-1229. Junny Gonzalez, contact person.

Meat and Charcuterie: Nueske Hillcrest Farms, Wittenberg, WI 54499; (800) 382-2266. Producers of an exquisite apple-smoked country ham and related charcuterie. Jim Nueske or Gilbert Thompson, contact persons.

Olive Oil, Olives, Vinegars: Nick Sciabia & Sons, P.O. Box 1246, Modesto, CA 95353; (209) 577-5067. Second generation family-operated olive vineyard, producing an exceptional line of olives, olive oil, and vinegars.

Kimberly Wine Vinegar Works, 290 Pierce Street, Daly City, CA 94015; (415) 755-0306. Produces several varieties of exceptionally fine vinegars and olive oils. Mrs. Ruth Robinson, contact person.

B.R. Cohn Olive Oil, 15140 Sonoma Highway, Glen Ellen, California 95442; (707) 938-4064. Very fine olive oil in a gorgeous etched-label bottle, and several fine vinegars. Ron Morris, Director of Marketing and contact person.

For information on Mediterranean-produced olive oil, telephone the Olive Oil Council, at 800-232 OLIVE.

INDEX
••

Magellan soup, 150
Magenta consommé, 88
Maintenon soup, 177
Majordomo soup, 177
Malakoff soup, 140
Mallorquina, 279
Malmsbury style soup, 154
Mancele soup, 140
Mancelle consommé, 108
Mandoline, 23
Marcilly soup, 177
Margaret soup, 177
Margot consommé, 88
Margot soup, chilled, 213
Maria consommé, 88
Marianne soup, 178
Maria soup, 177
Maria Stuart soup, 177
Marie Antoinette soup, 178
Marie-Louise consommé, 89
Marie Louise soup, 124, 178
Marigny consommé, 89
Market-gardener's style soup, 140
Marmite (def.), 287
Marquise consommé, 55
Marquise soup, 178
Marquise style soup, 128
Marrow, about, 44
Marseille style fish soup
       (bouillabaisse), 237
Marshal's style soup, 178
Martha soup, 179
Martinière consommé, 89
Mary Stuart consommé, 55
Masséna soup, 198
Mathilda soup, 179
Mathurine soup, 155
Meat glaze, 15–17
  in thickened soups, 122
Meatless stocks, 8–9
Medici consommé, 55
Médici soup, 150
Medici style cream of chicken soup,
    165
Medium dice (def.), 286
Meissonier consommé, 56
Meissonier soup, 148
Melke, Arthur, 209
Melonen-Kaltschale, 216
Memphis style soup, 179
Mercédès consommé, 56
Mercédès soup, 179
Messaline consommé, 89
Metternich soup, 150

Mexican soups, 281–282
  chicken *(cancha mexicana),* 281
  noodle, 281
  pot, 282
Mezze tubetti, 123
Mignon consommé, 112
Mignon soup, 155
Mikado style consommé, 89
Milanese style consommé, 90
Milan style soup, 179
Milk, in thickened soups, 122
Mille-fanti, 251
Miller's style soup, 155
Mimosa consommé, 90
Mince (def.), 286
Minestral:
  al pomodoro, 254
  Turinese, 255
  Veneziana, 255
Minestrone, about, 252
Minestrone alla Contadina, 251
Miramount soup, 179
Mireille consommé, 90
Mirepoix:
  about, 4
  def., 286
Mirette consommé, 56
Mise-en-place (def.), 286
Mistinguette soup, 140
Mock-turtle consommé, 56
Modena style soup, 180
Mogador consommé, 90
Mogador soup, 180
Moldavian style consommé, 112
Molière consommé, 56
Molière soup, 180
Monaco style consommé, 90
Mona Lisa consommé, 57
Mongolian style soup, 140
Monosodium glutamate, 197
Monselet, Charles Pierre, 57
Monselet consommé, 57
Monte Carlo style consommé, 58, 90
Monte Christo soup, 180
Montepsan soup, 180
Monterey Jack cheese, 39
Montesquieu consommé, 58
Montesquieu soup, 180
Montglas soup, 180
Montmorency consommé, 90
Montmorency soup, 181
Montmort consommé, 91
Montorgeuil soup, 181
Montpensier soup, 181

Montreuil soup, 181
Morel consommé, 211
Morels, about, 197
Morlaix soup, 181
Moscovite soup, 272
Mozart soup, 141
Mulligatawny soup, 224
Murillo consommé, 91, 112
Musart soup, 182
Mushroom soup:
  chilled cream of, 214
  consommé, 211
Mussel soup:
  chowder, 264
  Spanish *(al cuarto de hora),* 278
Mutton soup. *See also* Lamb
    (mutton) soup
  Barcelona style, 278
  Turkish, 283

*N*anette soup, 182
Nansen consommé, 58
Nantes style consommé, 91
Naples style consommé, 58
Napoléon consommé, 91
  about, 27–28
Navarin consommé, 59
Navarin soup, 141
Navarra style soup, 182
Navy beans, as thickener, 124
Nelson consommé, 112
Nelson soup, 155
Nelusko soup, 182
Nemours soup, 182
Nesselrode consommé, 108
Nesselrode soup, 151
Nettle shoots, about, 172, 273
Nettle soup, 273
New England clam chowder, 256
New York style consommé, 59
Nice style consommé, 91
Nilson consommé, 92
Nîmese style soup, 156
Ninon consommé, 92
Nivernais style soup, 141
Noailles consommé, 92
Nobleman's style soup, 199
Noisette, 21
Noodles, as garnish, 38
Noodle soup, Mexican, 281
Normandy style shrimp soup, 156
Normandy style soup, 182
North American soups, 255–266
  American style, 255